WINDS OF CHANCE

WINDS OF CHANCE

By

HAROLD ENSLEY

A division of Squire Publishers, Inc.
4500 College Blvd.
Leawood, KS 66211
1/888/888-7696

A division of Squire Publishers, Inc.
4500 College Blvd.
Leawood, KS 66211
1/888/888-7696

FOREWORD

THIS BOOK is a collection of short takes during 50 years of television and radio broadcasting, covering the outdoor scene. The scope of coverage on four continents , over a long period of time, makes it difficult to maintain a chronological order.

I dedicate this book to all the doctors, surgeons, nurses, medical technicians and caregivers who have kept me alive; to my family and the thousands of people all over the world who have touched my life; to my publisher, Tom Leathers; to David Glass, a special friend; and to Jeanne Boyd, my assistant and caregiver, without whose help I could not have written this book. My sincere thanks, and may God bless you all!

Sincerely,

Harold Ensley

Jeanne at work on the book

A closer look at a big snook taken in the Caribbean near the mouth of the Paquari River in Costa Rica (See story page 29)

A closer look at a tarpon taken in Angola, Africa, where the Quanza River empties into the Atlantic (See story page 169)

The Early Years

FOR MANY YEARS people kept asking me to write a book about my adventures in the broadcasting field. I'm not a writer, and I had no aspirations to write a book. I've been an active member of the Outdoor Writers Association of America since the early '50s and still carry a press card. There were four of us who pioneered the uncharted water of outdoor television shows in America: Charlie Davis in Los Angeles, Mort Neff in Michigan, Gadabout Gaddis in Boston, and myself in Kansas City.

Television was in its growing stages. Sometime in the mid '50s I was honored to speak to my peers in the outdoor field at the Outdoor Writers annual convention at Penn State University. After my speech I was approached by the Stackpole people about writing a book. My involvement with the media was through radio and television. They told me that if I ever wrote a book, they wanted to publish it. I did write a daily outdoor column for the *Independence, Missouri Daily News* for a couple of years, but my job was in radio and television. At that time I was hosting and producing a live 30-minute outdoor TV show, 52 weeks a year, and a 15-minute daily radio show, Monday through Friday. In addition to that, I was on the lecture circuit. That gave me little time to devote to writing a book.

After 50 years in the outdoor broadcasting field, I've finally decided to write a book, not a "How To," but a "Why Fish?" book. I awakened one night a little after midnight with a title for a book, "Winds of Chance." I got out of bed and started writing down things that I wanted in it. I finally went back to bed around 4 a.m. After all, life is a game of chance. Why are some people at the right place at the right time, and others are not? So, "Winds of Chance" seemed right to me.

The next day I called my secretary, Gloria, and told her that I had finally decided to write a book. She was almost in a state of shock, as I had always said I would not write one. Gloria has been my secretary and right hand for 30 years. She also is my daughter-in-law. She asked me about the title. I told her "Winds of Chance," and she said that sounds like a book of romance. Why not call it "Chance of a Lifetime?" She is a real sharp lady, so I kicked it around in my mind. Then I got to thinking that what I've been doing *is* a romance!

"Winds of Chance."

A romance with God's great outdoor world that started with me, as a freckle-faced, barefoot boy with a willow pole, a piece of string and a hook I had fashioned myself. It's a romance that for 50 years has led me to faraway places, fishing for Atlantic salmon and grayling in Finland, to the rivers of darkest Africa for tiger fish and tarpon; from fishing for the beautiful Arctic char of Canada's northwest territories, to the Amazon Basin in South America for peacock bass; from the salmon fishing streams of Alaska, to the jungle of Costa Rica for tarpon and snook; from the sky-blue waters of Bermuda for Allison tuna and bone fish, to the waters of the Pacific. Yes, it is a romance with God's great outdoor world that started on that little creek in western Kansas and will carry me to my grave.

So "Winds of Chance" it is! God created all things! God created fish one day before he created man. I'm sure God created fish *for* man! He created the fish for food, but there is more to fishing than fishing for food. Sir John Buchan, Scottish poet and one-time Governor General of Canada, said it best, and I quote, "The charm of fishing is that it is the pursuit of what is illusive, but attainable, a perpetual series of occasions for hope."

There is a certain magic about fishing that is hard to define. The great thing about fishing is that you don't have to be an expert, and you don't have to be rich or famous. I was born in western Kansas on a small cattle ranch. It was a working ranch with the bunkhouse and sometimes a few riders. No one knows how, or exactly when, I received my love and fascination for the outdoor life.

My grandfather from Illinois moved to western Kansas in 1887. He homesteaded in Scott County, which is some 90 miles northwest of Dodge City. My dad was seven years old at the time. His mother had passed away when he was a baby. Times were hard. Everyone in the family had to work. At ten years of age Dad worked around the mess camp, helping the cook at the chuck wagon. Most of that country then was rangeland.

When Dad got old enough, he became a cowboy. He worked until he had enough money to buy a small cattle ranch near Healy, Kansas, not far from his dad's homestead. In Texas they would call it a small spread, but it was a working ranch. When I was small, after supper, as we called the evening meal, I loved to go up to the bunkhouse and listen to the cowboys spin yarns. A small creek ran through our ranch from west to east and eventually into the Smokey Hill River, just above what is now Cedar Bluff Reservoir. It was not a real clear stream, but even in the real dry years it still ran. There were a few fish in some of the pools, mainly bullheads, carp, sunfish and chubs. Dad didn't fish, nor did Mom, but they didn't mind that I fished, as long as I did my chores. I milked cows, fed the calves, and the usual things you do on a ranch.

I don't remember my first fish, but strangely enough, I nearly always caught something. My tackle was crude! A little willow pole, with whatever string I could find, a short piece of a branch for a bobber, and a hook I fashioned myself. Dad fed the cattle cottonseed cake. It came in burlap sacks, which we called gunnysacks. They used a wire safety-pin-like gadget that held the ingredient tag to the sack. It worked well, except I couldn't put a barb on it. If I hooked a big fish, I had to drag it up the bank. If it was a small one, I would toss it over my head. In that day, many people used a bent pin, but I never did. I shall always remember the first real fishing line and hook that Dad bought for me.

In those days there was a stigma about fishing and hunting. If a person in the community spent a lot of time fishing, he was counted as the "no-good" of the area. I had an uncle that fit that description. When mothers wanted to correct their children, to get them to do their chores or go to school, they would say, "You don't want to grow up to be like Uncle So-and-So, do you? Then go to school and get your work done!" I thought my uncle was great and loved it when he would come to visit. However, Mother was just like the rest of them. I'll never forget one morning that I pretended to be sick, and as soon as the school bus had gone on, I sneaked out the back door to go fishing, but I didn't fool Mom. She worked me over pretty good and told me that she wanted me to grow up and amount to something. She said, "Anybody can be a nobody! I want you to be somebody!" Mom convinced me. I dug in and studied hard. You probably won't believe this, but when I graduated I was valedictorian of my class. I'll have to admit it was a small class, but my mom was proud of me.

I then went out into the world to make Mom proud of me. I am just like my uncle, getting paid to hunt and fish. My mom got to see me on television, and she got to see me win the World Series of Freshwater Sport Fishing. She was proud of me, in spite of the fact that I was spending my life hunting and fishing. "Winds of Chance."

50 Years of Broadcasting

YOU WONDER about the "Winds of Chance," and the way you traveled, at the cross-road. I think of the word "if" in the English language. *If* I had taken that way instead of the other, what would have happened?

If a friend of mine had not had a date and asked me to pinch/hit for him, I might never have broadcast sports on radio, and never have gone to television. "Winds of Chance." Bill Grigsby (who has done color on the Kansas City Chiefs radio football broadcast from the beginning) and I worked together on a small radio station in Joplin, Mo. Bill was sportscaster, and I was in sales. He had a date with a lovely lady, Fran, who later became his wife. He asked the boss, Brick Poyner, if he could have the night off and that I would call the basketball game, which happened to be a state tournament game. Brick asked him if I had ever called a game. Bill said, "Not that I know of, but he can!"

I shall never forget the terror I felt at the start of the game. Kenny Boyer played in that game and later went on to "star" for the St. Louis Cardinals. Thanks to Bill, I learned to broadcast basketball, and it saved me when I moved to Kansas City.

Another "if." If my boss had not sent me to the little town of Seneca, Mo., to sell a radio promotional package to the merchants of Seneca to welcome the Milnot Milk plant, I probably never would have had a television career. I sold a $10 radio spot to my fishing buddy, Wiley McGee, who ran a filling station at the intersection of Highways 43 and 60, in Seneca, Mo. He gave me a $10 bill for the spot and said, "This isn't worth it, what I want is a fishing show!"

The next week I went down to see Wiley. I asked what he meant. He said, "Someone should come on radio and tell the people when the fish are biting and where." I asked him if he would buy it. He said, "If you'll do it, I'd buy it!" He did, and I did! Out of this came a full-time career in radio and television outdoor shows. How did it happen? "Winds of Chance," or really the Chance of a Lifetime?

Years later, I received a letter at the television station from the TB sanitarium in Mount Vernon, Mo. It was from Wiley. He said, "I need a favor. All of us here in the hospital watch you every week on Channel 10 out of Springfield. When you come on TV, I say, 'I know that young man.' Everyone laughs at me! So, will you come on the air and tell them that we fished together?" The next week I read his letter on the show and said, "Not only did we fish together, but Wiley is responsible for my career!"

Radio voice of the K.C. Chiefs and special friend

Then I got another letter from him, saying, "You made an old man cry when you read my letter on TV. Now even the preachers come to see me."

I'll always be grateful to Wiley, and to my friend, Bill Grigsby. Wiley passed away, but Bill and I have a friendship that is special, to this day.

I moved from Joplin to try my hand in the big city, Kansas City. There were several radio stations at that time: WDAF, KMBC, KCMO, WHB and one other small station, the call letters of which I do not remember. I tried all of them for a job as a salesperson, with no success. An announcer named Henry Efforts worked at KMBC. I had worked with him at Joplin. He told me of a new 1000-watt daytime station in Independence, Mo., Harry Truman's hometown. Everyone I knew in the business told me not to try it, that it wasn't going to make it. Henry said, "Harold, I'd go. It just may work." "Winds of Chance," and again the Chance of a Lifetime. I went to Independence and met with the owner, Craig Siefried. He showed me the radio log. It showed very few sold spots on anything. He also owned two newspapers, *The Daily News* and a weekly pictorial shopper, tabloid size. He wanted someone to sell for the total package, saying also that was the only way he would take me was on a straight commission basis. I told him that was the only way I would work, and I took the job. I had never sold newspaper space, but his pictorial shopper was doing very well.

Radio was another story. I just couldn't find a breakthrough. Spring came, and with it the opening of their Little League baseball program. It was sponsored by the Kiwanis Club of Independence and took youngsters up to 15 years, as I remember. They had no lights, so they played Monday, Wednesday and Friday afternoon games. We were a daytime radio station. I asked the boss if we could broadcast these kids' games, live. He acted like someone had hit him over the head with a stick. He said, "Whoever heard of broadcasting Little League baseball, who will do it?" I said, "I will!" He said, "Did you ever broadcast baseball?" I said, "No, but I can!" He said if I would do it for nothing it was okay with him, providing I could sell it. I went from one business man to another, starting with the Ford dealer, Dwight Moody, who said no to the idea, although he sponsored an American Legion team and I helped coach them. So I went to the Childers Bros., who ran a prescription shop on the square. They also turned me down, but also sponsored a team in the Kiwanis League.

Years ago I made it a practice when fishing to always make one more cast after I quit, so I went back to Moody and asked him if Childers would buy one spot, would he? I think we only asked $10 a spot. He said if they would buy a spot, he would! I went back to Childers and asked them if Moody would buy a spot, would they? They told me yes, and the rest is history. It was pretty corny, but it worked! The mothers and dads loved it. Then the whole community loved it. I found that even people in Kansas City started listening. I did the games for nothing, but made a little commission for selling the spots.

Fall came, and with the Kiwanis League over, I approached the boss to broadcast the high school basketball games. He said, 'We are only a daytime station, and who would call them?" I suggested we tape the games at night and play them back the next day. He was sports-minded and gave me the go-ahead, if I would sell them and do them for nothing. There were schools all around, Wm. Chrisman, Raytown, Lee's Summit, Grand-view and Liberty, just to name a few. I went to their local merchants, banks, car dealers, and sold them spots at $10 each. The schools loved it, because they and the parents could hear it the next day. I remember doing a game between Wm. Chrisman and Lee's Sum-mit. A man came to me at halftime and asked me about the spots and said he wanted to buy one spot each game in the immediate vicinity. I told him to see me after the game. My engineer, Eldon Ryan, said to me, "Do you know who that man is?" He said, "That is Charley Oldham. He makes Oldham's Sausage. He bought the spots. Then came the Wm. Jewell Invitational High School Tournaments and the state tournaments. Then came the day games of the NAIA Tournament at the Municipal Auditorium. Then came the consolation games of the Big Six and Big Seven Tournaments. They were played in the afternoons. I would sell them and call them. Shades of Phog Allen, Sparky Stalcup and Bruce Drake, great basketball coaches in their day.

Thanks to Bill Grigsby and his date, it was off to the races, but I was suffering on my fishing schedule. I'd had to drive to the Lake of the Ozarks or Grand Lake in Oklahoma to do any fishing. I went to the boss and told him that I would like to do a fishing show on radio. He asked me what I wanted. I told him 15 minutes a day, Monday through Friday, in drive time around 5 p.m. He said I could have it if I would do it for nothing. I started not to take it, but there again, "Winds of Chance." I took it! I shall be forever grateful to this man, for this was the Chance of a Lifetime, and I almost blew it!

I lined up reporters on the different lakes, Grand Lake in Oklahoma, Lake of the Ozarks in Missouri and Lake Norfolk and Bull Shoals in Arkansas. I had no money for phone calls, so I told them that if they would call in their reports I would put them on the air. I told them I wanted the truth each day, or I would not use them. I had to work in Sales to make a living. This I would do, Monday through Friday. Then my wife and I would leave Friday after work and drive to Arkansas or Oklahoma to check on the fish-ing first-hand.

The program caught on, not because of any special talent on my part, but the public was hungry for this information. I did the program for nothing from early spring to August. I tried to sell it, but couldn't. In August of 1950, my wife and I drove to California for a two-week vacation. Before leaving, I called on Sears, one of my accounts. A man named Morrison was in charge of their advertising. They had two big stores in Kansas City and a big catalog business. Their main office was at 15th and Cleveland. They had an outlet store in Independence. That day, when I talked to Morrison, he said, "I can't do anything today, but come back in two weeks and we'll take a two-page ad in the *Shopper* for the Independence outlet.

Television in the Los Angeles area was new. A man named Charlie Davis and his wife did a live TV show, giving out fishing information in southern California, similar to what I was doing on radio in the Midwest. I called him, told him who I was, and that I would like someplace to try some saltwater fishing. He invited me to be his guest on his TV show, to share our experiences in the outdoor world. It was my first appearance on television. Charlie may have been the first to do an outdoor show on TV. His two sons, as I remember, were working on a charter boat out of San Pedro. He arranged for me to spend a day with them off the Catalina coast, fishing for blue fin tuna. My first time on saltwater, but I was hooked.

My wife and I drove home to Independence, Mo. It was back to work. Sears was one of my newspaper accounts. They had two great retail stores in Kansas City, one on the Plaza and one at 15th and Cleveland, and a Sears catalog outlet office. They had a small outlet store in Independence. Before I left on vacation I had called on Morrie Morrison in their advertising department about an ad in the *Independence Pictorial Shopper*. I started back to work on Monday morning after my vacation which, by the way, was the last one I ever took. You know how you feel, starting back to work the next day after vacation. I went to see Morrison, in anticipation of an order. Morrie was nice, but told me they had orders from Chicago to cut off all advertising temporarily, but to come back in a few weeks.

I started out the door and was about halfway out. I turned to make one more cast and said, "Morrie, is Sears big enough to buy my radio show?" He said, "What do you mean?" I told him about my fishing show. He asked me to come back and sit down and tell him about it! He picked up his phone and called the Sporting Goods Department. He talked to the department manager, Floyd Roberts. He turned to me and said, "Can you sell shotguns?" I said, "I can sell any good product, and besides my fishing, I'm an avid hunter!" He invited me down to Sporting Goods and introduced me to Floyd Roberts. Morrie asked me the cost and said to see him Thursday, that he had to talk to Ray Bjorkland, his boss.

I didn't tell anyone, not even my wife. I had been a salesman long enough not to count on a sale until I had a contract. Thursday I braced myself and went back to see Morrie. He asked me to take a seat and said, "You are not going to believe this! I went to the boss about buying a fishing show. He said, 'Before you buy one, I want to tell you about one I listen to all the time. It's at 5 p.m. on a radio station in Independence, Missouri. I go out to the parking lot to listen to him every night.' It was your show, and we are going to take it for four weeks to sell shotguns."

It was the right timing, just at the start of the hunting season in both Missouri and Kansas. Sears had their own gun, J.C. Higgins, made by Hi-Standard. It was a good gun and well worth the price. The first week of the show they sold more shotguns than they had ever sold in the same period of time.

It was ironic in a way that, as a 12-year-old boy in western Kansas, I had bought my first 22 rifle through Sears catalog in Kansas City, and here years later I'm selling guns for Sears. You may wonder about my first rifle. It was a Stevens, single shot, and sold for $4.20, plus postage. At that time, as a kid, I made my school money trapping and shooting rabbits. The county paid us a bounty of five cents for a pair of rabbit ears, one dollar for coyote ears. That winter a severe blizzard killed many of the jackrabbits. I collected enough of them to buy that 22 rifle, my first gun!

But back to the program — it was the Chance of a Lifetime — "Winds of Chance." Sears bought the show for four weeks and kept it for 15 years. Television was coming on. We had one station, WDAF, Channel 4. My wife told me that I'd better do a TV show, or someone else would. I went to Morrie and asked him if they would buy one. He suggested that I buy a movie camera and some film, in color, and start planning for television. He said that as soon as some more channels opened up they would plan to put me on TV. He said, "Be sure to shoot your stuff in color."

Time moved on. I'd almost forgotten about TV. The radio thing was going so well, and I was also writing daily fishing columns for the *Independence Daily News,* along with my sales work. In early September of 1953, two new TV channels opened up in Kansas City. KCMO, Channel 5 and Channel 9 was divided between KMBC and WHB. I called Morrie. He said, "Make your best deal, and we will move the radio show and put you on TV." I thought I had it worked out with WDAF. They were the old established station. They wanted the 15-minute daily radio show, but we could not agree on the TV part. So I left to make "one more cast." I went down 31st Street, a short distance, and talked to Joe Hartenbower, general manager of KCMO. He asked if I really thought I would go over on TV. I told him that I still had radio and could sell. He and I agreed on a contract, merely a handshake. I was so anxious to get on TV that I agreed to produce and host a 30-minute show, 52 weeks a year.

I went back to Morrie, and he had just received an order from Chicago to cut all advertising. He said, "We cannot do the TV thing, but we will keep the radio show and move it to KCMO."

I did two sustaining TV shows, and it was sold to Evans Electrical Company for 13 weeks. A guy named Morley Davies called Lee Martz, account executive for KCMO-TV. Morley was with J. Walter Thompson, who handled the K.C. Ford Dealers account. He had just been transferred from the Denver region to Kansas City and saw my show and wanted the right for first refusal if the program came up for renewal. He bought the show, and we were off to the races. "The Chance of a Lifetime" — "Winds of Chance." They kept the show for 25 years, until I went into National Syndication. The rest is history! We did the show, live, 52 weeks a year, for 22 years. I had a boss who believed in me. He kept me in prime, and prime access time, for all those years. The show was opposite such network shows as Ben Casey, Peter Gunn and Combat.

We then expanded to an eight-station network, touching eight states. In the rating books in February and March of 1971, we carried a 26% share on the audience on KCMO-TV in Kansas City; 39% share in WIBW-TV in Topeka; a 49% share in KTTS in Springfield, Mo.; a 29% share on KOAM in Pittsburgh, Kansas; a 28% share on the Kansas State Network; Wichita, Garden City, Great Bend and McCook, Nebraska; and a 33% share on KQTV in St. Joseph, Mo. Proof that a fishing and hunting show would work.

I'll always be grateful to the late Joe Hartenbower for his faith in me, and to the 250 Ford Dealers of the K.C. region who made it possible. It is difficult to put things in chronological order that happened almost 50 years ago. Names and places escape me as the years pass on. This started a chain of events. My television show was gaining momentum, in conjunction with my daily radio show. We found the television audience hungry for good, wholesome family entertainment. It is just as true today as it was 48 years ago. I used the term "we," because the whole family was involved. My wife, Bonnie, named the title of the show, "The Sportsman's Friend." Smokey, my oldest son, worked with me. He drove for me and helped produce the show for several years. Then Dusty, my youngest son, went to work for me. The three of us had some fabulous trips together. One in particular, floating the famous Gunnison River of Colorado in a rubber raft, an area that is now flooded by Blue Mesa Reservoir. Then came our daughter, Sandy, who was seven months old when I did my first TV show. We used her in her first fishing movie when she was three and a half years old, her first bass movie in Table Rock Lake in South Missouri.

A few short months after we started the TV series, I received a telephone call from a man named Nick Kahler of Minneapolis, Minnesota. He wanted to have a meeting with me about his project to start a boat, sport and travel show in Kansas City. We met and he told me of his problem. I'm not sure, but he may be the one who originated the idea of the big Boat, Sports and Travel Show. He had one in Chicago and the one in Minneapolis. He was going to do one in Kansas City at Municipal Auditorium. He said, "I just cannot get any media attention." He said that someone had told him abut me and my work in the outdoor field, and that I was the one who could help. I asked him to tell me about it, and that I would help if I could. He was bringing to K.C. what he called a Sports, Boat and Travel Show. It was to last 10 days, with two daily stage shows, top stage acts, many of them from Europe and Las Vegas, who had given command performances before the Queen of England. Many of them had appeared on the Ed Sullivan Show and the Gary Moore Show. He had animal acts and a trout pool in front of the stage. Around the auditorium were booths manned by travel people, big game outfitters, state fish and game people and resort people from all over North America and Canada, and tackle manufacturers and dealers. This ALL under one roof.

I thought, what a novel idea, to give the people of this area an opportunity to select their vacation spots and learn about new tackle and equipment. I asked him what he

Part of our TV crew on live show from Kansas City Sport Show, 1954 .

wanted. He said, "I simply want to tell the people what we have." I said, "We can use my radio show daily to promote it, and how would it be if I would telecast some of his stage acts live on my Monday night show? All I ask is that you give us the choice of your acts."

I'm not certain that KCMO had ever, at that time, done a remote broadcast, live. It wasn't easy like it is today with all the facilities and equipment we now have, but I had great confidence in my crew. So we made the necessary arrangements. Fortunately, the second stage show went on at 9 p.m., as did my live TV show. I called several of my reporters from Bull Shoals to bring in some big bass to show from the stage. Everett Crow, of Crow-Barnes Resort, John Wiggins of Lead Hill Boat Dock and others. They did, and I remember they brought in a tremendous string, including 10 that were at least 10 pounds each. We got quite a buzz for the full house. However, just before show time, Kahler called me up on the stage. He said, "We have a problem. The acts you selected will not perform without double pay. Even the band wants extra money! Two of the acts I wanted had been on the Ed Sullivan Show and the Gary Moore Show. One group, the Amandus Tumbling Group from Europe and Starkey the Seal, with his trainer. Nick called Gunther Amandus, the leader of the group, up on stage, and the seal trainer, who said, "I didn't let Ed Sullivan or Gary Moore show the seal in the tank, so why should I let this guy?"

Nick pointed to the stands, a full house, and said, "Why do you think they are here? If you don't go on his show, I'll cancel your contract!" Gunther Amandus turned to me and said, "What do you get out of this?" I said, "Nothing but a headache from you guys?" he said, "Why didn't somebody tell me? Sure, we will really put on a show for you," and they did, and we telecast Sharkey the Seal in the tank.

Nick had given me booth space in the extreme back end of the auditorium, with my Ford Country Sedan. After the TV show, he said, "Next year you are going to have space that I sell to no one! I want you and your station wagon at the front of the stage where everyone who comes to the show has to come by you!"

The show drew some 130,000 fans. Until the day he died, he kept me there. When Nick passed away, Phil Perkins, his right-hand man, took over and treated me the same way. Now the show is held in Bartle Hall. Phil passed away, and his son, David, very successfully carries on the tradition. Forty-seven years later, I'm still working with the Perkins family, with a red Ford station wagon. The difference, they get media coverage in the Sport Show. Yes, my meeting with Nick Haler started a chain of events that has led me to four continents! That's what I call "Winds of Chance."

In the summer of 1956 I got a call from Barney Laum, who owned Ontario Central Airlines out of Kenora, Ontario. He wanted to fly me to God's Lake in Manitoba to do a story. When I was a boy, I read James Oliver Curwood's books about the North Country. I remember two of them, "God's Country" and "God's Country and a Woman." I never dreamed I would ever have a chance to see that country, much less fish there. Barney owned a fleet of float planes and several camps. His main operation was out of his camp at Ball Lake in Ontario, but he also had two great fishing camps at God's Lake, one at Kanuchuan Rapids and Elk Island on the main lake at Elk Island, a former gold-mining camp. He also had an outpost cabin on God's River — a fly-in operation. In fact, the only way you could reach God's Lake at that time was by float plane. Barney not only flew his own customers in, but also flew for other camps. Bonnie, my late wife, and I left Kansas City after I did the program, drove all night to reach Kenora, Ontario, where the next day one of Barney's twin-engine float planes flew us to Elk Island to fish and to shoot a movie for our show.

We had fished at Lake of the Woods the year before. We had tremendous small-mouth bass fishing there. I was dedicated to bass fishing; it was easy to adjust. I had caught walleye in Lake of the Ozarks and on the White River chain, but was really a novice when it came to fishing in the North for walleye and northern pike, but we still caught lots of fish!

God's Lake was a different story. Too far north for bass, but plenty of walleye, lake trout and northern pike. Believe me, we had lots to learn! My first mistake was to throw a top water lure, with two sets of treble hooks for northern.

I can still hear Pete Burton as he told our guide to take us to Rat Portage on the east side of Elk Island. Pete was one of the most unforgettable and interesting characters I had met in my lifetime. A pioneer in operating a hunting and fishing camp, and a very colorful one. When he was 18, he ran away from home to work in the gold mine at Elk Island. When the mine closed down, he married and operated a hunting and fishing camp where the gold mining town was located. It's my understanding that at one time some 500 miners worked there. I don't know if Barney Lamm was the first owner of the camp, but he was at the time he flew us in. At that time you could see a lot of the remains of buildings, mine shafts, etc.

But back to Pete and Rat Portage. After 45 years of fishing the far North, I have learned that you could catch northern pike on a corncob, if it had a hook on it. They will hit at anything! So stupidly I cast a Lucky 13 into the waters of the Rat Portage Bay. My wife, Bonnie, was working the camera. I started working the lure in. There was an explosion, as two small northern pike ran together after the lure. They were only small ones, about 12 or 15 lbs., and only one of them got hooked. I played the fish for the camera, and the guide netted the fish and lifted it into the canoe. The fish flopped around, rolling up in the net. I think we were nearly 30 minutes getting the fish untangled from the net to release it for the picture. The fish had twisted and flipped in the net until the hooks were all bent. We decided right then not to use a lure with two sets of trebles around northern pike. My advice to everyone is, in that light, use a lure with a single hook. Another reason, if you catch a small pike, five or six lbs., on a crank bait on a lure with two sets of trebles, when you try to release it there is a chance of two things happening — you will either kill the fish or get hurt yourself. Besides this, you can catch as many on a single hook and not get hurt.

Since then, I have caught many northern out of God's Lake from 20 up to 30 pounds. This was during the summer of 1955 — can you believe during the summer of 2000 we were still fishing God's Lake and catching oodles of walleye and lake trout, and at the same spot in Rat Portage, big northern. Through the years we have been privileged to take many youngsters, including my grandson, to the same spot. You can be sure it will produce a good fish for you.

The next day they flew us to their outpost camp on God's River. What a beautiful stream and one of the premier brook trout streams of the world. We didn't do well, but finally caught a few. Since then, through the years we have caught brookies up to seven or eight pounds; four to six pounds are common. If I get time, I'll tell you about catching the two biggest ones.

Now I want to finish that trip. Walleye fishing was great, but they said you had to troll to catch the lake trout. We didn't even try for the lakers, but when we later learned how to fish for lake trout, we found it to be one of the great spots of Manitoba. I've become addicted to lake trout fishing, but we will tell you more about Barney Lamm. He was one of the pioneers of flying fishermen and hunters into the north land. A pilot instructor in World 2, he operated Ontario Central Airlines. He had several fishing camps with headquarters at Ball Lake. He and Warren Plummer, along with several others, were responsible for much of the fly-in fishing of Canada. Plummer, on Great Bear Lake in the Northwest Territory, and Barney in Manitoba and Ontario. If Canada were to have a Hall of Fame for bush pilots of the north, both of them should be there. I shall always be grateful for what these men did for me in exploring the fishing in these respective areas.

Our trip to God's Lake started a chain reaction of a relationship with Barney that lasted some 40 years. If I needed program material, I called Barney. He would say, "Just tell me where to pick you up." We would either drive to Kenora or Fort Francis and then fly in. I want to share a few of these with you. Producing 52 new TV shows each year kept me searching for program material.

We had a preacher friend, Layton Plaster, who loved to fish. We had used celebrities, athletic stars and people of most every walk of life. Youngsters, oldsters, whatever seemed best at the time. We thought it would be nice to feature a preacher and his wife, so I called Barney. He told me that would be fine, to bring all of them up at the same time that Milburn Stone, who plays Doc of Gunsmoke, had called me from California. He said that the weather was really hot out there. Could we take them to Canada to fish? We had fished together on Lake of the Ozarks several years prior to that. Doc and Kitty and Chester were performing at a rodeo near Camdenton, Missouri, where we fished with them. Can you imagine Miss Kitty fishing for catfish? She and Doc got up at 4 a.m. to go fishing with Bonnie and me. We started a friendship that lasted as long as both of them lived. It all happened at once; Doc called at the time we were going to take the preacher and his wife. I called Barney. He said to bring them all. One party one week, and the other the next. So Dusty, my son, and I met Doc and his pilot at International Falls, then drove us to Fort Francis, where Barney picked us up and flew us to God's Lake. We fished there four or five days and caught a lot of fish, then flew back to Ball Lake, where I left Doc, his pilot and Dusty.

I joined the preacher and his wife and Bonnie, who had driven to Kenora, Ontario, and had flown into Barney's Ball Lake lodge. The three of them were greeted by Barney at the dock when the plane landed. He said, "Mr. Lamm, I don't get to fish much, so I would like to fish as much as I can." Barney said, "You are with the right guy, but I want you to tell me about it after a few days with him." The first day Barney flew the two couples of us to Pine Needle Lake to shoot a lake trout movie. Big Jim McCullough was our guide. We stashed two canoes together for stability and had a fabulous day of lake trout fishing. Nothing of any size, mainly from four to eight or nine lbs. But that day I learned a method of catching lake trout when they are down deep. It was purely by accident, but it's deadly, and I still use the same retrieve as effectively as then.

The next day Bonnie and Wilma were going to fish walleye and small-mouth bass at Ball Lake. Big Jim came to me and said, "Let's take the preacher to Lennon Lake and try to set a new record of catch and release lake trout." He said that the last time he and I fished it, with two other fishermen, that the two boats of us had boated and released 96 trout. We would need to catch at least 49 to change the record. I have never worried about records, and I don't know of Big Jim's counting. I said, "Let's go." Lennon is a small, deep lake full of small lake trout. We had fished it many times and never taken anything over ten pounds. I don't remember ever catching a walleye or pike there.

Barney flew us in, and the pilot told us to be ready at 6 p.m. for the pick-up. We fished hard using my newfound retrieve, with one-half ounce maribou jigs, on 6-lb. test line and spinning gear. At noon we had four fish. We just couldn't find them. I suggested to Big Jim that we skip shore lunch and just eat whatever was in the shore lunch box. Jim exclaimed, "Somebody forgot to put the bread in." All we had was two big onions, some raw potatoes and a can of Spam. They always put in a can or two of Spam, just in case you can't catch any fish. We had caught enough fish for shore lunch, but I told Jim if we were going to set a record we would not have time to build a fire and cook. Guess what! He cut two big slices of onion, put a piece of Spam between them and handed it to the preacher. After our onion sandwiches, we moved to another part of the lake and found the fish. Then we didn't have electric devices to locate fish. It was simply trial and error. "Winds of Chance." We were fishing in 70 feet of water, and they rally turned on. The preacher, bless his heart, caught the largest. We took it in and weighed it — 11-1/2 lbs. While not a trophy at all, I had it mounted for him.

As the day wore on, we were catching small trout four to seven pounds, almost every cast. One I put in the boat to release it, and it spit up a minnow. It was a long, slender, silver-colored minnow, and its gills were still moving. I hooked it up under the chin on that maribou jig and immediately caught another trout on it. The wheels in my head started turning, and I planned to get some plastic when I returned to Kansas City and design bait. Big Jim claimed we caught 70 lake trout for a new record and released all but the preacher's and returned to camp. It had been a wonderful trip, and I'm so glad we made it.

Some years later Layton Plaster contacted Lou Gehrig's disease. He was confined to a wheelchair and preached from his wheelchair for the Church of Christ at Branson, Missouri, during his last years. A few short years later, his widow was brutally murdered near Branson.

When we arrived in Kansas City, I called the Marlynn Lure Company and asked for some lead jig heads and some plastic material that I wanted to design a new lure for lake trout. I called Barney and told him I had a new lure I wanted to test. He asked me when and where to make a pick-up. I told him that I would leave immediately after my show and drive all night and reach Fort Francis, Ontario, the next day. My wife Bonnie, my son Dusty and ten-year-old Sandy picked me up at the TV station. We drove all night and arrived safely at Fort Francis, then flew into Ball Lake. The next day we flew into Lennon to test the homemade bait. Big Jim told Barney that I wanted to spend the night at Lennon in the old trapper's cabin there. That was not exactly what I wanted, but to please Big Jim I said okay.

We fished that day and caught a lot of fish with the new lure and fought mosquitoes all night in that old log cabin. The next day we caught a lot of fish and returned to Ball Lake. Jim told Marian, Barney's wife, that I had designed a fantastic new lure and that we had boated and released 57 trout. She said, "Don't tell me about it. He can put a piece of a ribbon on a bare hook and catch fish."

Then I thought a moment about it and asked Barney if he would fly Dusty and me back to Ball Lake and take his 11-year-old daughter, Cheri, and our ten-year-old daughter, Sandy, to shoot a movie of the two girls catching lake trout. They each caught their limit of trout for the movie, and we had proof that a new lure had been born. "Winds of

Chance." Had that trout not spit up the minnow, I would never have designed the lure — the Chance of a Lifetime. We called it Reaper, as in Grim Reaper. We designed it for lake trout, but found it deadly for walleye, northern pike, bass and saltwater fish. We have been and still are using it on all kinds of fish that feed on minnows; from Arctic char in Canada in the Northwest Territory, to tiger fish in the jungle rivers of Africa.

A few years later Barney called me. He asked me if my son Dusty and I would help him with a group from Texas who wanted to fly to a remote river in Northwest Territory in Canada. He wanted us to help them catch lake trout. It as Lake Franklin where the Back River runs into the Arctic. It was there that the Franklin party perished on their way to the North Pole. Here was another Chance of a Lifetime, and we jumped at it. Barney had flown some small aluminum boats and motors on the wings of the old P.B.Y., and we were going to have to fish in shifts and camp out. We have fished in remove areas of four continents, but this was the wildest spot of them all. They called it Chantry Inlet, where the Franklin party perished. I told Barney to pick us up the next day in Kenora and fly us in to Ball Lake, which was the starting point of the expedition.

Chantry Inlet

THE FOUR OF US, Dusty, my wife Bonnie and our daughter Sandy and myself, left Kansas City after my TV show at 10 p.m. and drove all night to Kenora, Ontario, reaching Ball Lake mid-afternoon. Barney and his crew were feverishly packing things for the trip, food for 14 men for a week and small camp stoves to cook with. There was absolutely no wood or trees for firewood. They had tents for kitchen and sleeping quarters. The PBY is quite an airplane, but counting the food, camping gear, movie equipment and our fishing equipment, we couldn't get off the water to leave Ball Lake. Rex Kitely, one of the great pioneer bush pilots, taxied back to the dock, and we shed any weight possible. We made a second attempt to no avail. The third time we made it by flying up the river between the trees. Many of us had our wives watching from the dock.

We headed for Churchill or Hudson Bay to refuel. It was to be our only stop enroute. We arrived there safely, refueled and headed north. About 100 miles out of Churchill, we encountered such heavy head winds that Rex turned and headed back to Churchill. I asked Barney what the problem was. He said that if the strong winds persisted we had enough fuel to get there, but not enough to get back. So we returned and spent the afternoon and night in Churchill. This, too, was quite an experience, as we got to go into

Guiding at Chantry Inlet — one of Canada's most remote fishing spots.

Hudson Bay to watch them harpoon the white whales, and even watched them cut off the blubber at the processing plant. The next morning the wind died down, and we flew across the bay toward Chantry Inlet. It was a beautiful day, and flying low we could see the whales swimming about. I even got pictures of them from the air. We flew over the Kazan River rapids, a spectacular sight, and hours later made it to the Chantry Inlet. It was a remote, wild and rugged spot. The Franklin party had perished there, enroute to the North Pole.

Everyone was anxious to get to the fishing. Dusty and I ran the boats for the first shift, then the second shift, and then he and I fished a shift together. It was absolutely unbelievable, the number of lake trout you could see in the clear water. No giants, but fish from 18 to 40 lbs. Most of the guys couldn't cast, so we trolled. The rest of them had a pot up for the biggest trout. Two guys won it with a 58-pounder, but as far as I know, that was the only one of that size taken. Our trip home was uneventful, but we had been treated to some of the greatest lake trout fishing in the world. Dusty and I went back for Barney the next year with his group in the PBY.

The next year Barney wanted us to go back with another group. He told us that he lacked one to fill out the party, and would we mind bringing our family doctor, Dillard Eubanks, with us? Dillard had been a customer of Barney's at Ball Lake Lodge for many years. Barney said that he wanted to do something nice for him. Dillard was getting along in years, and Barney wondered if he could stand the trip. It really was a rough trip travel-wise, and then camping out in the barren waste was not for softies. Doctor was a tough one, and I thought he could make it. He was a colorful character, sort of those one-of-a-kind individuals you meet once in a lifetime. His parents had been missionaries in China and during World War II; Doc was in charge of the search and rescue mission into Tibet for pilots down while flying the hump from India. He was our family doctor for years and was loved by all the families whose lives were touched by him. He loved to fish and did fish a lot in Canada. He and other surgeons from Kansas City made a trip to Columbia, South America, with us for peacock bass. We had always enjoyed fishing with him and were thrilled to get the opportunity to take him with us. In earlier times he had introduced us to a great fishing spot at Crane Lake, Minnesota, and the boundary waters there. He kept telling me about a resort operator on Crane Lake that I needed to meet, a man named Bowser. He would tell me that Bowser was the best fisher man he had ever met. He would tell Bowser about me and say the same thing. We finally met and became close friends. We fished there many times and did many TV shows about the area. "Winds of Chance," and my thanks to Doc for this.

But getting back to Doc and our trip to the barren country of Chantry Inlet. We made our flight without incident and set up camp. Dusty and I would guide two eight-hour shifts, then fish together for a while. The daylight hours were long, and I'm not sure that we saw a sunrise or a sunset on the trip. The fishing was unbelievable, but strictly for lake trout. We probably could have caught some grayling if we had tried. We were trolling huge husky devil spoons which were about the size of a big bluegill. One day Dusty and his party came back to camp for lunch. He said, "Dad, you're not going to believe me, but we found lake trout feeding on 1-1/2 to 2-pound whitefish." I didn't believe it until I saw it myself.

I was guiding Doc one day; his fishing partner wanted to stay in camp and rest awhile. It is difficult to describe how it was to handle those small aluminum boats in that swirling water below the falls. There were whirlpools all around. Doc yelled that he had a big one; I reeled my line in. His rod was bent double, but it appeared to me that it was staying pretty much in the same place. After a while, I said, "Doc, you're snagged on a rock." He told me right quick-like that he could tell a rock from a fish. The fight went on for almost a half-hour. I said, "Doc, that has to be a rock, but holding the boat in one place in that swirling, twisting current was almost impossible." Doc finally realized that he was snagged and would just have to break his line. We were getting short of lures, so I told him to just hang on and maybe we could get the boat in position to just jerk it loose. It finally happened; the lure came free, and as Doc started to reel in a lake trout hit it. I said, "Doc, you have one now; just hang on." We fought that fish all around the whirlpools for a long time. That fish came to the surface, and I thought for a moment that a log was floating. There was no timber within 100 miles. I got the boat around where we could see it better. It was another big lake trout by the side of the one he had hooked. Actually the free fish was much larger than the one on Doc's spoon. We finally gaffed Doc's fish and took it back to camp. It weighed 40 pounds.

Doc said, "I've had enough for today," so Dusty and I went back out. We hooked and released several big trout. I said, "Dusty, maybe we better shoot some more footage for my show while just the two of us are together." We had two cameras in the boat. I hooked a decent-sized fish; he took pictures of me fighting the fish. I got the fish up to the side of the boat. I didn't want to gaff it, so I finally got my hand in one side of the gills, lifted the fish up for the picture. It flopped out of my hand and went back into the water. I got it up again and got it into the boat. Dusty was taking pictures; he said, "Give me a big smile." Then he said, "Hey, where are your glasses?" When that fish flopped back in the water, I was holding my casting rod with my left hand, the line whipped by my face and took my glasses off, in 30 feet of water, and I didn't even feel the glasses go. "Winds of Chance." I can't say that it made my day, but it was a beautiful fish, it weighed 37 lbs. We finished our stay, heard lots of stall tales and flew back safely to Kansas City. I do not know if there ever was or ever will be fishing like that again. The next year Dusty didn't make the trip, as Barney was just taking two of his friends.

The third year he asked me if I would go with two of his friends from Kenora. We were to fly in a Beach Baron, the five of us: these two men; Doug Cameron, the pilot; Ken Race, the co-pilot, and me. We had collapsible aluminum boats and a small outboard in the plane, plus our gear, tents, cook stoves and food. We flew to Churchill, then to Baker Lake, which was the nearest point of civilization, refueled there and went on to Chantry Inlet. The first day was calm and beautiful, and we caught lots of fish. The second day

Every day for seven days, every member of our party caught trout like this one in the swirling, icy waters of Chantry Inlet. This one knocked my glasses into the "drink" while I was landing it.

was one of the wildest moments of my fishing life. The wind was "not a tornado," just a straight wind that Doug estimated at 70 or 80 miles per hour. Waves four to six feet high tore the plane from its mooring and broke one of the anchor ropes. Kenny Race jumped in the boat and somehow got in the plane, started the engine before the plane crashed into the rocks. He somehow got the plane in the air, but could not land at the camp for the huge waves. He flew to the other side of the lake and found water to safely land. Doug Cameron, the pilot, told me that we had to get across to Kenny. Since I was the only one who could run a boat, it was my lot. We put on life jackets and got in the small boat. The two fishermen waded into the water and held the boat until I could start the motor. I started the motor, and in my excitement I left the coke on; the motor died. The huge waves threw us up on the bank. We tried again and made it. Never in my life have I ever put a small boat and motor through such water. Doug Cameron, a veteran bush pilot, had a white-knuckle ride. We had to go with the waves at an angle of 45 degrees, then come back at an angle toward the other side. We made it safely back to camp.

To show you how wild it was each day, our pilot would leave a note on the card table that we used to eat on. He would say, "My name is Doug Cameron, pilot of Beach Baron number so-and-so; Kenny Race is co-pilot; with three passengers flying up the Back River as far as the Meadow Brook, to look for char. If we are not back in by a certain time and anyone finds this note, start looking up the river to the Meadow Brook. We made it home safely, and I always regret that I didn't save one of Doug's notes.

Early on I became addicted to bass fishing. Week after week after week, my wife Bonnie and I could drive to some of the impounded waters of the Midwest to do a bass story for my TV show and to have material for my radio shows. At that time it was mainly either Lake of the Ozarks in Missouri or Grand Lake in Oklahoma. Then came Lake Norfork and Bull Shoals in Arkansas. Lake fishing was new to all of us, but we learned by trial and error, with crude equipment compared to today's bass fishermen. No trolling motors, no fish locators, no fast boats, we used small, heavy cedar-strip boats with small, slow motors. Yet we caught worlds of bass! We caught our first six-pound bass in Grand Lake in Oklahoma in the '40s, our first nine-pound bass in Bull Shoals in the late '50s, and our first 11-pound bass in Bull Shoals in 1961.

We thought this was a big breakthrough, that it took more skill to catch bass than anything else. We thought this until I saw my boss catch two bass on one backlash. He caught one while he was trying to pick out the first backlash. His plastic worm was motionless on the bottom of the lake. I saw his rod tip move, and I said, "Jerk." He did and reeled in a three-and-a-half-pound bass. He reeled right over the backlash. I took the fish off the hook and tossed the plastic worm over the side of the boat. He started again to pick out the mess, and I saw his rod tip dip again. I said, "Jerk." He had another bass and reeled it in right over the backlash. I took the fish off the hook, but put the plastic worm in the boat. I thought to myself that this guy caught two bass on one back-lash. If I threw the plastic worm back into the water, he might catch a third. I said to myself that this guy could ruin the lake. Tell me it takes skill to catch bass!

I doubt there is a bass fisherman who has not caught a fish accidentally. How many times have you started to leave a spot and have one of your parties reeling in his lure too fast to get it in the boat, only to catch a bass. They wouldn't have caught the fish had they reeled the lure in at a normal pace. Is that skill? I wouldn't have caught one of my largest bass had I not cast on the wrong side of the boat, and the other, if the guide's lure had not been snagged and we went in to get it. I soon learned that it didn't take more skill to be bass fishermen than for any other species, crappie, catfish, etc. That's the magic of fishing; it could happen to you. How much is luck and how much is skill?

I remember so many times unusual things happened that produced fish. Once four boats of us with native guides rode for some 45 minutes from God's River Lodge to little God's Lake. After several hours of fishing for walleye, we didn't have enough fish for shore lunch. One of our native guides suggested another area. We had a young native boy running our boat. About a mile out of little God's Lake our motor conked out and we drifted into a rock reef about the shape of a loaf of bread. The other boats stopped to help the kid with the motor. I wasn't going to just sit there, so I dropped a reaper over the side of the boat in about five feet of water. I felt a little peck, but missed it. I told my buddy, Jim Higgins, that I had a walleye peck my reaper. I dropped the reaper back and had a four-pound walleye. The fixed the motor and started to leave. I said, "No way, just back out away from the reef. The four boats of us caught limits of walleye, up to six or seven pounds. We made our movie and had shore lunch in just a matter of a few hours, all because the motor stopped on us. We had never fished that spot before and would not have fished it, had not the motor quit on us. Was it skill? Certainly not! It was an accident, but we adapted to it.

"Winds of Chance."

Along the Tournament Trail

SINCE THE LATE 1800S, fly casters and bait casters have been holding competitive tournaments. They were not fishing tournaments, but contests for accuracy and distance. Maybe first just fly casting, but later came the bait casters. Those of us who fish today are deeply indebted to these people What we have today in fishing equipment, fly rods and reels, bait casting rods and reels, fishing lines and then, last but not least, spinning rods and reels, came from their dedication to improve their skills. Yes, today we have better rods, reels and line, because of them. Many people today think that the bass tournaments were the beginning of the tournament trail, but far from it. To my knowledge, the first professional fishing tournaments were held by the Junior Chamber of Commerce of Hot Springs, Arkansas.

I was invited to fish at Hot Springs in the mid-'50s. The tournament may have been by invitation only, I just don't remember. There was no entrance fee and purse was small. Most of the contestants were men involved in the tackle industry. A few were members of the casting world. There were only two of us involved in the television side. It was a three-day tournament, one day on Lake Ouchita, one on Lake Hamilton, and one on Lake Catherine. It was all strange water to me, but I enjoyed it. I placed in the money, taking fifth place, enough to pay my expenses. They invited me back the next year, but I declined.

Many years ago I was privileged to fish with Joan Wulf. Joan is probably one of the greatest woman fly casters for accuracy of all time, winning 17 national championships and one international championship. I don't know if she holds the women's record for distance with a bamboo fly rod, but I do know that she has cast a fly 161 feet. To me, that is almost unbelievable. She is the author of many books on fly casting and fishing. We were both under contract to Abu Garcia when I first met Joan. One year Abu Garcia brought some of their people from New York to Missouri and we fished on Lake Table Rock, and Joan was one of them. A few years later we fished together on Lake Bull Shoals in Missouri. In fact, Joan had fished in the boat with me the morning that I caught my 11-pound bass. She wasn't with me when I caught the fish, as she and her companion had gone on to the dock while my guide and I stayed out until dark. It was just at dark that I caught the fish under a most unusual circumstance. I have that in

Joan Wulf, women's champion accuracy fly caster, in action

another chapter of this book.

Before I started writing this book, I called Joan to ask her about the history of casting tournaments. She put me in touch with the proper people. I asked her if she had a picture of her in a tournament competition. I wanted to use it as a tribute to what she and others have done to make it possible for me to do what I've done. If you are looking for a fly-fishing school or books on fly-fishing, just write to:

Wulf School of Fly Fishing, P.O. Box 948, Livingston Manor, New York 12758.

But back to the Tournament Trail. It seems difficult to pinpoint the beginning, but it appears to have been in England and Europe. It then spread to the East Coast of the United States. Casting clubs were found in the New York area. Then perhaps Michigan, then Chicago and on west. When I first started my radio and TV shows, Kansas City had a very active club. We did several shows with them and for them. The only names I could remember were Steve Aleshi, Ronnie and Bob Miller, and Fred Conally. I think Steve won several national titles and maybe some international ones. As far as I know, Fred was the first person in this area to use a spinning reel. He promoted spin casting so much that they called him "Spinner Fred."

Late in the summer of 1960, I received a call from Hy Peskin, a *Sports Illustrated* photographer in New York City. He was planning what he called the World Series of Freshwater Fishing. They had already signed fishermen from Sweden, Iceland, Canada, Mexico and Costa Rica. It was to be a ten-day tournament touring the state of Michigan in October. He asked if I would come either as a reporter or as a contestant. He told me of his format. It seemed okay to me, and since I had never fished in the great state of Michigan, I thought it a good opportunity. I told him I would come as a contestant and try to win the thing! There was no entry fee and no purse, just a title and a huge silver trophy. He then asked if he could fly to Kansas City and be a guest on my TV show to promote the idea and also to use my radio show. I'll never forget his words to the television audience. Into the camera, he said, "Ensley, if you don't win this, you can't come back and tell these people that you are the best fisherman in the world." I told him I had never said that! He said, "Maybe not, but all you guys think it." I agreed to go.

My son Smokey and I drove to Dearborn, Michigan, where the tournament was to start. It was to be strange water and a different lake each day. There was no pre-fishing, no guides, no trolling motors and no fish locators, two contestants to each boat to share boat-handling chores. It was tough fishing! We had to handle the boat in the wind and waves and still be competitive with our fishing. We had waves three feet high or more on Lake Michigan. That day my companion gave up at noon. He didn't want to fight the waves and cold. No one was allowed to fish by himself. I was stuck with a problem. I was just barely in first place and needed to stay on the water to be competitive. It just so happened that the big contestant from Sweden had the same problem. So the rules committee allowed us to fish the rest of the day together. He was from Stockholm, and the cold didn't bother him. I wish I could remember his name. I was running the motor, and we hit a big wave and water splashed all over him. He shook himself like a big dog and said, "Harold, isn't this invigorating?" I caught enough fish to remain in first place and eventually win the championship. I was using jigs and won it on walleye and small-mouth bass. It was as tough fishing for ten consecutive days as I had ever experienced in my life. It was especially tough on the contestants from Mexico and Costa Rica.

We fished ten grueling days in nine different lakes, from 8 a.m. until 4 p.m., in a strange new lake each day. We fought the elements, sleet, wind and cold. They would hold an awards banquet each evening, then drive that night to the next location. I don't remember all the lakes and places, but we started at Union Lake near Dearborn. We worked our way through the state to the Upper Peninsula, where we fished Lake Michigan and returned for the last day at Union Lake. It was a tough battle, but I did win it! They had a big awards banquet, and it was attended by dignitaries and their wives from all of the countries represented. Smokey and I then drove back to Kansas City, where we were met with a police escort to the television station, and then rode with Mayor H. Roe Bartle in his limo to the Lincoln Memorial, where in a ceremony Mayor Bartle presented me with keys to the city. As long as Roe Bartle lived, I never received an award that he

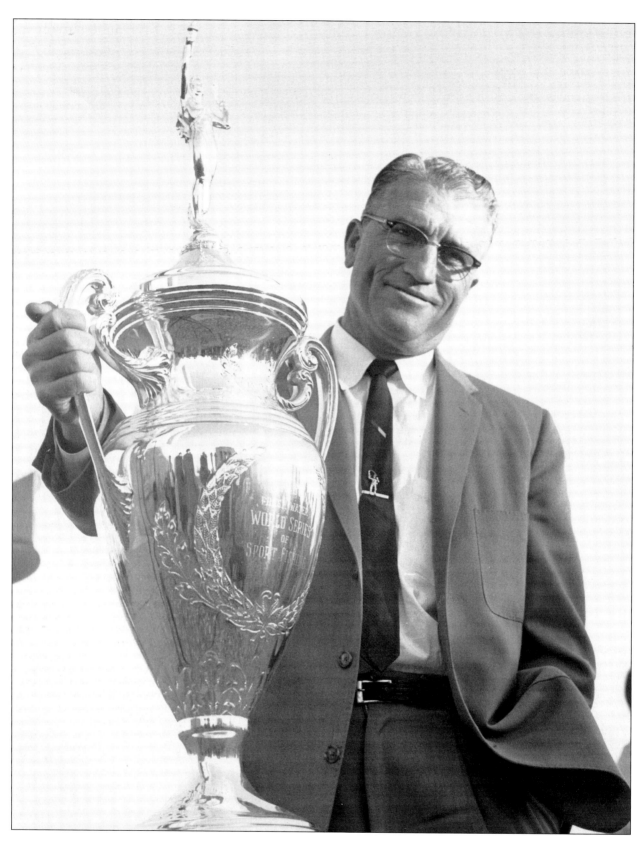

Winner of 1960 World Series of Fresh Water Fishing in Michigan

didn't send me a letter of congratulations.

In winning the first World Series of freshwater Fishing, there was no money involved, only a title and a big silver trophy. A similar situation in today's market would probably mean a million dollars. Hy Peskin started it all, but somehow couldn't make it go. Several years later, Ray Scott picked it up and made it a bass tournament trail and started the bass organization. Ray took it from almost nothing and parlayed it into a multi-million dollar operation. Today, fishing tournaments are all over the country, bass tournaments galore, crappie tournaments, catfish tournaments, you name it — they have it! In today's market a young man may make it a successful career, and countless thousands of fishermen are enjoying fishing in big and little tournaments. While I didn't get any money, it did mean a lot in endorsements and opportunities to fish all over the world.

Catching bass for Universal Pictures news reel

Tarpon and Snook — "The Pride of Costa Rica"

ONE OF THE GREAT THINGS was meeting three fishermen in the series from Costa Rica. Carlos Barrantes, one of the three, owned a fishing camp in the little village of Parisimina, Costa Rica, on the east coast. He invited me down to fish for tarpon and shoot a movie for TV. I had almost forgotten about it.

One day in the spring of 1966 I received a telephone call from a man who had just returned from fishing Costa Rica. He said, "Ensley, you just must break out of your heavy schedule and go down to fish at Carlos' Place. He sent word to invite you down." He also said, "Carlos has the wildest tarpon and snook fishing you ever saw, and he also said this is the perfect time to go."

My son Dusty and I called Carlos, packed our bags and headed south. Then, airline connections were bad. I don't think any American carrier flew to San Jose. We had to fly to Miami, Florida, spend the night, and board Lacsa Airlines early the next morning for San Jose. We had one stopover at Grand Cayman, then on to San Jose. I remember the stop at Grand Cayman. The young man who was steward on the flight insisted that we go into the small airport building. He said that the girl who worked at the counter was the most beautiful woman he had ever seen. We had only a 30-minute break, but to please him we went in with him. She was a pretty girl, but his taste and mine were a little different. I only tell you this part of the story because several years later I needed to use the incident.

We arrived safely in San Jose at their then tiny airport facilities, where Carlos met us. He also owned a tackle shop in San Jose. He said that he was tied up on business, but could possibly join us later in the week to fish. He hired a pilot in a Cessna 180 to fly us over the mountains, across the jungle. We took off from a soccer field. The flight was smooth and the scenery across the mountains, then across the coastal jungle, was absolutely breathtaking! As we passed the huge banana plantation, we could see the outline of the coast and the little village. As we circled the village, I couldn't see an airstrip, so I asked the pilot where we were going to land. He said, "In that cow pasture between the village and the beach. But first I have to buzz the pasture to scare the cattle and horses out of the way. The pasture was about one-quarter mile from the camp. When the plane stopped, I looked out to see my friend, Ted Williams, sloshing through the mud to greet

us. At that time Ted and I worked for Sears. He was excited and said, "Ensley, you have never seen anything like this tarpon fishing." Ted and Vic Dunaway had arrived a day earlier to do a story for *Sports Illustrated*. We had known Ted for some time, but it was our first time to meet Vic. As we sloshed through the mud to the lodge, Ted remarked, "Ensley, I'd give my eye teeth to catch a 25-lb. snook." He had no sooner spoken the words than a barefoot, skinny native boy walked up with a 24-lb. snook which he had taken from the river, off the dock on a hand line.

The accommodations were adequate, the food excellent, but the water situation was not the best. We had to drink distilled water which really was not a problem, but finding a way to shave and shower was a different story. The little village of Parisimina was situated on the banks of the Parisimina River, where it emptied into the Caribbean. We had good native guides, boats and motors that were adequate. The water in the river was clear, and the tarpon came in to spawn by the hundreds. You could catch them right in front of the lodge, but the largest concentration was up a lagoon toward California Creek, and just as the river hits the tidewater. There were six of us in the camp — a couple from Chicago, Ted, Vic, Dusty and me. It was too fantastic to even believe. Words can in no way describe what the fishing was like — hundreds upon hundreds of tarpon, not big ones, mainly running from 50 to 100 lbs. We were using bass equipment and top water lures.

The fishing in the lagoons was safe, but fishing in the shark-infested waters of the cut could be risky. We would anchor in the current of the river and cast toward the spot where the river met the tide. It was difficult because of the current and the sharks to land any size tarpon in this area, but who cared as long as you could get four or five good jumps.

To rest up from tarpon fishing, Dusty and I worked back in the small jungle streams. I thought to myself, this is God's garden, and as long as I live I want to come back! We really didn't fish for snook, but made two movies for our TV show, one with Ted and Vic, and one of the jungle life and scenery.

Ted and Vic left one day before we did. The young native who had guided Ted was my guide the next day. As Ted's plane took off from the cow pasture, with stars in his eyes my guide said, "There goes Teddy Baseball." I don't think you can put it any better than that.

The morning after Ted left, we found the

My biggest snook casting in surf at Costa Rica

My friend, Ron Loveless, from Bentonville, Arkansas, fighting his first tarpon in Costa Rica

Bud Walton, co-founder of Wal-Mart, and I take a breather from snook fishing in Costa Rica

good spot! We anchored in the river in the current just above where the current met the tide, a treacherous and dangerous spot but great for fishing! I honestly believe that you could have dropped almost any top water bait over the side of the boat, let it drift in the current to the edge of the tide a hundred times and had a hundred tarpon hits. It was unbelievable!

Dusty and I fell in love with the place and its people. We have been back every year for 34 years. Changes came, but to me it is still "God's Garden Spot." "Winds of Chance."

The first few years we were there, only the camp had boats and outboard motors; the natives used dugouts. In fact, there was a native in the village who made dugouts. We would see families coming and going on the river and in the lagoons in dugouts. You'd see children in small dugouts with hand lines, fishing for food for the family.

We have many snook stories, but will just bother you with a couple. I first met Sam

Walton at Bentonville, Arkansas, before he and his brother Bud started the Wal-Mart stores. My mother was den mother for Rob, Sam's oldest boy, when he was a Cub Scout. She kept telling me about Sam Walton, who ran a small Ben Franklin store on the square in Bentonville. One day when I was visiting Mom and Dad in Bentonville, Mom wanted to buy some thread and asked me to drive her down to the Ben Franklin store. She introduced me to Sam, and we started talking about quail hunting and our bird dogs. We began hunting together, and he brought his brother Bud along. We had some great hunts and hunted together until his health took him down. Sam didn't fish much, but Bud started making trips with us. He loved to fish and made several trips with us to Costa Rica.

This particular year, my wife Bonnie, Gloria, Dusty's wife, and Bud and his wife Audie made the trip. That one day we came in early at siesta time. Dusty and Gloria started fishing for snook around the treetops that had washed down the river right in front of the camp. Dusty yelled that he had a big snook. Our guide took us over to take a movie of his fish. He landed it and we took it to the dock, which was just 100 yards away. It weighed 32-1/2 lbs., and he had taken it on a top water bait. It was his largest at that time, but in later years he caught a good many that size. Bonnie, who had cancer at that time, walked up to the lodge. It was siesta time, and I mean when that time comes, the guides head for the barn.

Bud and Audie were still casting in the shallow water for snook in front of the camp below the dock. I decided to wait at the dock until they came in. I was standing on the dock and made a cast across a big tree that had washed down the river in a flood. The branches had been gone for a long time. It was a huge tree trunk with its bottom end stuck in the mud, but the main trunk of the tree upstream was just above the water line back toward the top section, which stood out of the water a couple of feet. About three feet from the base of the tree, the water poured over the trunk, maybe 10 inches deep for a couple of feet down the submerged trunk. I wasn't going to just stand there to watch for Bud and Audie. I cast a creek chub darter about 10 feet past the log and worked it slowly in. Nothing

Dusty's 32-1/2-lb. snook taken on top water lure in front of Lodge at Parisimina, Costa Rica

33

happened, but I thought to myself that looks pretty good! I cast across the log for 12 consecutive times. I had about given up, but as always try to make one more cast after I quit. Then I made the 13th cast. I thought, I can't quit on 13, so I made one more cast. Just as the darter came over the log, there was an explosion as a good-sized snook took the lure. Fourteen casts for one fish, but it paid off! "Winds of Chance."

About that time, Bud and Audie came up to the dock. Bud said, "Where did you get that fish?" I told them right there off the dock. That week, every day I caught a snook around that old tree. Even the Saturday we were supposed to fly out and were supposed to have our gear packed very early that morning, I ran to the dock and caught one more snook. The next year the log was gone, having washed away. The snook is a tremendous fish, really an exciting one, especially on top water baits and bass tackle. Dusty and

My biggest guapote taken on buzz bait at California Creek in Parisimina, Costa Rica

I were trying to get a snook picture one year where the Paquari River runs into the Caribbean, some seven miles down the coast. We were casting creek chub darter into the surf to no avail. A little native boy was fishing next to us. He was using a hand line and throwing a creek chub darter into the surf. He had his line wound around a bottle. He would lay the bottle down on the sand for a while and take off 10 or 12 feet of line, whirl the lure as if he were trying to lasso a steer. He was a skinny, scrawny boy about 12 years old. I asked my guide what the kid would do if he hooked a big snook. He said, "He'll land it!" After a bit, I heard him grunt and saw that he had a fish and a good one! I yelled at Dusty to get the camera. That kid was in and out of the water with line running through his hands. Finally our guide went over and gaffed the fish — 27 lbs. You should have seen the grin on that kid's face as he held up the fish for our picture and started home with food for the entire family! I later caught one near there that weighed 25 lbs. and had to work hard with my good equipment to land it. I still can't understand how that skinny kid hooked and landed a 27-lb. snook, barehanded. "Winds of Chance."

Florida Trail

BEFORE OUR START in television, my wife and I drove to West Palm Beach, Florida, for the second time, to check out the fishing and fish with a man named John Oltmer. His brother owned a little bait and tackle store two doors down from the TV station, and through him we met John who invited us down to fish. I don't even remember what time of year it was. The first day he took us out to Lake Okeechobee to bass fish. We had heard about the big bass there and were really excited about it. The first year we had fished mainly for snook. John was a dedicated snook fisherman. He called them "snuke" as in Luke. John had one arm off halfway between his wrist and his elbow, but with a spinning rod he could cast a Zarah Spook and work it like crazy.

We fished the canals at night but didn't accomplish much, but to all you snook fishermen out there, you owe a lot to this man. He was one of the early champions of saving the snook. He worked zealously with others to get snook on the game fish list. The snook is a great fish, and thanks to him and others, they probably were saved from extinction in Florida waters. I told him that I had never caught a sailfish and wanted to try it the last day. He couldn't go, but told me a marina where I could book a trip. I booked the trip for the next day. My wife wanted to go shopping while I fished. She loved to fish but didn't want to get out on the ocean. The next morning I was to be at the dock at 8 a.m. I was all fired up and excited about the prospects and arrived at the dock a little early. No one was there at 8, 8:30 came, then 9, and still nobody. About that time an elderly gentleman from Baltimore showed up. He said he wanted to try for sailfish. I told him that I had booked the trip the day before, but can't seem to find anyone. About that time, the skipper of the charter sauntered up. He said, "I'm sorry I can't take you out, because the rest of the party canceled out." I was really disappointed; I'd been standing around for almost two hours for nothing. I told him that this elderly gentleman wanted to go also. He aid, "I'll take you two out for a part of a day for so much." I don't remember for sure, but I think it was $80. I didn't have a lot of money, but I would go if the other man wanted to go. We went offshore, and it was a beautiful day. The ocean was calm. He aid, "We'll have to fish for some blue runners for bait, which we did with small jigs. I had fun just fishing for bait, but I wondered how I got into a deal like that. By this time, our outing was pretty well shot. We were trolling with live blue runners. The guy with me said, "I don't care if I catch anything or not, I just get a thrill out of being here." He then caught one of the biggest amberjacks I ever saw. I thought, isn't that the way it goes? I'm just dying to catch a fish and can't! He doesn't care and caught one! I don't get too excited about trolling, but that was the way it was done. I decided to reel the line up to see if the blue runner was still alive. I had it almost to the surface when I saw the sail coming. That sail took that blue runner and headed for the deep blue yonder. It was stripping off line like crazy. I said to the skipper, "Tell me when to set the hook." He said, "Let it go a little longer because it was a good-sized blue runner." Then he said, "Now let him have it!" I did and that beautiful fish came out of the water three or four times. It was really a thrill! We landed the fish and I told him to release it.

The Atlantic sail do not compare in size to the Pacific sail, but this one was about average for those waters. He said, "We're not going to release it. We're going to take it to the dock. That's the first sail I've had in my boat for six weeks!" "Winds of Chance."

Since then I've fished for sail around the Pearl Islands of Panama, the west coast of Costa Rica and around Cozumel on the Gulf, but I'll always remember that day at West Palm Beach. The next year John invited us back to bass fish in Lake Okeechobee. I had caught lots of bass in the impounded waters of the Midwest and had several in the 9-lb. class and one 11 lbs., but I'd heard all about the 15 or 16-lb. bass in Florida.

One winter my wife and I drove to check out the big bass with John. The first morning we went out, John told me we would have to use big shiners. While he put the boat in the lake, he told me to buy some shiners from the marina bait shop. He said for me to buy three. I thought, man, I wouldn't start out with just one apiece, so I bought six! When they told me they were seventy-five cents apiece, I nearly fainted. At that time in our part of the world, you could buy a dozen minnows for little or nothing. I wasn't flush with money, times were still pretty tough, but I splurged and bought six shiners. We were at the south end of the lake. John's boat wasn't the fanciest in the world, but sufficient for our needs. We motored out to one of his pet spots where he anchored the boat and we started fishing. The sun was shining, but a front had just moved in to chill the air. Bonnie and I had left the cold of Kansas City to enjoy some of the great Florida weather and really didn't dress properly for the drop in temperature. We sat there for some two hours with nothing. Bonnie said, "Honey, I've had enough of this shiner fishing, why can't I cast a top water bait?" I told her that I didn't even bring a tackle box and asked John if he still had that Gilmore Jumper I had given him years before. It was a stick bait made in Arkansas and one of our favorite top water baits. John dug around in his tackle box and found it. He said he had never used it, and the hooks had rusted pretty bad. I tied it on for Bonnie, but cast it out in an open spot in the grass to see how it worked. There was an explosion as a nice bass hit it, but I missed it. I handed the rod to Bonnie and asked John if he had any top water baits. He had some baby Zarah Spooks and gave me one. We each tied on a Zarah. He pulled anchor and started paddling the boat around through the weeds and grass. We would cast into any open spot we could find. Bonnie was just catching bass, one after another, mostly in the 4 to 7-1/2-lb. range. John was catching them,

Robert Fuller, star of "Wagon Train," "Laramie" and "Emergency," with Florida bass

too. I couldn't get a strike! In those days, we kept the bass. Bonnie and John had a stringer of fish. I had caught nothing! Bonnie was getting tired and said, "Let's call it a day." John was putting the stringer of fish in the boat. Bonnie handed me her rod with the Jumper on it. I always try to make one more cast after I quit. I saw a little opening in the grass and cast the Jumper into the spot. The water exploded. I said, "I finally got one." Would you believe it got off before I got it to the boat? John and Bonnie gave me a big laugh, but it had been a great day! Sadly, we never got to fish with John again, but the memories still linger. As the years rolled by, we had many wonderful trips to Florida from the Keyes at Islamorada, up the west coast and a ways up the east coast. A fishing buddy of mine, Fred Morrison, moved to Marco Island and sold real estate in the development of that area. He asked me to come down and explore the fishing in that region. We had some great trips there and shot many TV shows in the Thousand Island region. We had some great bass fishing trips near the little town of Okeechobee.

In a celebrity tournament at Lake Table Rock in Missouri, one year they paired me with Robert Fuller. Bob starred as scout on Wagon Train and Laramie. He also starred in the series, "Emergency." We had a good time buzzing for bass on Table Rock. He said that sometime he would like to go Florida to catch a big bass. A few years later, I met a Western Auto dealer, Bill Coble, at a dealer show in Jackson, Mississippi. He was from Tennessee, but also had a place in Okeechobee in Florida. He invited Dusty and me down to bass fish. That summer I called him and told him I needed to do a TV show wading in Okeechobee. Dusty and I flew down and had a great trip, no bass over 8 lbs., but lots of fish. I told him about Bob Fuller wanting a big bass. He said, "When can you bring him down?" The next year I called Bob and asked him if he would like to meet Dusty and me in Florida to catch a big bass. Dusty and I drove down to the little town of Okeechobee where this guy lived. We picked Fuller up at the airport in Miami, and drove to the lake. We had three or four days of great fishing, wading and casting buzz baits. Fuller made it fine until he saw an alligator. I'm sorry that I cannot remember the name of our host. He was a good fisherman. He was a good fisherman, about 6 ft., 5 in. tall, and though not a young man, he was strong. With a rope around his waist, he pulled the boat behind him and cast as he waded. When Bob saw that alligator, he was in the boat in short order. I wasn't as worried about the alligator as I was the cottonmouths. It was a great experience, and Bob caught a good bass. "Winds of Chance."

In all my wonderful memories of fishing in Florida, one of my most embarrassing fishing experiences came about in Florida. We were shooting movies for our show at God's Lake in Manitoba, fishing for brook trout on God's River, and lake trout, northern pike and walleye on the lake. One night after dinner a nice-looking young man from another group came to me. He said, "They tell me you are catching lots of fish. This fishing is strange to us; can you tell us what to do?" I said, "I can, but you probably won't listen!" I gave him some of our Reapers and told him how we fished them. The next night he came and asked me if I ever fished in Florida. I said, "Yes, almost every year since 1950." He asked me if I ever had ever heard of Amelia Island Plantation. I told him no

Big kings off Amelia Island — Jack Healan and Wilson Tennille

and asked him where it was. He told me and, believe me, I'm still embarrassed! I told him that the years that we drove down we went down the west coast. He said that Amelia Island Plantation was a famous golf and tennis operation, but they also had a fishing program. He said, "Why don't you call our fishing pro, Terry LaCoss, and come down to fish. He said, "Better still, I'll have Terry call you." He handed me his card. He was Jack Healan, president of Amelia Island Plantation. Terry LaCoss called me and we arranged a trip. We have been down every year since. It's one of the garden spots of North America, whether you play golf or tennis, fish or just enjoy being in a beautiful spot with beautiful people. I've fished with a lot of guides on four continents, but you won't find a nicer person or a better guide than Terry. That's how it happened. Jack and I met almost 3,000 miles from Amelia. "Winds of Chance."

I'm still embarrassed that I hadn't heard of Amelia Island Plantation. I found a new home with some great people. Thank you, Jack Healan.

Terry LaCoss and his son Terry

Live TV Was Fun

LIVE TV was fun, but also a challenge every time you stepped in front of the camera. If you made a mistake, it went out over the air. Early on we used a boom mike. A stage hand would operate the boom to keep the mike in front of the one speaking. I remember one night while we were doing the show, Vic Anderson was handling the boom mike. I had been seated and decided to stand up to demonstrate something. Vic was so engrossed with what I was saying that he didn't move the mike. When I stood up, I hit my head on the mike and it nearly knocked me out. All you could do was laugh, rub your head and go on. I'm sure that in doing a 30-minute live show 52 weeks a year for 22 years, I made every mistake you could make in front of the camera. Taping a TV show in comparison to doing a live show can cover a multitude of mistakes.

Years ago at a tackle show in Atlanta I ran into Roland Martin. He told me he had a young man who wanted to meet me. It was Rolando Wilson. In the course of our conversation Rolando said, "Roland tells me you did a live fishing and hunting show for 52 weeks a year and are now doing shows 13 weeks a year." He also said, "I couldn't do a live show every week."

Of course, we didn't have the equipment to work with that we have today. I started out using a small Revere magazine-loading movie camera to shoot the work in the field. It was a turret camera with three lenses. You had to use a light meter and set the lenses for light and distance, no automatic eye. I started out shooting Eastman 16 mm color Kodachrome Two. We would go out on the shoot and bring the film in Sunday night, take it to the Calvin Co. for processing early Monday morning. They would have it ready by mid-afternoon. The projectionist and I would edit it and have it on the air at 9:30 p.m. It would make for a wild day. Sometimes we would get our film in by Friday morning and not be so rushed. Our second cameras were Eastman K. 100 with the same lenses. In its day it was a great camera. It used 100-ft. rolls of film and had a 40-ft. wind, but you had to set the lens for distance and light. You should try it sometime, with a man in a boat at five feet and the fish jumping out there at 30 feet. It took some doing! We stepped up to Canon Scoopic, a new battery-operated camera with an automatic eye. Almost everyone else is using sound now, but we prefer silent film and voice-over narration.

But getting back to the studio production live, we had an excellent crew all those

Editing film the old-fashioned way, over the shoulder of my projectionist, Jack Von Englen

years, men who were dedicated to making me look good. I wouldn't feel right not to mention my television crew at the CBS affiliate, KCMO-TV in Kansas City, who did so much to keep my show going. It seems trite, but it became almost a "family affair." They seemed to be as anxious to do my show every week as I did. Some of them have passed on. Ken Heady, Steve Mills and Harry Francis were my first directors. Bill Kerwin was my first announcer. Then Don Warnock became my announcer in 1964 and is still with me in 2001. Ken Young and Leo Kallenberger were my camermen. Ralph Friend and Jack Von Englen and a man whose name I do not recall were the projectionists. Marion Honker, Bob Bowen, Alvin Young and Clem Meyers were the audio and video technicians. Bill Junkins, Floyd Finch and Bob Taylor were the stage hands. This was my crew for 22 years. Then I went to National Syndication over KSN-TV, the NBC affiliate in Wichita. There, Don Davis was my director for about ten years, and Buck Bonner finished the remaining 16 years. To all you men, my sincere thanks for your great work and for a very special friendship.

We were constantly searching for program material. Many times people would call me about a big fish that they had taken and wanted to show it on my television show. You just can't imagine what this led to. I started having guests come on for maybe three or five minutes, depending on how much time I had aside from my film. Three to five minutes goes pretty fast, and I know that sometimes they were disappointed that they didn't get more time. I finally reached the point where I would tell them my program was pretty full, but would they bring their fish in for 60 seconds of air time. They would come in and I would give them five minutes, and they would be happy. I remember in 1961

Kansas was celebrating their 100 years of statehood. They invited Smiley Burnett to appear for the big celebration in Kansas City, Kansas. They called me and asked if I would have him on my show to promote the Centennial. I was thrilled with the opportunity, for I had used his song, "Well, I might have gone fishin' " for my radio theme song. Steve Mills, my director in the studio, asked me how much time I wanted to give Smiley. I said, "Five minutes." We moved a piano into the set. Smiley was so great that we used him for the entire 30 minutes. He played and sang the fishing songs he had written and used with Gene Autry, "Well, I might have gone fishin'," and "Catfish took a look at my worm," and others. It was just pure fun! They asked me if I would take him fishing while he was in town. We arranged to pick him up at his hotel at 4:30 a.m. during a terrible thunderstorm. The rain eased off and we drove out to Peculiar, Missouri. My friends, Buddy and Denny Baier, owned a shooting preserve and had just built a new 37-acre lake. We caught and released a lot of bass. I think maybe it was the first time Smiley had caught a bass on top water bait. "Winds of Chance." He had a great day, and as I let him off at his hotel, he said, "May the good Lord take a likin' to you, and don't let me lose track of you!" As long as he lived, he sent me a Christmas card every year.

I had fun and my crew had fun! Bob Taylor, Bill Junkins and Floyd Finch, our regular stage hands, were always doing something! Taylor was something else. One night as I was doing the show I kept hearing somebody whispering. It was Taylor behind a cameraman with a small fish bowl with a couple of small goldfish swimming around in it. He had a short stick and a piece of string, making out like he was fishing. He would whisper, "Boy, is my fishin' fever high!" Each day I would get ready to close out the show, I would say, "When I get to thinking about those big Arctic char at the Tree River, it gets my fishin' fever up. If anyone wants to know where Ol' Harold is, tell them the last you saw of him he was headin' out in that red Country Sedan. He's gone fishin','' and I would put my "gone fishin" " sign on the mantle of my fireplace. The stage hands were supposed to put my sign at the edge of the fireplace. One night I went through my close and reached for my sign — it wasn't there! I turned to the camera and laughed and said, "Maybe I've not gone fishin'!"

One other time I heard Taylor whispering; I looked back of the cameraman, and there stood Bob with a fly swatter in his hand whispering, "Harold, I'm fly fishing!"

No one book is large enough to cover everything that has happened down through the years. Some people called in from Excelsior Springs, Missouri, about a pet St. Bernard that performed magic and wanted to show some of its tricks on my show. They brought the dog in. It was a beautiful creature and seemed so gentle. As we went on the air, I wanted Steve, my director, to get a shot of the dog's head. The dog had turned its head to the side. I put my hands up on each side of its head, and without warning the dog grabbed my right arm just above the wrist, tore my shirt and the flesh of my arm. The wound started to bleed, but we just kept on with the show. It wasn't a serious wound, but I still have a scar there. "Winds of Chance."

Me, hanging "Gone Fishing" sign, to close my TV show

The coon hunters were constantly after me, saying you do shows on quail hunting, duck and goose hunting, why don't you film a coon hunt? I told them that if they could figure out a way to follow those dogs in the dark, and keep up with them, I'd do it. Finally I got a call from Sedalia, Missouri. Someone there had a world champion coon dog and wanted to show it. I had what I thought was a brilliant idea. I had a friend, Sam Williams, who had a minnow farm in southwest Missouri. He was also my reporter for the cowskin arm of Grand Lake in Oklahoma. His wife had a pet coon. I asked Sam if he and his wife would bring that live pet coon in for my show. I would have her lead the coon across the floor of the set, and they would then see if this champion dog trailed it and barked. We would not let the dog harm the coon. Everyone agreed that it might work. Sam and his wife brought the coon in. We let her put the coon through some of its tricks. She led the coon across the floor. Then the man with the champion dog put his dog down on the trail where the coon had walked. Nothing happened; the dog didn't even sniff. This all took place on the air. The man with the dog said, "My hunting buddy's out in his car with a young dog. We brought the young dog in, and when it smelled where the coon had walked, pandemonium broke loose. The dog made a run toward Mrs. Williams and the coon. It scared the coon, and it jumped out of her arms and ran up the boom mike and perched there. The studio was just one small unit. You never heard such a racket in your life. I was trying to get my director to get a shot of the coon perched on the boom mike. I knew we were running out of time. All he got was the seat of the hunter's pants. By the time we got things sorted out, it was time to go off the air. "Winds of Chance."

I received a telephone call from a lady in Clinton, Missouri. She told me that this 80-some-year-old doctor had killed a trophy buck deer, and because of the age and size of the deer, she wondered if he could show the head and skin on my show. I told her that my program was pretty well filled, but if he wanted to bring it in for a few minutes, it was okay. She called me back and told me that they would plan to be there. I learned early on when interviewing someone not to ask a lot of questions beforehand, because they would be worrying about what they had said the first time. I would rather have them come out with it fresh. They arrived at the studio in time to go on the air. It was a real trophy. They had cut off the deer's head as they skinned it, so they had the deer's head and skin intact. They moved it across the floor, and I reckon a thousand ticks came out of its skin. I didn't count them, but there were a bunch! When it came time to have him on the air, I said, "The good doctor's wife called me about his trophy deer. He said, "That wasn't my wife; that was my nurse." I asked how long he had been hunting. He said, "Since I was a baby!" I said, "What did you hunt when you were a baby?" He said, "Nourishment!" He was a great old man and was proud to show his deer. My crew learned to stay loose.

A farmer called from Hiawatha, Kansas, some 100 miles northwest of Kansas City. He told me that he had caught a big catfish and would like to put it on my show. I asked him what kind of shape the fish was in. He told me that it was still alive and he had it in a small horse tank. He told me that they had weighed it, and it weighed 72 lbs. My show was full, but I told him that if he could bring it in alive, to be on for just a few minutes, okay. He told me that they would bring it in. They brought it in a small horse tank in the pickup truck, which fortunately was a Ford. At that time the Ford Dealers of the Mid-west sponsored my show. We had him drive the truck right onto the set, and we started the show. After the first commercial when he and the stage hands brought the fish up out of the tank, it started thrashing and flopping. It splashed water all over the set, me and the cameramen and their cameras. It is difficult to handle a fish that size, and it gave us all a good soaking. Live television, you go right on with the show. "Winds of Chance."

A few weeks later I received a telephone call from a fishing buddy of mine, Dewey Scott, from Osceola, Missouri. One of his friends had taken a 119-lb. blue cat on a trotline. They had weighed it for the record books. It was officially recognized as a new world record for blue catfish. I think that this record has been broken since then. They had iced it and were saving it to put on my show if I wanted it. Dewey told me that they didn't let anyone release a picture and story of it until I had a chance to put it on my show. Again I had a full program, but certainly would not pass this story without showing the fish. They brought the fish, and we showed it on the air. It was a tremendous fish, and every-one loved seeing it. "Winds of Chance."

Most of our shows were voice-over movies that we shot in the field, but it was also for people to show off their big fish. Speaking of big fish, I was invited to fish for alligator gar in the White River in southern Arkansas. When you tell people about alligator gar, they immediately think of the long nose gar, commonly found in the rivers and lakes through-out the country. The alligator gar is entirely different. It has a head shaped just like an

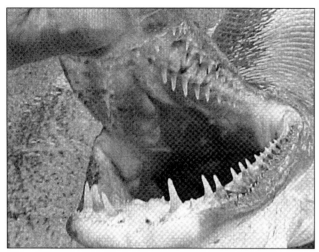

Missouri alligator gar taken by David Smith in Mississippi River

alligator and grows to enormous size, possibly up to 200 lbs. The first one I caught weighed 118 lbs., and the second trip we caught one that weighed 122 lbs. We froze it at a cold storage plant, wrapped it in a tarp with dry ice and brought it to Kansas City. We showed it on television and then displayed it in the Sears store at 15th and Cleveland. It created quite a stir. It looked like some prehistoric monster.

When Nick Kahler, owner of General Shows in Minneapolis, heard about it, he called me to see if I would help him get one to have mounted to go with the rest of his display of fish. We made the necessary arrangements, drove to DeWitt, Arkansas, and fished for three days. It was terribly hot, but we managed to get Nick his fish. At one time the White River was a tributary of the Red River, but the year after a flood it cut a channel into the Mississippi. We fished all the way down to the Mississippi, even fished for a short time in the Mississippi. For me it was a big thrill. "Winds of Chance."

It wasn't always fish that we put on one show. A fishing buddy of mine, Jim Higgins, a deputy sheriff at Holden, Missouri, called me about a man who had raised some big watermelons and wanted to show them on TV. Jim told me that the man couldn't come to be on the show, but Jim would bring them in. The Yankees were in town for a series with the A's. Bobby Richardson, Yankee second baseman, and Tony Kubeck, the shortstop, had been fishing with me that day. I asked them if they would mind being guests on my show, adding that they could bring on these two 90-lb. watermelons. They brought them in on a cart. I had each of them hold up a melon. They did, and I heard that Casey Stengel and the rest of the Yankees were watching at the hotel, and Casey nearly fainted for fear Bobby and Tony would hurt their backs. I don't know if that story was true, but I know that Bobby went two for four, and Tony went two for five the next day. After the show someone called in that his dad had a 100-lb. melon and would like to show it the next week. His name was Wendt, and he had a big truck garden in the Kaw Valley across the Kaw River near Bonner Springs, Kansas, and a few short miles from Kansas City. The next week they brought the 100-lb. melon to the show, and we put it on for a few minutes.

Can you believe it, a 119-lb blue cat and a 122-lb. alligator gar and a 100-lb. watermelon on live television? "Winds of Chance."

Television and radio were fun! I wanted viewers and listeners to feel like we were members of their family and that they were part of our family, simply to share what took place as a family affair. We developed a grapevine of helpers all over the world. People would call and suggest ideas and places that would make good program material. I owe so much to so many people. No way, in one book could we cover all the things that came by "Winds of Chance."

For many years, we did programs from Bus Hartley's fish hatchery near Kingman, Kansas, which is about an hour drive west of Wichita. As far as I know, Bus Hartley and a professor Kansas State University pioneered the hatching of channel catfish and also fish farming. I really don't know when or how our paths first crossed, but we developed a friendship that lasted until he passed on. Bus was one of the great minds to come along in my generation with regard to hatching, rearing and stocking farm ponds and man-made reservoirs. Bus and his wife Irene had four children, three boys and a girl. Wallace, the oldest, then Billy, and a pair of twins, Jerry and his sister Janet. The boys have followed in their dad's footsteps in a real professional way. They were all a great help to us. We have fished and hunted at their place and did many programs from there. I'll always remember the first time I fished with Wallace, the oldest boy. We were fishing in one of the rearing ponds. Wallace caught three or four fish before I had hardly gotten started. I was shooting a movie of the kid fishing, and his dad came over and said something to him. After his dad left, I asked him what his dad had told him. He said that he told him to slow up, that I probably wouldn't like it if he caught more fish than I did. I really got a kick out of that! The years wore on; we had lots of fun together.

In 1973 Bus was named National Fish Farmer of America at their national convention. Bus called me after one of the conventions and told me that he needed a favor. He said that he attended their national convention in New Orleans and was in a cafe when a young man came up to him and started a conversation. He told Bus that he had seen an outdoor TV show of Bus and his fish hatchery and wondered if there was any way we could get that man to come to Florida and do a show on the Seminole Indians at their fish hatchery and fish farming ranch near Okeechobee. They also had a processing plant to dress fish and sell them. He asked Bus if he knew me well enough to get it done. Bus told him that we had been good friends for a long time and that he would call me. He had the man's telephone number and said that he would consider it a personal favor if I would call him. I called the man to check on the possibilities. In the course of our conversation I told him that I would be honored to do a story on their operation on one condition, that one day I be allowed to shoot a show of fishing with their chief. I told him that I had done a story fishing with the Apache chief and wanted to do one with theirs. Their chief, like Ben Oliver of the Apaches, was an elected chief. He agreed to arrange it and told me that their chief's name was Mike Tigre, and we could do the fishing on Lake Okeechobee, out of Buckhorn Marina. My wife and I drove down to the town of Okeechobee and covered the story. They were doing a fine job with their operation of fish farming and processing the fish for the market. I don't know if they are still in business. You may have gotten some of their fish at a supermarket.

Some people look down on what they term lowly catfish as being a good fish to eat. I'm a little partial to crappie and walleye, but I'm here to tell you that I think fillets from farm-raised catfish are as fine as any you ever tried. If you go to the supermarket to buy catfish, just be sure to buy fillets. For almost 20 years we have been doing demonstrations in the Wal-Mart stores, teaching people how to take care of their fish and how to fillet fish so there will be no odor. Lots of people, especially women, don't like the smell of fish in the house when they cook it. My wife used to make me cook fish in the garage until I learned how to fillet and cook the fish with no odor. In fact, there is no odor in the fish's flesh. In fact, there is no odor in the flesh of anything God created — man, beast, fowl or fish. People put the odor in with the way they clean the fish. We would do these demonstrations in the sporting goods department and also help people select fishing tackle. When Wal-Mart started their super centers and were selling meats and produce, one of the stores where I was demonstrating came up with the idea of cooking fish in the department while I was filleting fish. I think it was Charlie Bezoni's district at Jefferson City, Missouri. I told them that it would not be possible to use the crappie fillets, but that they sold farm-raised catfish at the meat counter. They brought some farm-raised catfish fillets, the demo lady cut them in small pieces and dipped them in buttermilk and rolled them in a fish mix we have on the market and deep-fried them. I learned a lesson; those catfish fillets are as good as anything I ever tasted, and the public agreed. It proved so successful we started doing it at all the super centers where I gave demonstrations. "Winds of Chance."

Had Bus Hartley not attended the fish farmers convention in New Orleans, he would not have met the man from the Seminoles, and I would never have known about the Seminole fish farming and processing. I fished with Mike Tigre, their chief, for two days on Lake Okeechobee. We caught some nice fish and had a good time. Late in the afternoon of the last day, he asked me if I would like some pictures of a big alligator. He told me where this big alligator generally stayed and took me there. The alligator was sunning himself on the sand at the water's edge. He eased the boat in close for my shots as the big rascal slithered into the water. It was the largest alligator I ever saw, in captivity or in the wild. Mike knew where that creature stayed, as though it were his own pet. What a thrill it was for me to be there and get the pictures. "Winds of Chance."

As I mentioned beforehand, our choice of programs came from many unusual sources. Max Sklower, the general manager of the ABC affiliate in Albuquerque, New Mexico, called me about doing shows about the trout fishing facilities on the Vermejo Ranch near Santa Fe. I've always had a special feeling about the West and was always fascinated about its history. I flew to Albuquerque to meet Max, who then drove us to the ranch. He got me a brief rundown about the ranch at that time, as I remember. It had been a Spanish land grant, and I think it covered a million acres of land. It has since been purchased by Ted Turner. At that time they had many man-made lakes stocked with trout. Max was using a bubble and a fly. He had never seen anyone throw a crappie jog. We caught a lot of nice trout and made two shows. Max did a great job for us, using our show in that part of the West.

Besides being a fisherman, I was a jogger, so for all my jogging friends, I had a chance to run in New Mexico.

A few years later they had me back to do some shows on the Chama cattle ranch, near Chama, New Mexico. The fishing was similar to that at Vermejo. It was another good trip.; I never had a chance to fish with Max again, but a few years later I received a call from him. He had been trout fishing in Montana on the Missouri River. He was all excited about it and suggested that I go to do a show there. He told me about a friend of his in the television business, Thor Myhre. Thor had retired and bought a home on the Missouri near Craig, Montana. Max had told Thor about my work and me, and he also told this guide about me and my TV show, and that I should call them.

I have been a Lewis and Clark buff since high school days. I had fished up the Missouri from Yankton, South Dakota, on to Oahu at Pierre. Then Sakakawea above Garrison Dam. I was thrilled with the opportunity to make another stretch of the trail. However, I could not in my mind picture the Missouri River with rainbow trout. For over 40 years we had driven on highways along the mighty Mo, from St. Louis through Kansas City, St. Joseph, Omaha, Nebraska, Sioux City, Iowa, and on to South Dakota. Trout in that muddy river? No way!

We made the necessary arrangements. I flew to Great Falls where Myhre met me and drove me to his house. It was a beautiful home, right on the banks of the Missouri River, and the water there was as clear as a mountain stream. According to history, Lewis and Clark and their party had camped on the point across the river from their house.

That first night I awakened sometime after midnight and looked out the bedroom window. The moon was shining as the water moved silently along. What a great moment! I almost had to pinch myself to be sure I was not dreaming!

The next day I fished with Thor and his son-in-law whose name I can't recall. He was at that time Attorney General of Montana and loved to fish. They were fly fishermen and were using a top water mouse. They would cast to the edge of the grass along the riverbank and work the bait out a couple of feet. The trout were feeding close to the grass, and I suppose if the mouse fell in the water it didn't make it very far. We didn't fish a long stretch of the river, but the next day we were scheduled to drive some distance up the river and float down. I was to fish with a special guide and they were to fish together. We had dinner that night in the little town. They invited the guide to eat with us and sort of make plans for the next day. I told the guide how thrilled I was to be there to fish. I told him that from the rocks along the riverbank I had shot some movies of trout surfacing after Mayflies, and that at one time I had four rainbows in one picture!

He said, "Tomorrow I'll show you Mayflies hatching in such numbers that it looks like a snowstorm. I'll show you places where over 100 trout are rising at one time."

When we got home, Thor asked me what I thought about it. I said, "If he can do what he said he could do, we are in for a heck of a day!"

The next morning we pulled the boats up the river some distance and started drifting down. I never saw so many Mayflies in my life! I got movies of them, so thick that it did look like a snowstorm! Thor and his son-in-law started ahead of us, and we never saw them again until that night. I don't think our guide wanted any other boat near us when he was fishing. I have never in my life seen that many rainbows surfacing at one time. He would wade some and fish from the boat some. He was as good as you'll ever see, catching rainbow on a fly, and released them all. I didn't fish, but just filmed him at his work. However, I asked him if he would get some pictures of me, just to show that I was there. I fished with him one more day and flew home. It had been another great trip! It was a fabulous fishing spot, and beautiful, on the mighty Missouri, and I don't think it will ever be fished out. In three days we were on the river we only saw three other boats.

In the late '60s I received a call from North Dakota inviting me to come to their state to fish in Lake Sakakawea. I was thrilled at the thought of another stretch of water on the Missouri River along the Lewis and Clark trail. In fact, the lake was named after the Native American girl who guided Lewis and Clark through several miles of their trip along the Missouri. The lake was a big one formed by Garrison Dam. I had heard of its reputation for big northern pike and walleye. We were to fish out of a marina at the upper end of the lake, operated by Mark Slater and his wife. Mark was a former professional football player. He played offensive center for the Philadelphia Eagles when they won the Super Bowl. I'm not sure that Mark had fished much at that time, but he and his wife did a good job with the marina.

I had met a young man at a Wal-Mart store promotion. He impressed me with his work attitude. He loved to fish and told me that if I ever needed a helper he would like to go with me on one of my trips, provided he could get off work. The store manager was very gracious and let him off. It was almost a two-day drive for us, and we arrived at the marina the second day about mid-afternoon. It was my first trip across that state. North Dakota has a vast, wild beauty about it. I am amused when I hear people talk about the dullness of traveling across the plains states. To me, the states of Oklahoma, Kansas, Nebraska and the Dakotas have a beauty of their own. The same God that created the grandeur of the mountain states created the beauty of the plains.

I'm not sure that we fished that first evening, but the second day Mark had a guide for us. He was a local middle-aged former oil field worker. While working during a thunderstorm gauging an oil storage tank, lightning struck the tank. The explosion blew him off the tank and he was badly burned, but managed to survive, and after his recovery he started guiding on the lake for Mark. He had become a successful walleye guide and made a special kind of trolling rig to use with a spinner and a minnow.

We fished hard for two days but didn't get enough walleye for a show. We were using the guide's lure and method, a thing we try to do on waters new to us. It is a matter of respect for their judgment. Wind can be a factor on that lake as it is everywhere. However, we had been blessed with two nice days. The third day it was almost dead calm. We had not done well and were coming back to the marina. As we started across a big bay, I saw a boat right out in the middle of the bay. I asked our guide what those people were doing right in the middle of the lake. He told me there was a shallow spot out there. He called it a sunken island and that the fellows were probably fishing for sauger. I suggested we go see what they were doing, and we eased our boat up to them. They had anchored their boat and were fishing with minnows. We asked them about their success. They told us that it had been slow, but that they had caught a few nice saugers. We asked them about the depth of the water. If I remember correctly, they said that it was 15 to 30 feet deep and that depth covered an areas of several acres. I asked them if we would be in their way if we backed off a ways and started fishing. They were very nice and said, "Help yourselves, there is lots of room here for all of us." We thanked them and had our guide move away from them a good bit so that we would not interfere with them. Our guide anchored the boat in about 20 feet of water and we started fishing. I told him that we wanted to try our method of fishing with a lure I had designed and used successfully everywhere we had fished for walleye. We were using ultra-light spinning gear and 4-lb. test line. I tied on one of our reapers and gave one to my companion. The guide said he would just watch us for a while. In short order we caught seven or eight nice sauger, and the guide decided he wanted to try one. He did, and the first drop down he caught a 3-1/2-lb. sauger. He couldn't believe it. It was getting late and we needed to get back to the marina. On the way back to the dock, I asked the young fellow with me if he thought we could fish one more day and drive all the next night to get me back in time for my TV show. He jumped at the chance.

The next morning early we had our guide take us back to that spot. In a matter of four or five hours we each caught our limit of sauger from 2-1/2 to 4 lbs., made our movie and headed for Kansas City. If we hadn't seen those guys fishing right in the middle of the lake, we would have gone home empty-handed. "Winds of Chance."

Before going to Lake Sakakawea, the lure company suggested that I take a lot of reapers, in case we caught fish on them. Maybe the marina would buy them and get them started in that area. They threw a couple dozen cards of them in my station wagon. The guide told Mark of our success on the saugers with the reaper. I asked Mark if he wanted to buy the reapers I had with me. He said, "No, it might ruin my minnow and leach business." So we drove back to Kansas City with enough material for one TV show.

Two years later I received a call from Mark telling me that they were having a run of big walleye, and he'd like me to come up and do a movie for television. I called a fishing buddy of mine, Blair Flynn, who lived at Overbrook, Kansas. He and I had hunted and fished together for years, and he just might be one of the best all-around outdoorsmen I've ever met. He helped me with a lot of pictures for television down through the years. His wife was extremely ill with cancer, as was mine. In fact, she lost her battle, and a year later my wife lost hers.

We wanted to do something nice for Blair, so I asked him to go with me. We drove to Fargo, North Dakota, spent the night, and drove on to Sakakawea. Mark had arranged for two of his fishing buddies to help us. They had been catching numbers of walleye in the 8 to 10-pound class, but they'd been trolling crank baits. I told Mark I didn't want a picture trolling, and I was sure we could catch some fish casting with reapers. Mark didn't think so, nor did the other two guys. I said, "Mark, all I ask is for you to locate the fish for us." We put Blair in the boat with his two buddies, and Mark and I fished together. It was a beautiful day with no wind. Blair and I rigged up with reapers. I think I was using 1/4 oz.-3" and Blair was using 1/2-oz.-5" reapers. Mark looked at me and asked what weight line I had. I told him 4-lb. test. I think Blair had 6-lb. line. I started to cast, and Mark said, "You'll get that thing hung up in the rocks!" But I made the cast and let the reaper sink to the bottom. As I lifted the reaper off the bottom, I felt pressure and thought to myself, Mark is right; I'm hung up on my first cast. Then I felt the fish shake his head. Blair had one of my cameras in his boat nearby. I yelled at him to come and start filming. After a good fight, Mark netted the fish, a 7-1/2-pound walleye. He said, "I still don't believe it!" A few casts later, Blair said he had a fish, so Mark and I went there to film the fight. They landed Blair's fish, which was larger than the one I caught. I told Mark we needed to go to shore, as I wanted to dress the walleye and put them on ice. He said, "Why, we'll lose the school of fish!" I told him that was all right; I needed to show the TV audience how to take better care of the fish they plan to eat.

For years I had demonstrated in Wal-Mart stores using crappie or bluegill, put them on ice without dressing them and traveling to different stores; we had to keep the fish for several days. We would keep the fish alive, and we'd put them on ice with about four inches of crushed ice in the bottom of the cooler, then a layer of fish, a layer, of ice, etc. It had been working, but I got to thinking that maybe that was wrong. I got the telephone number of the fish market in Kansas City and dialed it. A man answered, "Fish market, may I help you?" I said, "Yes, this is Harold Ensley,' and before I could say more, he said, "Oh, you couldn't catch any fish so you want to buy some!" I said, "Do you know who I am?" He said, "Harold, I've watched you since I was a little boy, what do you need?"

"I need information! I've been keeping crappie and bluegill without dressing for up to a week, putting them on ice and keeping the water drained off." He said, "Harold, you are right on target! You can do that with the sunfish family, bass, bluegill and crappie. But walleye and channel cat should be cleaned immediately and put on ice." I wanted to show this, and that's one reason I came up to catch some walleye. We went to the shore, gutted and grilled the two walleye and put ice in the cavities of both fish and covered them with crushed ice.

We went back out to fish and, needless to say, we lost the school of walleye. Mark said, "Didn't I tell you what would happen?" and I said, "Yes, but this part was more important to me than catching more fish."

We proceeded to fish that day and two more, caught lots of nice walleye and sauger.

Mark even put on a reaper and put a leach on the reaper and caught fish. We made two movies for television and had three great days of fishing.

We were getting ready to leave, and Mark said, "Did you bring any extra reapers? If so, I'll take them!" I can have the best of both worlds; I can sell reapers and leaches at the same time!" "Winds of Chance."

In the late '60s, my son Dusty came to work one Monday morning. He told me that he and his wife Gloria had just returned from a bass fishing trip to Lake Table Rock. He told me they had hit it just right and that the bass there had gone crazy over a new buzz bait called Pomme Special. It had been designed by the Mar-Lyn Lure Company for muskie in Pomme de Terre Lake. Consequently came the name "Pomme Special." It was a single spin with a large spinner blade, a plastic skirt and a fiberglass weed guard. He said, "It's just the right time to make a good bass picture. Let's plan it next week." I told him a better plan, "Let's go tonight after the show."

We called J.D. Fletcher at Devil's Dive Resort near Eagle Rock and drove down. We didn't have a guide, but Dusty had already located the fish. Abu Garcia had just sent me a new 5500-C casting reel. It had a higher gear ratio than the 5000. They wanted us to test it. Dusty used it the first day. He caught his limit of bass, including two in the 7-lb. class. I didn't fare that well with the 5000 and slower retrieve. The second day I used the 5500 and caught my limit, including two over 7 lbs. We made our movie, weighed the fish and released them at the dock. "Winds of Chance."

The wheels started turning in my head. I told Dusty that we should try it on snook in Costa Rica on our next trip. The reason I thought it would work was an incident that happened in Costa Rica the year before.

This particular day, my buddy, Wayne Brower, had been catching lots of tarpon on topwater baits, up in the lagoon off the Parisimina River. You could just catch one after another, no large tarpon, but mostly from 65 to 95 lbs. It was hot and muggy on the lagoon. I told our guide, Goya, that I would like to go down to the mouth of the river, where we could feel the cool breeze from the ocean, and I would like to fish for snook until noon. Goya was happy to make the move. Number one, it would be cooler and, number two, he wouldn't have to paddle the boat. He stopped at an eddy near the edge of where the river current hits the salt water. He dropped his anchor over the stern, leaned back and propped himself against the motor with his bare feet on the boat seat. He put his hat over his face as though he were going to take a siesta. He told us to cast off either side of the boat.

We were using topwater baits, small Heddon Creek Chub Darters. We had each made eight or ten casts with nothing. We would cast to a spot, let the bait float a moment, then twitch it, sort of finesse it. Without moving his hat from his face, Goya calmly said, "Why don't you just try reeling the lure in?" I did on the next cast. I had reeled the lure steadily about 6 ft., when the water erupted like someone had tossed a hand grenade in! I set the hook and yelled for Wayne to grab the camera and start rolling. We got the picture and got the fish in. It was not a big snook; it only weighed 15 lbs. Wayne got a picture of my next cast, and it happened again. This time a 14-lb. snook! He got the picture and said for me to make another cast. I did and it happened again! This time it was an 8 -pounder. He got the picture and told me to make another cast. It happened again, but only a 7-pounder. We weighed them all at the dock, so it wasn't just guess weight. Wayne said, "That does it; I'm putting the camera down. I haven't been able to fish since you caught that first one!" I had already made another cast. This time it was a tarpon. It just jumped all over the place. I yelled at Goya to pull the anchor and start the motor, that we were going to have to follow this one! He did, and we pulled the fish up the river, out of the current, and landed it not far from the dock. All this time we had been in sight of the dock and the lodge. The tarpon only weighed 81 lbs., but on a light bass rod in that river, it was a handful.

We kept the snook for the camp, and Goya took the tarpon for the village. Five casts; four snook, one tarpon, all because our guide in sleepy fashion said, "Why don't you just try reeling the lure in as you would a buzz bait?"

When Dusty and I had such a great trip buzzing for bass on Table Rock, I thought of the day in Costa Rica, of the snook; we caught fish just reeling the Creek Chub Darters. Just maybe using that Pomme Special in Costa Rica to buzz for snook might be just what the doctor ordered!

The next year, we took some Pomme's with us. Bud Walton, the co-founder (Sam's brother) of the Wal-Mart Stores went with us. We had caught a lot of tarpon on Creek Chub Darters. Believe me, catching an 80 or 90-lb tarpon on a light bass rod and a top water lure and that, just cast after cast, is as near Heaven as you can get.

Bud and I had just about worn ourselves out on the tarpon. Bud suggested that for a break in the action we should try one of the creeks off the canal for snook. We had been fishing at the mouth of the Paquari River. On our way back to camp, Goya took us back into a creek off the canal. We caught several small snook when I happened to think of the Pomme Special. I tied it on and rolled it across the water. We called the sound of its gurgle "Champagne Music." I don't think there is another buzz bait that gives off the same sound. In fact, the first time I used one in front of my friend, Terry LaCoss, was at Amelia Island in Florida. When he heard the sound, he exclaimed, "Where did you get a buzz bait that sounds like that?"

But getting back to Bud Walton in Costa Rica, our guide Goya nearly fell out of the boat seat laughing at the sound of the gurgle. I said, "Goya, don't you think that will catch snook?" He said, "No way!" I saw a submerged log at the edge of a weed bed. As I rolled the Pomme across the water, there was an explosion as if someone had tossed in a grenade. I set the hook, but missed the fish! Goya yelled, "Big guapi." He said, "Reel in and we will go in for lunch. After lunch and a siesta I'm going to take you to some fishing you won't believe." I said, "Snook?" He said, "No, big guapote!"

After lunch he took Bud and me up through the lagoon to Californio Creek way back in the jungle. I mean this was really jungle! Some places the guide had to hack his way through the green cover with a machete. We came to a fork in the creek, and Goya asked

Capturing the beauty of the Tree River as it flows into the Arctic Ocean in Canada

how heavy was the line I was using. I told him 17-lb. test. He told me it was not heavy enough. I asked him what he used, and he said 60! I said, "Goya, you've seen me land hundred-pound tarpon. How big are these guapote?" He said, "Maybe 5 lbs."

Bud said, "I'm not going to fish; I've got to see this, so I'll just watch." We were in a small channel not much wider than the boat. Goya asked me how many lures I had. I told him that I had five of them. He just sort of grinned but didn't say anything. He spotted a small alligator, maybe 5 ft. long. I thought I would see what a gator thought of the Pomme. I rolled it by its head, and that was a mistake! Goya told me that I was now down to four baits. I tied on another Pomme. Goya paddled the boat quietly up the creek. He pointed to an opening on the water about 10 inches wide and some 5 or 6 ft. back in the jungle growth. He said, "Cast to the back of that slot and roll that bait out." Again there was an explosion as that guapote smashed into the lure and headed back into the jungle cover. I couldn't stop the fish, and it broke my line. Goya said, "Now you are down to three baits." He paddled a little farther, same explosion, just like a hand grenade and the same results, a broken line! Then a short time later it happened again. Bud Walton chuckled and said, "You are down to one bait and you haven't landed one yet!" I tied on my last Pomme. We came to a fairly open spot in the creek, maybe 10 ft. across with five or six logs about 5" in diameter lying parallel to each other, extending out halfway across this opening. Water was pouring over these logs about 8" deep. The water was crystal clear. I cast the Pomme about 5 ft. beyond the logs and rolled it across them. A guapote came up through the logs and just exploded the water as it grabbed the lure. That was my last Pomme, so I just let out line and didn't try to force it. I heard a racket behind me; Goya stripped off his clothes, grabbed my line and dived in. We could see him in the water with his hand on my line. He followed it out of our sight and came up out of the water with a 5-lb. guapote. As he put on his clothes, he said, "I wasn't about to let you lose that last bait! I wanted some guapote for my dinner tonight!" Bud Walton said, "Ensley, we have just been introduced to something special!" "Winds of Chance."

Not many people fish for them; the casting is so exacting, and in those narrow streams it's best if you fish one person at a time. After 30-some years of fishing for this feisty rascal, it still excites me to fish for them and remember the "good old days." The largest guapote we ever caught was 10 lbs. 2 oz. We used to catch lots of 4 to 6-lb. fish. Things have changed. When they opened the canal, it brought an influx of natives from Limon, fishing with cut bait and heavy line and even spearing them; it took its toll. We have caught many kinds of fresh water fish in our lifetime, North America, South America, Central America, Africa and Finland, but nothing compares to that powerful guapote in its own jungle home. In open water it does not have that great advantage that it has in deep cover. In his hometown, the guapote is the toughest of them all. My wife Bonnie and I and Dusty and his wife Gloria have spent many wonderful moments back in the jungle of Costa Rica, pursuing this illusive and exciting creature. "Winds of Chance."

Hollywood Connection

ONE MONDAY MORNING I came to my office at KCMO TV. The boss called me in and said we have a new assignment for you. Next week, they want you to come to Hollywood for a cameo appearance on Gunsmoke. I said, "Boss, I'm not a movie actor. What would they want with me?" He said, "I don't know, but we're flying you, your wife and little daughter to California next week, right after your show. We had fished with Doc and Kitty and had become friends. Gunsmoke was one of my favorite TV shows, but not in my fondest dreams did I think I would walk down the street of Dodge City on the Gunsmoke set, much less have a bit part.

We were met at the Los Angeles airport with a big limo and taken to our hotel. The driver said he had orders to pick me up the next morning to take me to the Gunsmoke set. He gave me the time, but told me I couldn't take my wife and daughter. I was ready the next morning, and at the scheduled time he took me to the Gunsmoke set. Not being an actor, I was a little apprehensive about what would take place. At the set we were met by a publicity man who took me to the make-up room. The make-up artist said, "What do you want me to do with him?" He said, "Make him up!" The make-up man said, "I can't make him any better. He's as brown as a bear now! He must have spent a lot of time in the sun." The publicity man said, "Act like you are making him up for a couple of pictures, then dress him in Western garb." Then, dressed in Western gear with a big hat, they had me walk across the street to the Long Branch.

Kitty was sitting in a rocking chair, going over her script. She didn't see me until I said, "Hi, Kitty!" She jumped up, gave me a big hug and said, "What in the world are you doing here?" She said, "Does Doc know you're here?" I said, "Kitty, I don't know what's going on, but I'm supposed to do a big part on your show. She said, "I'll go get Doc." She came back with Doc. We visited a moment when Doc asked, "Where's Bonnie and Sandy?" I told them that they said they couldn't come on the set. Doc said, "We'll see about that." Thirty minutes later a limo drove up in front of the Long Branch with Bonnie and Sandy.

They gave me a script. I was to be a waiter in the Del Monico. There were just a few lines between Festus and me. Just before production time, they told me they were going to change the script and write in a part for me as a fisherman. They stopped everything

Harold and Festus visiting

and wrote the part. I was to be standing in front of the jail. Festus and a 12-year-old boy rode up on Festus' mule. The boy was holding a tree branch stringer with some small fish. I was to tell the boy I knew where he could catch the big ones, but wouldn't tell Festus. After we did it, they said, "We want you to do the water part just in case we want to use it." They again gave me the original script. The episode was called Deputy Festus. His cousins were in jail for some reason or other, and Festus was to come to the Del Monico to get them some food. After I took his order, I was supposed to ask if he wanted some coffee. He was supposed to say yes, black. I saw his script book and noticed that where I asked if he wanted coffee he had scratched out, "Yes, black," and written in, "Yeah, about a gallon!"

They started production; I took his order and asked if he wanted coffee!! He said, "Yeah, about a gallon." I said, "What are you going to do, take a bath in it?" The director yelled, "Cut, cut. I don't want you guys ad-libbing." Consequently, we did it over. "Winds of Chance." It really didn't amount to anything, but Bonnie, Sandy and I were thrilled just to be there with the crew.

Some years later Doc and Kitty were to perform at the American Royal Livestock show in Kansas City. We were invited along with a few of their friends to meet them at the airport. We visited for a few minutes, and then Doc said, "What time is your TV show?" I told him. He said, "Kitty, we can make it!" I asked him what he was talking about. He said that he and Kitty had planned to be guests on my show if they could. I said, "Doc, I don't have any money to pay you to be on my show." He said, "Who said we had to be paid to be on your show?" Kitty had said, "One thing for sure, we want to be on Harold's show!" They were on, and we had a good time, and we got to spend some time with them throughout the week. I will always treasure their friendship!

Sometime in the '60s, I received a telephone call from Paul Henning. Paul created the Beverly Hillbilly show and was the executive producer. I have no idea how he knew who I was and where he could reach me. He said that they had planned to do a series of episodes at Branson, Missouri, and asked me if I would come down and fish with the crew. He gave me the dates, and I told him what week I could be there. We arranged to work it in. I drove to Branson.

Eddie Fausett operated a marina at Fall Creek below Table Rock Dam. Eddie and I fished some that afternoon, just to check out the fishing. Then I drove to the hotel to meet the cast. I had met Granny, Jethro and Ellie Mae when they performed at the rodeo in Camdenton, Missouri, a few years back. But I had never met Buddy Ebson, better known as Jed Clampett. I'm not sure whether Paul Henning was there or not, but we had a get-acquainted session and I started to leave. Someone from the production crew, it may have been Paul himself, said to the director, "What time do you want Ensley down at the Marina?" I asked what they wanted me for, and they said, "We are planning to use you for a few minutes in the episode, but be sure to come in your fishing clothes." I told them they didn't need to do that. I just came down to fish with the cast. The next morn-

Harold visiting with Kitty on the Gunsmoke set

Harold and Matt talking fishing

ing they had Jed and me get in a boat and start fishing. Phil Silvers was to come down to the water's edge and yell for Jed. I heard him and said, "Jed, someone is yelling at you." He didn't say anything, so I said, "Who is that yelling at you?" He said, "It sure ain't no bass. They won't talk to me!" That was my brief appearance on Beverly Hillbillies. However, I got more mileage out of Jed. He would say, "Granny, I doggies, I'm going to call that Harold Ensley. He knows where the big ones are." We had a great time fishing with him and Jethro. I think Eddie Fausett and I fished three days with Jethro and caught a lot of fish. Jethro was something else in a boat. He never wanted to quit! He wanted to catch a trophy trout, and I told him if he did I would have it mounted and shipped to him. He did hook a big rainbow. I told him to be careful, that he had his trophy fish. We were using either 2 or 4-lb. test line on ultra-light spinning reels, casting small jigs. He was so strong, and I kept telling him to ease off, but the fish broke his line.

I recently called Eddie Fausett to see if he remembered the dates. He said, "It must have been late '60s or early '70s. We remembered what a good time we had! He said, "Do you remember when he got his jig caught in a tree and almost fell in trying to get it? He

Doc and Kitty, guests on my TV show

said, "Both of us were telling him to break his line off, that we had plenty of jigs." He could have turned our boat over. Jed liked to fish and we had a good time. He caught some trout, and we started to go in. I said, "Everybody make one more cast." We all made a cast and caught nothing.

I saw a trout swirl after a bug. I made seven or eight more casts but didn't get the fish. Jed said, "Ensley, when you say one more cast, when do you start counting?" It was pure fun, and to think that I got to appear briefly on two of my favorite TV shows, Gunsmoke and Beverly Hillbillies. "Winds of Chance."

Thirty years later I was giving a fish cleaning demonstration in the Salem, Missouri Wal-Mart store. A crowd had gathered to watch. Someone in the crowd said something about the Beverly Hillbillies. A man said, "Ensley, last week I saw you on a rerun of Beverly Hillbillies. I asked him what I was doing. He said, "Guiding Jed." I told him that I did a bit part in one of the episodes, but had never seen it. He said, "I taped it and will send you a tape." He did, and I lost his name and address and could not thank him. Maybe he will read this and write me. "Winds of Chance."

In the early days of television, three networks dominated the scene: NBC, CBS and ABC. I cannot remember, nor could I find any source as to the first big Western to hit the air lanes. Just recently I called my friend, John Mantley, in California about it. John produced over 100 Western movies during his career. Among the movies were "How the West Was Won." He had produced Gunsmoke and he thought that it might have been the first of the big Westerns to hit the screen. Be that as it may, Gunsmoke was an immediate big hit. With the success of Gunsmoke came a rash of Westerns on the networks. I have been unable to learn in what order they came, but I remember Wagon Train, Laramie, Bonanza, Rawhide, Cheyenne, Wyatt Earp, Big Valley and possibly other frontier shows, like Fess Parker in the Wild Frontier. All were great shows and we loved them all. In fact, today I enjoy the reruns and wish the television industry would produce shows of like quality today.

Everyone was talking about Matt Dillon, Doc, Miss Kitty and Chester. At our home, Gunsmoke became our favorite TV show. I never in my fondest dreams thought that I would meet these stars, much less have them as guests on my TV show. Nor did I ever dream that someday I would be on the Gunsmoke set of Dodge City in Hollywood for a cameo part. It all started at Camdenton, Missouri, on the Lake of the Ozarks. I did not recall the exact date. My wife Bonnie and I drove to the Niangua arm of Lake of the Ozarks for our annual spring walleye fishing trip. At that time we had reporters in the area who called daily Monday through Friday. They would give us reports of water conditions, fish catches and general information about the fishing outlook for the week. These reports were used on our daily radio show.

We also would be searching for opportunities to shoot movies and gather material for our weekly TV show. That particular week while we were fishing, our reporter paid us a visit. In the course of our visit we were asked to drive into Camdenton to see their new rodeo arena. I told them that I had been raised in rodeo country and that I enjoyed them,

On the Gunsmoke set

but at the moment I was busy with a fishing movie. In the first place, I couldn't visualize a rodeo of any consequence in the hill country of the Lake of the Ozarks region. The reporter insisted that this was going to be big time. So out of courtesy and respect we drove the few miles to Camdenton. I could hardly believe my eyes. A promoter named Harry Nelson had built an arena that would grace any rodeo facility. Unless perhaps you would mention Frontier Days in Cheyenne, Wyoming, and Calgary Stampede. The bleachers would perhaps seat 12,000 fans; the whole facility was first class with adequate parking spaces. Then, of course, with all the resorts on the Little Niangua, the Big Niangua and the Grand Glaze arm, the area offered the motel and hotel accommodations that would be necessary. The place was to be completed for the first big rodeo in the fall. Harry Nelson was a promoter. He thought what he was planning would work, and he said he was going to make it work! He said that he was going to bring in the professional cowboys and the best rodeo livestock in the nation. Also, for each rodeo he planned to bring in stars of the TV Western shows to perform each night. He asked me if I would work with him. He suggested that we come down for the rodeo and fish with the stars. It made sense to me, and an opportunity for new and exciting program material. "Winds of Chance."

Autumn came and Harry called and gave me the dates. He was having Rex Allen, the singer, and Casey Tibbs, the saddle bronc rider. He would like to have them in as guests on my TV show to promote the rodeo. Then we were to attend the rodeo and fish with Rex and Casey. It all worked out. They had tremendous crowds. The stands were filled, and Harry was off to the races. The next year he called to tell me that Doc, Kitty and Chester of Gunsmoke were to be there for the rodeo. I could use them on my show, and then Doc and Chester wanted to fish with me. Everything came to pass, except Chester had to go to Joplin for something. When Doc told me that, he said that Kitty wanted to go. I told him that it would be hot on the lake and we would have to fish for catfish. I also told him that we would need to get on the lake around 4:30 or 5 a.m. He said, "That's fine, Kitty and I will be ready." I told him my wife would go along to fish with Kitty. When I told Bonnie about it, she said, "You've got to be kidding me!" But it happened! The next morning Doc and Kitty were ready and waiting. We drove to the lake and had a great time. Kitty caught more fish than anyone, and they let me shoot movies for my TV show. This started a friendship with them that lasted as long as they lived.

The next year Harry called me and he was bringing in more stars. I'm not sure as to the order, but we used many of them on our show and fished with them all, except one year. That year he brought in Hoss and Little Joe of Bonanza. I could not do it, as Chevrolet sponsored Bonanza and Ford sponsored my show. I wasn't going to play two ends against the middle just to satisfy my ego. The next year it was Clint Walker, who played Cheyenne Bodie. We fished with Clint and had him as guest on our show.

Several years later I fished three days with Clint in the Bahamas, but we will deal with that later on. The next year Harry had Fess Parker of King of the Wild Frontier. He was a guest on our show, but we did not get to fish any. The last time we worked with the Nelsons they had Granny, Jethro and Ellie Mae. This time he was having a special skeet and trap shooting tournament. You should have seen Granny at that. She was a great lady! The three of them were great! In my fondest dreams I never thought some day I would work with them at Branson. "Winds of Chance." But this closed out the Camdenton Rodeo, as Harry became seriously ill.

A friend of mine, Don Walker, had a cabin on Indian Creek in southwest Missouri. He asked me to teach him how to catch small mouth bass and goggle eye around the rocks in the clear waters of Indian Creek and Big Sugar. He was Warner Bros. rep for Kansas City region, and before we were to fish on the streams, he called me about a press junket to Jackson Hole, Wyoming. They were releasing a new film with Henry Fonda and Maureen O'Hara, called "Spencer's Mountain." There were some scenes in the movie of Henry Fonda fishing, and they would like for me to represent the Kansas City region at the Press Premier. He told me that they might want me to fish with Fonda, "So take your fishing gear with you."

Jimmie McArthur also had a role in the movie. I had never been to a bash like that, and I had never fished Lake Jackson or the other mountain lakes in the Tetons, so I accepted their invitation. They also invited writers from the newspapers from St. Louis, Omaha, Des Moines, Tulsa, Dallas and others. I think there were about a dozen of us in the group, but I was the only one of our bunch in the Midwest from television. Press came from all over the world and big-time stars from Hollywood. Arthur Godfrey were there to film a bear hunt. I never dreamed that they would let me fish with Fonda or anyone else. I wasn't accustomed to all the glitter of a bash like that. However, since I had never fished Lack Jackson, just to be safe, I went to the marina on the lake to rent a boat and pre-fish the waters. The marina told me that Warner Bros. had all the boats rented. I told them that I was with the Warner Bros. group, but still they refused me a boat. After the big press banquet that night, I was informed that I was to fish with Henry Fonda and his agent the next morning. I was almost in a state of shock, but promised to meet them at the marina. They had a boat and a guide ready when we arrived. The guide told us we would have to troll to catch lake trout at that time of year. We trolled all morning with nothing. I had some 1/2-oz. Maribou jigs with me that I used to catch lake trout in Canada. However, the guide didn't want me to use them. About eleven o'clock, Fonda's agent told him that they had to get back to the lodge for a big press conference. Henry told him that he would rather stay out and fish. He said, "Maybe we can find the fish!" However, the agent prevailed and we headed for the dock.

When we came to the dock, Jimmie McArthur and his wife, Joyce Boulifant, were waiting for us. She asked me if I would take the two of them out. I said, "Don't you want to be at that luncheon?" She told me that they had brought box lunches for the four of us, so let's go! The guide told them that they would have to troll with live bait. She told him that she would rather cast with artificial lures. Nonetheless, he rigged up a trolling outfit for each of them and started the motor. It is difficult to try to cast in a boat with two others trolling, but I tied on a 1/2-oz. Maribou jig and started casting. I was using one of my 6-ft. spinning rods with 4-lb. test line. With a hard cast I could almost reach the shoreline, with the motor running and with two in the back of the boat with lines out. It forced me to reel the jig a little faster than usual. I knew that, generally speaking, a lake trout likes a fast-moving bait. I had made four or five casts when I got the first strike. I yelled at the guide to cut the motor, that I had a fish. He did, and I lost the fish! He turned to them and said, "That guy doesn't know when he has a stick or a fish." He started the motor and started them trolling again. A few casts later I had another strike. This time I made sure that I had the fish hooked. I yelled for him to cut the motor, He did, and when he saw that I did have a fish, he had them reel in their lines, then netted the trout for me. It was a small laker, compared to what I was accustomed to catching in Canada. I suppose that it weighed 6 or 7 lbs., but it made my day! "Winds of chance."

Joyce said, "I thought you said that you couldn't catch trout casting an artificial lure." He told her that I had just lucked into one, but after I had caught two or three more, she told him she wanted to cast! I had two extra rods and spinning reels with me. We rigged them up to cast jigs, and they started catching trout. We caught a good string of fish, and they were happy! They both loved to fish. Her dad was a charter captain on a fishing boat in Miami, Florida. She was a beautiful and gracious lady. We took the fish in and gave them to the chef at Jackson Lodge. The next morning he prepared them for our breakfast, and we shared them with Arthur Godfrey and the group at his table. Godfrey's cameraman asked where I was going to fish that morning. I told him that I didn't have much time, but that I planned to go down to Jenny Lake to make a few casts. He went with me and took his movie camera and I had mine. I made a few casts but caught nothing. It was a beautiful morning, and what a beautiful setting! Jenny Lake is one of the most beautiful mountain lakes I've seen in the Rockies. The peaks of the Tetons were majestic in the background! There was a cut bank, maybe 20 ft. high above the lake, but with enough room at the water's edge for me to stand and cast. I was casting the white Maribou jig across the lake. I asked him if he would mind to take my movie camera and get a shot from the cut over my shoulder casting the white jig across the lake. He did and asked me if I would mind if he took the same shot over my head with his camera. He said, "That is a spectacular shot!" We went back to the lodge and all went our separate ways.

The next week someone told me that they showed Henry Fonda on the Jack Paar Show. He was casting a white lure across the lake at Jackson Hole, Wyoming. So I made the Jack Paar Show for a few seconds, once in my lifetime. I had only one regret, that we didn't get to put Henry Fonda in fish, the way we could have. I never saw him again in person, nor McArthur or Joyce, but Don Walker told me that Fonda was always asking about my welfare and would say that he wanted to go fishing with me again. That was another of my missed opportunities! "Winds of Chance."

A few years later, Don called to see if my wife and I wanted to fly out with him and his wife to Hollywood for the big bash on the release of the movie, "The Great Race," with Tony Curtis, Jack Lemmon, Keenan Wynn and Natalie Wood. I couldn't think of any reason why I should go to Hollywood, but I thought my wife Bonnie might enjoy it. We arrived at the set, and the first thing they asked us was, "Where is your fishing gear?" I asked why I needed it. They said that I was to pull Natalie Wood out of a pool. I told them that Milburn Stone, Doc of Gunsmoke, had a set of my rods and reels. They called the Gunsmoke set, and shortly after a limo drove up with the rods and reels. It never developed for me to fish Natalie out of the pool, but I really didn't expect it anyway. That night Jack Warner threw a party for the press. The press took turns with interviewing the stars. Keenan Wynn saw me with the fishing rods and told the girl in charge that he wanted me next. So I did an interview with him. Henry Mancini and Johnny Mercer furnished the music for the affair. You can imagine the glamour and glitter of the evening! Almost too much for an ol' country boy and his wife. "Winds of Chance."

The next time Don called me to go to Cheyenne, Wyoming, for the opening of the film, "Cheyenne Autumn," with Jimmy Stewart and Carol Baker. We were to fish in the Laramie

River. My wife and I flew with Don and his wife to Cheyenne. The water in the river was so low that we couldn't fish it. However, I got to teach Jimmy Stewart to cast with spinning gear. There were stars and dignitaries all over the place. The Cheyenne tribe had a spectacular presentation, making Jimmy and Carol honorary members of the tribe. It was a beautiful ceremony around a campfire, and I don't think anyone filmed it. My wife Bonnie was shy and reserved, and I almost fainted when she went over to Carol Baker. Carol was in Western garb and on her horse. My wife asked her if she could get a movie of me interviewing her. She was very gracious, and we did the interview. When we walked away, Bonnie said, "Carol is the most beautiful woman I've ever seen !" That, coming from another woman, is quite a compliment. The tragic part of the interview was that someone stole our film. I have one other regret; when the Cheyenne chief heard that I had just done a story on the Apaches, he invited me to the Cheyenne reservation to promote their tourist facilities. I never could make it! It was another of those missed opportunities! "Winds of Chance."

The next time Don called me, it was for a world press premier. He asked me how I would like to fish with Bill Holden, Kirk Douglas and Deborah Kerr. I said, "You've gone far enough. I'll go !" I asked him when and where. He told me that it was to be in the Grand Bahamas and gave me the dates. I told him that the only way I could go was if I took my wife, because I had been gone too much. He said, "Nobody takes their wife on this trip!" I told him to forget it. He said, "Don't get all stirred up, I'll call Ernie Grossman in New York." He did, and Grossman, who could never remember my name, told him, "If that fisherman wants to take his wife, take her !" Don and the two of us flew to Miami and across to the capitol of Grand Bahamas. I was certain that it would not be likely that I would fish with Bill Holden or Kirk Douglas. When we got off the plane, I saw Clint Walker in the crowd. I knew he liked to fish, and he had been a guest on my TV show in Kansas City. I told Don that I would like to fish with Clint. About that time, Grossman came up to greet us. He asked Don who I was fishing with. He told him Clint Walker. Ernie said, "Don't let him get by with that. Get some starlet to go with them. Go around to the pool and introduce him to Barbara Rhodes." She was a beautiful woman.

When he introduced us, she looked up and smiled. She said, "I understand that I'm to be in a fishing movie for you." I told her, "That is fine, but I want you to put on a few more clothes; I have a family show." She smiled and said, "Bless your heart for that!" The next day they arranged for her and Clint and my wife and I to go out on a charter boat for giant tuna. We didn't catch any fish, but I got some pictures of her and Clint fishing. Both of them were very gracious and a pleasure to be with.

That night I told Don of a great bone fishing spot, and that Clint and I wanted to try it. It was the Deep Water Cay, and undoubtedly one of the top bone fishing spots of the world! I had fished for bone fish in the Florida Keys, the flats of Belize and Bermuda, but never in my life have I seen bone fish in the size and numbers of the Deep Water Cay. They furnished us transportation and a native from Jamaica to pole the boat for us. They gave us some box lunches and some cold drinks to spend the day on the flats. I had my

Teaching Jimmy Stewart to cast at Cheyenne, Wyoming

camera and asked Clint if he would mind if I took some pictures for my TV show. He told me that he would be honored! I gave him one of my spinning rods with 4-lb. test line, like the one I was using. I had learned from other bone fishing trips that a 1/16 or 1/8-oz crappie jig worked better than anything else. I tied one on for Clint, and we started working the flats. Clint could get plenty of distance, but had a little trouble hitting close enough to the target. Our guide had brought along some live shrimp for such an emergency. I never saw so many large schools of big bone fish. The guide put on live shrimp and cast out. He hooked a big bone and handed the rod to Clint. Clint said, "What's this for?" The guide told him so I could get a picture. Clint politely told him that he would not do that and said, "Harold will not take a picture of me fighting a fish that someone else has hooked!" Clint caught his own fish, and we had a great day! He was dressed in short, tight swimming trunks. His biceps were almost as big as my thighs. He is a huge man and was almost twice the size of our small Jamaican guide. Clint was in the front. The guide tapped me on the shoulder and said softly, "Boss man, is that your boy?" Clint amused me when we ate our sandwiches. Like me, he is sort of a health food nut. He would throw the bread away and eat the lunchmeat. When we finished the day, he said, "Let's come back for more of this tomorrow." We did and had another great day. "Winds of Chance."

That night Bonnie and I sat at a table with six members of the press form Sydney, Australia. One lady was a writer for a ladies magazine. When she learned that I had fished that day with Clint Walker, she invited the two of us to come to Sydney to fish. Clint and I could never get our schedules to work out. Another missed opportunity! I never saw Clint after that, but I'm sure he will always remember our bone fishing trip to the Grand Bahamas!

To My Jogging Friends

I WOULD FEEL that I had neglected my jogging friends if I failed to write about running. I really cannot remember when I started a dedicated jogging regimen. When I was a boy, I loved to run just to be running. While our school didn't have a track program, I lettered in three sports — baseball, basketball and tennis, which, of course, required some running. But that's not my point; I just loved to run. I've had people tell me that walking is just as good as running, as far as fitness is concerned. That may be true, but you cannot convince a runner of that. Some runners get a high from running, but I had never thought of it in that light. I liked to run for the fun of it. I ran for some 50 years and would still be doing it, if it were not for a broken knee. I was not a marathon runner, but occasionally I ran in 10K races to raise money for charity. Most of the time I would just run 3-5 miles a day. Someone may have been making running shoes 50 or 60 years ago, but I ran mostly in what we called "tennis shoes." New Balance made my first real pair of running shoes, and I used them for thousands of miles all over the world.

When I ran in the Arctic regions, I ran in my fishing boots. Sometimes I ran barefooted on the beaches when we were fishing in Costa Rica. One time Dusty and I were fishing in the surf where the Parquari River runs into the Caribbean. It was hot on the sand, so I took off my shoes and fished for a while. I told Dusty I was going to get my running in, so I took off down the beach. The sand felt good to my feet. I ran what I thought was six miles, three miles down and three back. I had a good run and decided to start fishing again in the shallow water, casting into the surf for snook. The water felt good to my feet and wading on the soft sand, so I didn't put my shoes back on. I never thought of sun burning my feet. I got the worst sunburn you can imagine! I couldn't fish for three days. Believe me, I learned a lesson. Naturally your feet would be tender, and the tropical sun made me pay. There I was in some of the best tarpon and snook fishing in the world and laid up in bed with severely burned feet. It was a painful way to pay for my stupidity! "Winds of Chance."

We had a lot of interesting things happen because of our running. My wife and I were invited to Finland to explore their fishing. They wanted to import my rods and make my fillet knives. We arrived in Helsinki in mid-afternoon. We were assigned an interpreter and guide, a young man called Esko Altio. He was a brilliant young man. He spoke five

Jogging in Canada above the Arctic Circle and Hawaii

different languages and just happened to be a jogger. He stayed with us almost day and night for the three weeks we were there. He became like a brother to us. They were gracious to us and suggested we rest that first afternoon before we started a whirlwind series of trips throughout the country. After checking into the hotel in Helsinki, I told my wife Bonnie that while she rested I was going to look for a place to jog and get my running in. I asked the desk clerk, "Where would be a good place to run?" He said, "Just run anywhere out there; we have miles and miles of jogging trails throughout the city." He also told me that it would be safe to run on those trails, day or night. I remember when Helsinki was host to the Olympic, and that they had a distance runner, Paavo Nurmi, who had become a world-famous runner. I had a good run.

The next day we started our tour and fishing expedition, visiting the Rapala Plant that became world famous for its lures. We fished with Mr. Rapala, and he too was a jogger. We fished their state parks, visited the Martini knife factory. They market the knife that everyone calls a Rapala. The next time you use your Rapala knife, look on the blade and you will see the Martinez name. Mr. Rapala and Martinez were our hosts as we drove

north to fish for Atlantic salmon on the Tana River. I have not been able to recall Mr. Rapala's first name, but Mr. Martinez' first name was Lori. He was a real outgoing character. He wanted to learn to speak English, and we drove to Lapland. I rode with Lori and Bonnie and Esko; our interpreter rode with Mr. Rapala. Lori had his Berlitz English-Finnish book on the car seat between us as we drove along. Reindeer were running across the road. He was driving 60 mph with one hand and trying to read something from his book. He said, "Harold, how you say this in English?" I said, "Lori, it say to slow down and watch out for the reindeer." He laughed, but he did put the book down and we didn't hit any reindeer. We stayed in private homes, and our host could not believe that neither I nor my wife drank or smoked. From what they saw at the movies, they thought all Americans drank or smoked. We drove to the Arctic Ocean, and I told Esko I wanted to jog there on the rocky cliff overlooking the Arctic.

We fished and shot movies fishing for Atlantic salmon and Arctic grayling. Esko and I were fishing with a Lapland guide, a young fellow who could speak no English. They had a strange way of fishing for the salmon. They used a homemade wooden boat, 14 ft. long. The stern was almost as pointed as the bow. They used a small outboard to go up the river, and then drift back with the swift current, with a fly rod out on each side of the boat with a special fly. The guide held the boat with a set of oars at the stern. I sat on a float seat in the middle, and Esko was in the bow facing back toward us. It was most uncomfortable for me, sitting so low with my cameras. I had my casting rods rigged up with a potato bug daredevil and a 3/4-oz. spoon. It was the spoon I used to catch Arctic char in the Tree River. We were not doing any good. We had made three or four runs up the river and drifted back. Each time he would change patterns of flies. Finally I asked my interpreter if I could cast on the next drift. He asked the guide, who said something in Lapp language and they both laughed. I asked my interpreter what he said. He said that "he didn't have his hard hat on." I nearly fell out of the boat! We were in an area as remote as it gets, and he talked about hard hats. I told my interpreter to tell him that I would not hit him. He gave me the go-ahead, and I started casting. It was difficult to cast with two fly rods out and me sitting practically on the bottom of an unstable boat. After the first drift, the guide said something to Esko in Lapp language. My interpreter told me that the guide said, "The American could catch a fish if he had the right bait." We went back upstream for another run. He pulled the boat out on the bank, drug a Swedish Pimple out of his box and handed it to me to tie on. It is a thin, long, lady-slipper-shaped spoon, but the hooks were real rusty. I told my interpreter that a salmon would straighten those hooks out. He told the guide that, but the guide evidently told him that it would hold. On the second drift I hooked a salmon. I asked Esko to take my camera and get the picture. He was busy getting the two fly lines in and nearly turned the boat over. You talk about a Chinese fire drill, we had it! Esko was getting the movie, and we had the fish up ready to net it. It made another run, straightened out the hooks and went free. We had worked 22 hours for one fish and lost it! "Winds of Chance."

All this time Bonnie was stuck at the hotel where no one spoke English! We drove back to Ravenna and then flew back to Helsinki. In Helsinki I wanted to run at least one lap in their Olympic Stadium, and my interpreter got permission to do it. However, they wanted to take us to the Baltic Sea. We did, and what a thrill it was to fish where people had fished since 800 A.D.

But back to the jogging. Fortunately, I've been privileged to do my running in many places of the world. However, during 50 years of jogging I only had three scary moments. Once in Alaska, with a mama Kodiak bear and her two cubs; once in Louisiana, with a big cottonmouth on a pasture runway near the Lodge of Pecan Island; once at Bella Vista on the blacktop about two miles from our lodge just before dark one evening. A copperhead was right in the path. I'll not bother you with the details, but in each case it could have spelled disaster!

I've had many exciting moments. Topping the list would be one in Cincinnati, Ohio, and one in Springfield, Massachusetts. I was to work the National Farm Show in Cincinnati for a client here in Kansas City. We flew there, arriving at the hotel downtown late in the afternoon. After dinner I wanted to stretch my legs and get my running done. I asked the bell captain if there was a park nearby where I could run. It was almost dark. He said, "Don't run now, you might get mugged. Wait until early morning if it will work into your schedule." I didn't have to work the booth until 10 a.m. I got up early and started jogging up the hill toward the river. I met another jogger, a young man, and asked him about a place to run. He said, "If you like, come run with me." We took off together and went down by the baseball field. I thought of Johnny Bench and other great baseball stars who had played there. It was a great place to run. In the course of our conversation, he asked me what I did. I told him that I produced and hosted an outdoor television show, but was there to work the National Farm Show. Then I asked him what he did. He said, "I'm with the FBI." I said, "Man, you just made my day!"   "Winds of Chance."

I've jogged many times in bear territory, but prudently, I hope. At least I never had to outrun them and only once had a scare. The other incident I treasure was in Springfield, Massachusetts. I was there to work the Western Auto Dealer Show. At that time Western Auto had 4800 stores and was one of my major national sponsors. The first day before they started the show, I left the hotel to do my running. While looking for a place to run, I had to cross a freeway. The traffic was fairly heavy, and I was waiting for an opportunity to cross over. I was about ready to make a move when I saw a patrol car coming on the other side of the street. I didn't know if they had any jaywalking regulations, but decided not to take a chance. The officer saw me, stopped his vehicle and stopped the traffic for me to cross. I thanked him, and he told me that he was also a jogger and told me a good place to run.

One summer I was invited to fish in Wisconsin for the annual Governor's Fishing Trip. Governor Knowles was a jogger. We did some fishing in Lake Superior and caught enough fish for their cookout. However, I enjoyed jogging with the Governor as much as I did fishing! One morning the Governor couldn't go, so I took off through the back streets of this little town. It was just after sun-up. I saw this pack of dogs, with one big dog leading the pack. He laid his ears back and started after me, with about 10 or 12 smaller dogs right behind him. I knew that I couldn't outrun them and had nothing with which to defend myself. I saw a morning paper rolled up in a yard that a paper boy had just thrown. I picked up the paper just as the dog came up behind me. I kept on running, and just as the dog was ready to get me I hit him right between the eyes with that rolled-up paper. You never heard such a racket in your life! The big dog let out a big howl and stopped. The rest of the pack ran right over him. It started a dog fight to end all dog fights. I didn't stay around to see the outcome! However, people were coming out of houses up and down the street to see what had caused the commotion. "Winds of Chance."

I never jogged down that street again! To tell the truth, I don't think I ever jogged in the state of Wisconsin again. A broken kneecap ended my jogging career. I can't complain, because for 50 years I had been privileged to run in many parts of the world. To all my jogging friends out there, May God Bless You with many miles of happy running!

Military

IN THE EARLY '50s, I worked at the radio station in Independence, Missouri, and for Siegfried's two newspapers, the *Pictorial Shopper* and the *Independence Daily News.* I wrote a daily fishing column for the *Daily News* and sold advertising for the shopper. Each special day like Mother's Day, Father's Day, Memorial Day and Labor Day, an elderly lady came in and sold a promotional page or two to the business firms of the area. I can still hear her on the telephone to some executive, "There is no love like the love of a mother," and proceed to sell them a spot to honor mothers. She was a great lady and very successful at her job. We became friends as we worked together. When I left Independence to go to work on television, I lost track of her. Years later at work I received a telephone call. It was a lady's voice, and she said, "Is this the banker?" She was the only one who ever called me that, and why I do not know. Anyway, it was good to hear from her. After brief conversation about her welfare, she said, "I have a favor to ask of you. My son-in-law has seen you on TV and wants to go fishing with you." I was busy with my radio and TV shows and started to tell her it might be some time before I could, but I would see what I could do. I asked her what he did. She told me that he was a B-47 bomber pilot for S.A.C. out of Schilling Air Force Base in Salina. I immediately thought of those vapor trails in the sky, as these brave men risked their lives every day to make our country safe.

If they weren't in the air every day, flying all over the world, I might never have a place to fish. It would be a small thing to take one of them fishing. We arranged for the trip, and I took him to Bull Shoals Lake in Arkansas to bass fish. I had never met him, but the six-hour drive to Arkansas gave us a chance to get acquainted. He was a handsome young man about 6' 3" tall and had made a career in the Air Force. If I remember correctly, he was from Virginia or somewhere back there. At 18 he had enlisted in the Air Force. At enlistment they asked him what he wanted to do. He told them that he wanted to become a pilot. They told him that with his background he didn't have the credentials to become a pilot. They asked him for his second choice, and he repeated that he wanted to become a pilot. He made it and was one of the survivors of the raid on the Ploesti oilfields. He was pilot of one of the Liberators, when we lost so many planes. He told me that he could see his buddies being shot down all around him. I think maybe he had to make an emergency landing in North Africa. Anyway, he made it safely and was now a Major, flying a B-47 bomber for S.A.C. He was married but had no children. The first morning we went over to the dining room early. The other fishermen had not come to breakfast, so for the moment Bob and I were the only ones at the dining table. Crow-Barnes didn't serve their breakfast family style, but there was just one long table where you could come and go. We ordered ham, eggs and hash browns. The waitress brought out a platter with the two orders on it. She placed it on the table. Bob moved his plate to the side, put the platter with the two orders on it in front of him. He said, "Boy, they sure serve big breakfasts here, and started to pitch in. I said, "Wait a minute, half of that is mine!" He did divide it with me, and if I were to see him today after all those years, we would still both get a big laugh out of it.

He loved to fish and we had a great time. We caught bass on the lake and floated on the White River for trout. He said that his wife didn't fish and wondered how he could get her interested. I told him to buy her a new rod and reel, and suggested what kind he should buy her. It was an honor to get to fish with him. A few years later he called and wanted to know if my wife and I would take him and his wife June fishing at that nice place on Bull Shoals in Arkansas. He said that his wife didn't want to fish, but just to lie around the swimming pool, get a suntan and brag to the other officers' wives. We set a date, and they drove to Kansas City. We took them out to dinner that night, a sort of get-acquainted affair, and they made a handsome couple. During our dinner June said, "When we get there, I don't want you to ask me out on the lake to fish." I just let the matter pass for the moment. Then she said, "Guess what Bob bought me for Mother's Day!" I told her that I didn't have any idea. She said, "A new rod and reel, and guess what I got him for Father's Day!" I asked her what, and she said, "A new washing machine."

The next morning early we drove to Bull Shoals Lake. Bob and I let the girls rest, and we went out on the lake. At that time fishing was a little on the slow side. For the first time ever, heavy rains in the watershed and floods on the lower White and Arkansas Rivers around Little Rock forced the Corps of Engineers to hold as much water above the dam as possible. The water had backed up to flood stage. The lake level stood at 40 feet above power pool level, and they had opened the floodgates. Water was pouring off the dam, and it was a spectacular sight. In the lake proper, the water had backed up covering the timber. Some of the shoreline and trees were completely covered; farther up the elevation just the tops of the trees were visible. It really changed the fishing picture. Bob and I caught some nice bass.

The next morning at breakfast I told June that I wanted her to go fish with us. She said, "Just don't ask me to go!" I told her that we wouldn't stay out long, but as a special favor I wanted her to try. She finally agreed. I told her I wanted her to fish with me, and that Bob would fish with Bonnie. The lodge fixed box lunches for us, and Bonnie made me promise not to keep June out too long. I didn't know that June had a fear of being on the water. At the dock when I took her by the hand to help her in the boat, she was trembling all over. The guide took us to Jimmy Creek, and the two boats of us went along, one ahead of the other, close by. I tied on a top water bait for June, and I was using a jig and six-inch black eel. I taught her to cast, but had her cast on the lake side of the trees. She was coachable, and with her new bait casting rod and reel soon was doing very well. She was casting over open water, not toward the shoreline. I was catching a few nice bass, and Bob and Bonnie were also catching some. June said, "When am I going to get to cast where you are catching fish?" At lunchtime the guide tied the boats to the treetops and dug out our lunch. As we ate our sandwiches, I saw a bass swirl after a minnow. It was within June's casting distance. I told June to cast that top water bait to the spot. She did, and the water exploded as a bass hit the lure. I yelled, "Set the hook!" She didn't, but in the excitement the bass came out of the water several times and literally got rid of the lure. Dejectedly June said, "I could cry!" I told her that I could, too, but that would not bring the fish out. It was about a four-pound bass. I told her to reel her line in and asked the guide to untie the boat, that we were going back to the dock. June wanted to know why. I told her that we were through for the day, and that I had promised Bonnie I wouldn't keep her out too long. Therefore, we were going back to the dock. June said, "No way, I'm just getting started and we are not quitting now." We fished until almost dark, and June caught several nice bass.

That night at dinner June asked me when we were going to fish the next day. I told her that she and Bonnie were going to stay around camp, that Bob and I were going on the river below the dam for rainbow trout. She said, "No way, Jose, we are going with you!" I told her we had to be ready at 4:30 a.m. the next morning. She told me that they would be ready. I called my fiend, Rick Pace, who operated a float service below the dam. I told him that we were going to need another boat. We all fished the river the next day and all caught fish.

The last day Everett Crow, the lodge operator, told me they didn't have guides for us. He said, "You don't need a guide, and if Bob can run a motor, we can get you two boats and motors." June got in the boat with Bob, and Bonnie fished with me. Of course, since Bob had only fished the lake one time, he said, "Take off and we'll follow you!"

We took them up the lake to Big Music Creek, one of my favorite spots. Everett had packed some box lunches for us. We had taken several fish before lunch. After lunch, Bonnie noticed that June was having trouble and was getting discouraged. In the flooded timber she was getting snagged a lot. Bob wasn't used to handling a boat and fishing at the same time. Bonnie suggested that we make a switch. She would fish with Bob and I could help June. It worked very well; June started catching fish. She did well, and when it came time to go in, I was snagged in a tree. Bob said, "Bonnie and I will start in, and you can catch us with that faster motor." I asked if he knew the way in. He said that he did and they took off. June and I were about a half-mile behind them when I saw Bob stop and start messing with his reel. June saw it and wondered what had happened. I told her Bob was lost! She said, "He has flown all over the world, no way could you lose him!" I told her that might be, but he doesn't have any instruments in that boat! We stopped our boat by them, and I asked Bob what the problem was. He said, "Bonnie said go straight ahead, and I told her no, that we needed to go left." I told him they were both wrong, you have to go right. The lake split three ways there, and it was easy to get lost. However, I'll guarantee that you couldn't lose Bob in the air. They were great people, and I'm thankful that our lives crossed on the pathway of life. "Winds of Chance."

We fished two more days on the lake and came home. It had been a great experience for all of us. We lost track of them after that. One day sometime later Bonnie and I were driving to Grand Lake, listening to the news on the radio. It was reported that a B-47 bomber from Schilling Air Force Base had crashed, hitting an oil derrick near McPherson, Kansas, but the crew had parachuted to safety. Bonnie said, "I wonder if that was Bob." In the paper the next day it gave their names, and it was Bob's plane and crew. I saw him later and he told me about it. He ordered his crew out and was going to try to get the plane back to Schilling. He saw that he couldn't and just barely got out in time. He was so low that his crew couldn't see his chute open and thought he had gone down in flames. Again we lost track of them. About 25 years later I went with my boss on his annual trip with the Saddle and Sirloin Club of Kansas City. This particular year they made their headquarters at Shangri-la Resort on Grand Lake in Oklahoma. The boss liked for me to go along, for they usually had a one-day fishing contest with the rest of their activities. After dinner they were to have their card-playing time. I told the boss that I would get my running done. I did my five miles and had just taken a shower when the telephone rang in our room. I usually answer the phone by just saying "Ensley." A lady's voice came on with, "Harold Ensley?" I told her yes. She said, "This is June." I said, "June who?" She said, "June Hughes!" I said, "Major Bob Hughes' wife?" She said, "No, Col. Hughes' wife." I asked where she was calling from, and she said, "Bob and I were just walking across the parking lot and passed your Ford wagon with your name on it. We would like to come by and visit." They did and we had a great visit. Bob had retired as a Colonel. They were living in Tulsa and had a condo there near Shangri-La and had just come up for the weekend. You think of the odds of our meeting after all those years! "Winds of Chance."

Taking Bob fishing started a chain reaction. We received a call from Forbes Air Force Base in Topeka. They asked us if we would take their top bomber crew fishing. I told them I would be happy to, as soon as we could work it into my schedule. We took them to the Lead Hill area of Bull Shoals. They all caught bass, and we made a movie for TV and everyone was happy. A short time later we received a call from the Naval Base at Olathe, Kansas. Their top crew wanted a fishing trip, and we were able to schedule it and again took them to Bull Shoals down by the dam. A few weeks later we received a call from Whiteman Air Force Base. Their bomber crew had won some kind of contest and wanted a fishing trip. We felt honored to take them and we did. To me, every one of every crew was a hero. Some years later I received a long distance call from Wichita, Kansas. I answered as I always do, saying "Ensley." The caller said, "This is Staff Sgt. so-and-so," I can't recall his name. He told me that he watched my TV show and wondered why he saw nothing but brass. How about some enlisted men? I told him I guess it was because no one had asked me. Then I asked him what he did. He told me that he was crew chief on a B-52 bomber out of McConnell Air Force Base in Wichita. I told him that we would be happy to take him if we could work out a time. I asked him how many there would be. He told me six, but they would want to take the Colonel. I got a kick out of him wanting to take the Colonel. I called Everett Crow at Bull Shoals and told him I needed to take a B-52 bomber crew from Wichita somewhere. He asked me the dates and we worked it out. I called the Sgt. and asked him if his crew could meet me at Bull Shoals on that date. It worked out for all of us. It wasn't a problem for me; in fact, I felt honored that they would want to fish with me. We had a great time and caught a lot of bass. The Sgt. lost the biggest bass of the trip. He was in the boat with me and we were using plastic worms. I saw the fish hit and yelled for him to "Set the hook!" He didn't, but just started reeling the fish in. The fish jumped two or three times and just spit the hook out. Honestly, I believe it would have weighed eight pounds or better. It was the big one that got away, but I got the movie! He said, "That okay, I'll catch another that size." However, he didn't! "Winds of Chance."

I don't remember if the Colonel caught a big one or not. They were a great bunch of guys! We have produced our TV series at KSN, Channel 3 in Wichita, for 25 years now, and every time I see a B-52 in the air, I think of that Sgt. "Winds of Chance."

Match the Hatch

WE HEAR MUCH of fly fishermen catching their first fish. They would cut the fish open to see what it was feeding on. Then they would proceed to match the hatch. We made our first trip to Great Bear Lake in the early '60s. We caught a lot of lake trout at Plummer's old camp at Sawmill Bay. Warren Plummer was one of the pioneers in fly-in fishing in the North. In the late '60s during the winter he moved his camp from the south side of Great Bear Lake to the Dease arm on the northwest side of the lake. Warren invited us to come up and explore the fishing there. He had built an airstrip that would accommodate a DC-3. We flew with commercial airlines to Yellowknife, and then he flew us in with his DC-3. Warren was a good operator and pilot. The accommodations were adequate, the food and service excellent, the fishing almost unbelievable, almost like fishing virgin waters. Nearly every boat daily came in with the lake trout in the 30 to 40-lb. class. Everyone was trolling with heavy gear using big Daredevil spoons. I'm not particularly fond of trolling and would much rather cast. My fishing buddy, Wayne Brower, had never been into big lake trout, so we decided to join the trollers. Our guide, Moses Bird, was a native from the Kenora, Ontario area. Warren had brought his guides from southern Canada. Moses liked to troll. I had just invented the reaper and wanted to try it. I told Moses that I wanted to cast. He stopped the boat and said, "Cast." I asked him if he would troll at this spot, meaning to see if we were in the right kind of water to catch fish. Moses said, "Oh, so you want to troll," and started the motor. I told him I wanted to cast in a place where we might have a chance to catch some fish. Moses wasn't too happy with me, I think mainly because he didn't want to paddle the boat. I learned a long time ago that they would rather run the motor than paddle the boat. I had a bass rod with an Ambassador 5500-C and 20-pound test line and one of my ultra-light spinning rods with 4-lb. test line, but Moses didn't take to my using the light line. In fact, he seemed to think I really didn't know how to fish. The days were long; the sun didn't set until midnight and came back up about 2 a.m. I asked Warren if Wayne and I could take a boat after dinner and fish. He told me we could, but that if we tore up a motor on the rocks we would have to pay for it.

So each evening we went out and caught a lot of lake trout casting reapers. However, nothing over 20 lbs. One evening one of the other fishermen, a man from Muskogee,

Oklahoma, with his son, told me that he had found a shallow bay where lake trout were surfacing, evidently feeding on water bugs that were hatching and coming to the surface of the water. He told me that it appeared to be the kind of water for my method, using the reaper and ultra-light gear. He told me that if we wanted to do it we could follow his boat and they would take us to the bay. He had a 16-year-old native guiding him, and as we left the dock the next morning, I asked Moses to follow their boat. He aid, "You mean that kid is our leader!" I said, "That's right, he's our leader!" I could tell that it didn't make Moses very happy. Several other boats went with us, but Moses had a master motor and took off in front of their boat. I told Moses to slow down and follow the kid. He said, "That's right, he's our leader!" When we reached the bay, Wayne told me that we should troll for a ways with our heavy gear to see if he could catch his trophy. This made Moses happy again. We put on our heavy spoons and started trolling. I saw a nice trout surface after a bug, but the boat scared the fish and put it down. I put my ultra-light spinning outfit with the five-inch white reaper on a 1/2-oz. jig head on the boat seat by me. In case it happened again, I would have Moses stop the boat and try to catch the fish. Wayne caught a trout about 15 pounds; Moses netted it and released it. As he started the motor to troll again, he turned to me and said, "One to nothing," as though he was making a contest of it.

I was concentrating more on watching for surfacing fish. Wayne caught another nice trout, and when Moses released it he smiled and said, "Two to nothing." A short time later I hooked a trout, and Moses said, "Two to one." He got the net hung up on the spoon, and the fish got off. Moses put the net down and said, "Two to nothing." I said, "No, Moses, it's two to one, bad guide." As we trolled on a bit, I saw a trout rise for a bug within casting distance. I yelled, "Stop the boat." Moses thought something had gone wrong and cut the motor. I picked up my ultra-light and made a long cast to where the trout had taken the bug. Almost instantly the trout took the reaper. It wasn't a large trout, about 15 or 16 lbs., but with 4-lb. test line it was a good fight. When Moses netted and released the fish, he turned to me and said, "You really can catch fish. I'll take you to them!" We would wait for a trout to rise for a bug, and if you could cast that reaper within a foot or two of the swirl, the trout would take it. Moses was amazed. We had caught a lot of nice trout, mainly from 12 to perhaps 20 lbs.

Other boats were trolling in the area and would put the trout down. One of the boats had a couple of young men from Pennsylvania, and one of them hooked a trout not far from us. He knew that I was taking pictures for television. He yelled over that he had a big fish on light line and wanted to know if I wanted a picture. I asked Moses to run over close to his boat. We did, and you could hear the line singing on the reel. I got the cameras ready for the picture, and Moses asked him how light a line he was using. He told us 8-lb. test. Moses started the motor and took off! He said, "My man gets them on 4-lb. test." Needless to say, we didn't get the picture. Moses was happy and we didn't troll any more, but caught lots of trout. It was fascinating to see a 20-pound trout take a bug the size of your fingernail and throw to it with a five-inch reaper and catch it!

Landing on dirt runway in 737 jet at Plummer's Artic camp

From then on, year after year for 25 years, we went back to Plummer's and caught our trout on reapers. During that time Warren expanded his airstrip to handle DC-6s. What a thrilling sight to see that four-engine plane land on a dirt strip. We would fly commercial to Winnipeg, spend the night, and the next morning early we would take his charter DC-6 in. Then he started using jets. If I remember correctly, the first ones were F-28s, and then he went to 737s. The landing strip was across the bay from the camp. We would walk down the hill to a boat ramp, where they would ferry us across. Later they built a

Beautiful trophy char with my fishing buddy, Jim Higgins, at Canada's Tree River

Bonnie's 32-lb. laker taken on a 5" reaper while feeding on tiny water bugs.

road around the side of the bay and had a school bus to get us to camp. The trail made a great place for me to run, and I used it almost every evening. During that time we caught our trout on reapers using light stuff. My wife got the largest one, 32 lbs. That is, the largest one taken on surfacing flies. She saw the fish feeding on a water bug the size of your little fingernail. She threw to it and got it on a five-inch reaper. However, she was using an ultra-light rod with 6-lb. test line. Our guide killed the fish or we would have released it. We weighed it at the camp, an even 32 lbs. Since then, we have caught them on reapers much larger than that on 4-lb. test line. "Winds of Chance."

In addition to the great lake trout at Plummer's, we had many days of fabulous Arctic grayling. I doubt if you can find a better grayling spot in the world. Year after year we had taken grayling from three and a half to four pounds. We kept thinking we would get a five-pounder. The Arctic char fishing on the river is above and beyond anything you could dream of. I don't think we ever made a trip that we didn't catch a char of 20 lbs. or better. Twenty-three pounds was the largest I hooked, but took a picture of one that weighed 27-1/2 lbs. A Canadian from Peterborough, Ontario had it. I believe he caught it on a blue five-inch reaper. The first few years we used a 3/4-oz. potato bug spoon. One day when we came in for lunch the manager of the resort asked me if I had any extra reapers. He said that's the best lure he had used on char. We started fishing with 1/2-oz. jig heads threaded with five-inch white reaper tails. We caught more and larger char than ever before. "Winds of Chance."

Baseball Experiences

In THE EARLY DAYS of television most stations kept their switchboards open with an operator on duty. At that time there was no taping; everything was done live. Viewers could call in for information about programs and voice their opinions in a little different manner than the talk shows of today. MY TV show in the beginning came on live at 9:30 p.m. for 30 minutes on the CBS affiliate, KCMO, Channel 5. My boss, Joe Hartenbower, kept my program in prime or prime access time for 22 years. Then there were only three channels available. Many times after my show the switchboard would light up with calls. I always took every call that came in! It gave you a special closeness with the audience. My program preceded the 10:00 news, weather and sports.

One night as I was taking my calls, Tony Williams, the sportscaster for the station, came by the switchboard. Enos Slaughter, former Cardinals star, had just been traded to the Kansas City Athletics and had been Tony's guest. Tony introduced me to Slaughter and said, "Enos loves to hunt and fish, so maybe you guys should get together!" It was a happy occasion for me to meet Enos. We became friends, hunting and fishing together. He was more of a hunter than a fisherman, but loved to do both. Enos hunted and fished just as he played ball, and with the same intensity. I'll never forget the time when the State of South Dakota invited me to bring Slaughter up for a pheasant hunt. They put a new crew with us each day, but it didn't slow Enos down. I can still see him chasing a crippled pheasant across the field. I saw the bird, then Enos, then the Labrador retriever. Enos was close behind the pheasant, and the dog behind Enos.

One evening at dinner while we were there, the head of their Little League baseball program at Aberdeen, South Dakota, came to me and asked if Enos would mind speaking to a special meeting of all their teams on Saturday morning before we went hunting. At that time you were not allowed to hunt pheasant until noon. I told him I was sure that Enos would be honored to do it. Enos did speak to a huge group of fathers and sons. He signed autographs, answered questions and delighted the crowd. I noticed a man and his boy standing in back of the crowd. I went to them and asked the man if his boy didn't want an autograph. He said, "Yes, but he is too shy and bashful to ask for it." I took the kid and his dad to Enos and introduced them. Enos signed an autograph for the kid. I've been with Enos a lot and have never seen him turn anyone down. The kid's dad asked me if we had plenty of places to hunt. He said that he didn't allow much hunting, but he owned several thousand acres and would welcome us if we wanted to hunt. "Winds of Chance."

Later, Enos was traded to the Yankees. Their first trip in to play the Kansas City Athletics, Enos called me. He asked me if I would take him fishing. He said, "We have a rookie second baseman, Bobby Richardson, who wants to come along. We drove out to Peculiar, Missouri, to Baier's Den Kennels. They had a shooting preserve, but had just built a new 37-acre lake for fishing. The lake was new and full of bass. Enos fished with Buddy Baier, and Bobby fished with me. I don't believe that Bobby had fished much, but he caught a lot of fish. This started a chain reaction of fishing with members of the Yankee ball club. Bobby and Tony Kubek were good friends. Each time they came to Kansas City, we would take them fishing and have remained friends to this day. I had always been a baseball fan, but it was a big thrill to get to fish with them. Tony and Bobby liked to Hunt, Bobby for quail, and Tony for ducks and geese. I have some good hunting stories but will save them for a book on hunting that we are planning to write.

About that time a red-headed outfielder named Bob Martyn who played with the Yankees then came to the Kansas City A's. We became fiends. He was from Oregon and loved to fish. He told me of their great steelhead fishing. When he retired, he called me from his home in Beaverton, Oregon, and invited me to come fish with him. Producing a 30-minute TV show kept me constantly looking for material. We scheduled a trip, and I flew to Portland, where he met me and took me to his home. I had never fished for steelhead, and I was excited about being there with him. The first day we each caught our limit of nice steelhead on ultra-light tackle and spoons. Fishing from a boat, we fished either the Nestucca or the Wilson River. I'm not sure which, but the next day we waded one of the streams. Bob would point to the likely spot and tell me to cast there. He always gave me the first shot. I would say, "There has got to be a fish there." He would make a cast and get a fish. I asked him what I was doing wrong. He told me he didn't think I was feeling the fish hit. When you are fishing from a boat, you need to cast overhand, which I could do accurately. When we waded the streams with willow and trees overhanging water behind you and the same kind of cover on the opposite side of the river, you needed to cast side-arm. I was having problems getting my spoon close enough to the spots he showed me.

I'll never forget, he showed me a good spot and I got my spoon caught in the willows on the opposite side. Bob calmly handed me his rod. He said, "Cast this, and I'll get yours loose." He saw that I was going to cast his spoon under some willows across the river, about where my rod was snagged. He told me not to cast under the overhang, that I would get snagged up. I had already committed my cast; the spoon hit the water flat and skipped back under the willows. I felt the line tighten and thought to myself, he was right. I thought I'd gotten his lure snagged, and then I felt the fish shake its head. I yelled at Bob to get the movie camera off the bank and film the sequence. It was a nice steelhead, and Bob filmed it for my TV show. Bob and I had some good trips together. He's an excellent steelhead and salmon fisherman. In all the trips I made

Bob Martyn, former Yankee outfielder, with Oregon steelhead

with him, he never tried to show how good he was. I was his guest; he always gave me the first shot. It was a special courtesy he extended to me, and I'll always remember it.

I was talking to Bobby Richardson recently and was telling him about my book and that I plan to name a team from the players I had fished with. When I mentioned Bob Martyn, he said, "We played together at Denver, then a Yankee farm team, and then we both went up to the parent club in New York.

I was thinking the other day, we could put a pretty good team together with players we have been privileged to fish with! We could use our friend, David Glass, owner, and Whitey Herzog and Joe Gordon as co-managers; Darryl Porter and Buck Martinez as catchers; Catfish Hunter, Ralph Terry, Ernie Knevel, Bobby Shantz, Tom Bermeir and Preacher Rowe as pitchers; Pete LaCock at first base; Bobby Richardson at second; Tony Kubek at shortstop; Cletis Boyer and George Brett at third; Ted Williams, Mickey Mantle

Whitey Herzog and Bill Grigsby in conference on the mound

and Joe DiMaggio in the outfield; Enos Slaughter, Bob Martyn and Jerry Lumpe as D.H.'s; Harry Craft and Hank Bauer as coaches at first and third. Quite a line-up!
"Winds of Chance."

Bass Fishing Deluxe

WHEN THE CORPS OF ENGINEERS started building dams and impounding waters in the Midwest, it changed our pattern of fishing. In northwest Arkansas, they built Norfork Dam on the Norfork River near Mountain Home, Arkansas. The Norfork River was a tributary of the White River. The source of the White River was in the Boston Mountains south of Fayetteville, Arkansas. It flowed northward into southern Missouri, then eastward to Branson and Forsythe, Missouri. It then flowed back into Arkansas, and it was a tributary of the famous Red River from Texas. In the early '50s during a flood it changed its course and flowed into the Mississippi in south Arkansas. Lake Norfork became one of the hottest big bass lakes in the country. Bull Shoals Dam on the White River was just a few miles from Mountain Home, Arkansas, and Lake Norfork was built in the early '50s. It formed Bull Shoals Lake. We were privileged to fish it as the basin filled. I have a special feeling for Bull Shoals Lake, for there with G.O. Tilley, one of the best all-around fishermen I've met in my lifetime, we learned to bass fish in impounded waters. Because of the great trophy bass fishing on these two reservoirs, the dedication to bass fishing erupted; we thought it was the ultimate.

People who fished got to thinking that bass fishermen were smarter than anyone else! I would hear people say, "You have to be smarter than the fish and you have to think like fish to be good!" My observation over the years has convinced me that if that's what it takes, none of us will make it. Certainly we have made great strides in equipment and techniques that have changed the picture, but I'll still maintain, until the fish learn to read and write and talk, we will not have all the answers. If we had all the answers, there would not be a fish left to catch. Fishing would lose its charm if you knew it all. I've seen so many things out fishing that prove my point.

My boss at KCMO TV, the CBS affiliate in Kansas City, Joe Hartenbauer, loved to go fishing with me. He was entertaining some dignitaries from Chicago and wanted to take them to Bull Shoals fishing. Just before time for us to leave, the engineers went out on strike. He told me to take the group on to Bull Shoals and take care of them. He was to follow later. He aid, "Be sure you have a good guide for you and me." Rack Pace was my guide, and I told him we needed to put the guests in fish, but I also wanted to save a good spot for the boss. We had located several places that we thought would work. When he came, we took him to one of my favorite spots near Barnes Hollow. Joe was having a little problem casting. At that time we were using braided line, but we did not have free spool reels. We usually used about five or six feet of synthetic leader and were using a six-inch plastic worm on a 3/8 -oz. jig head. In desperation, I had Rack anchor the boat at the edge of the timbered bluff. We had Joe cast off the deep side so that he could limber up his arm casting and not get snagged. He was doing fairly well until he really cut loose with a big heave. He had about as bad a backlash as you can get. The plastic worm went about 15 feet from the boat and sank slowly down. He started picking out the backlash. Naturally, you don't watch your boss pick out his mess or say anything. Out of the corner of my eye I saw his rod-tip bounce. I yelled, "Set the hook." He really didn't, but hooked the fish anyway. He just reeled the fish in, right over the backlash. It was about a 3-1/2-pound bass. I netted the fish, took it off his hook and put the fish on the stringer. I tossed the plastic worm back over the side of the boat into the water. Joe stripped off line down to the backlash and again started picking out the mess. Out of the corner of my eye again I saw his rod-tip bend down. I said, "Joe, you have another one." He reeled that fish in right over the old backlash. It was another bass about the same size. I netted the fish, took it off the hook and put it on a stringer. This time I didn't put the plastic worm back in the water. I thought to myself, this guy could ruin the lake. I said, "Joe, you just set a new record, two separate bass on one backlash!" We both laughed about it. I'm sure there is not a bass fisherman anywhere who hasn't caught a fish on a backlash. Proving my point that doing the wrong thing sometimes produces a catch!

That afternoon Joe really got with the program! He caught a lot of fish and said to me, "Why does it take you all week to make a bass movie, when we have caught a boat load in one afternoon!" I laughed and said, "Boss, there is more to it than that!" He fished all morning without a fish, and then accidentally caught two bass. "Winds of Chance."

If he hadn't had a backlash, he would not have caught those two bass. I'll always have a warm spot in my heart for Joe. He believed in me and kept my program in prime and prime access all the 22 years we worked together. We fished together many times, but I must tell you one more incident.

We were fishing out of Baxter boat dock on Table Rock Lake. Ernie Knevel, former Yankee pitcher, and roommate, a Mickey Mantle, was our guide. It was just by chance that I met him, first at the old K.C. ball park on Brooklyn Ave. That was before Kansas City had a major league team. The St. Paul Saints were in town for a series with the Kansas City Blues. I had taken my boys, Smokey and Dusty, to the game. We liked to go early and watch hitting practice. The boys liked it because they could run down foul balls in the stands before the fans all gathered. I was sitting by myself back of home plate. I heard someone yell, "Hey, you!" I looked all around and couldn't see anyone, and then I looked on the field. A player in a St. Paul uniform yelled for me to come down. He said, "I'm Ernie." I told him that I knew who he was. He asked me if I would take him fishing sometime. He told me that he spent the winters in Kansas City and had watched my TV show. I told him to call me when the season was over and we would schedule something. "Winds of Chance."

That winter he called me. We drove to Grand Lake in Oklahoma to crappie fish. We were fishing one night off the boat dock on Honey Creek when a car pulled up and stopped on the road above us. Someone yelled at us. Ernie said, "Harold, that's Mick." I said, Mick?" He said, "Yes, Mickey Mantle!" Mickey came on down to the dock and fished with us. He was visiting his family in Commerce, Oklahoma, and had heard that Ernie and I were there. He stayed and fished late that night. It was a real thrill for me. "Winds of Chance."

By the way, I have a 9 x 12 picture of Mickey. On it he said, "To Harold Ensley, the world's second-best fisherman, Mickey Mantle #1." But getting back to Knevel, we caught a lot of big crappie. We brought them back to Kansas City, and he showed them on my TV show. At that time he was pitching for the Yankees. He retired to Table Rock Lake and started guiding on Taneycomo, as well as the lake.

But back to the day he guided Joe and me on Table Rock Lake. The lake had just filled, and the crappie were around the cedar trees in numbers you would hardly believe. Big crappie, the black species with the black stripe from the top of their head to the dorsal fin. Some of the cedars were still green and partly submerged. We were catching lots of big crappie on jigs. Ernie had tied to a green cedar top and we were casting toward another. Another party tied to the cedar near us and started catching crappie on minnows with a bobber set three feet deep. We had brought a bucket of minnows in case we needed them, but hadn't used them. Joe said, "Ernie, why can't I fish with a minnow?" Ernie rigged him up with a minnow and a bobber. Joe made a cast. The minnow and bobber went into a cedar tree. Joe gave a big jerk. The minnow and bobber came flying back by us and hit in the cedar tree to which we were tied. Without looking around at Ernie, Joe said, "Ernie, how's my minnow?" Ernie answered, "Joe, that minnow is pretty nervous. I'll put on a fresh one," and he did. But that Ernie Knevel was a funny man. We fished together many times until he passed away. Those are things that bring out the charm of fishing!

It isn't always the orthodox way that produces. You who fish just think of the times you were fishing and decided to move to another spot. Everyone starts reeling in their lure to make a move, and someone reeling in at a speed faster than normal would catch a fish. They wouldn't have caught a fish had they not accelerated their retrieve. Sometimes you fish the shoreline, while the fish are in the middle of the coves. I remember a time at Bull Shoals Lake we were casting Zarah Spooks. It's a lure that requires finessing, and it gets to be work after a while. We had fished from early morning until almost noon with nothing, pulled into one of our favorite coves, working the shoreline with long casts. The Zarah is a lure that makes you think you're a good caster. It goes so far so easy. I made a long, hard, heavy heave to reach the shoreline. The reel backlashed, and the Zarah fell about 30 feet from the boat and was motionless on the water. After a few minutes with the lure motionless, there was an explosion as a bass smacked that motionless Zarah. It wasn't a big bass, about 4-1/2 or 5 pounds. I had been finessing that Zarah all that morning with nothing, and then caught a bass on a motionless lure. That's not the way it is supposed to happen, and the fish wasn't supposed to be in the middle of the cove in 30 feet of water. I said to my fishing buddy, "We have been using the wrong retrieve and fishing the wrong water." Let's start casting the middle of the coves and let the Zarah be dead motionless. We proceeded to do so and caught our limit of good bass and made our movie. Sometimes we outsmart ourselves. I've seen it happen on all kinds of fish in many parts of the world.

People will ask how much of fishing is luck and how much is skill. You've heard the expression, "I'd rather be lucky than good!" If I had my way, I would like to be lucky AND good. If I hadn't seen that bass hit a motionless bait, I do not think I would have caught enough fish for my program — what's the answer? "Winds of Chance," and adapting to it. To me, that is the mystique of fishing.

I remember fishing out of the Buck Creek area of Bull Shoals. It was a cold winter day, about six inches of snow on the ground, but no ice. I was with two top bass fishermen; we were fishing up Big Creek, just across the Missouri state line. We hadn't done any good all morning. I was using a 5-oz. jig with a 6-inch pork eel. I had missed one strike and caught one small Kentucky. We were casting to the rocky shoreline, but for some strange reason I cannot explain I cast on the other side of the boat, toward the deep side away from the bluff. I let it sink to the bottom, and I felt a little pressure and set the hook. I yelled, "Boy, I finally got one, get the camera!" One of the men got the camera and got pictures of me fighting this fish and landing it. We weighed it when we went in for lunch, and it weighed 9-1/2 pounds. I'd always said I would not have a bass mounted until I caught a 10-pounder. After lunch we went back at it. I was so happy with my big bass, I really didn't work at it. Just at dusk across from Big Creek I was using a Twinspin out in deep water. I felt a gentle peck, set the hook and landed the bass, almost identical to the other one. We took it in to camp. It weighed an even nine pounds. I had them mounted, and they are on display in the Missouri Sports Hall of Fame at Springfield, Missouri. I had caught a 9-lb. bass in two different states the same day. One was on the Missouri side and one was on the Arkansas side. If I had first made a cast on the wrong side of the boat, it wouldn't have happened. Why? "Winds of Chance."

As I look back, I think of another story that wouldn't have happened if my guide hadn't snagged into a tree along a buff bank. This happened on the 10th of March in 1961. I had scheduled a personal appearance at Miami, Oklahoma, for the American Legion Boat and Sports Show. I told them I had to first go to Bull Shoals to shoot a bass picture for TV. They said, "Bring us a big bass." It so happened that a famous newspaper columnist and author was scheduled to be at the resort at the same time I was to get there. Everett Crow, who operated Crow-Barnes Resort, called me and asked if I would be willing to fish with these guys. I told them that I would be honored. We both arrived the same afternoon and the next day went out to fish. It was a windy, chilly day. He was a famous fly fisherman. The bass at that time were in about 25 to 30 feet of water. We beat the water to a froth to no avail. I was casting and he was fly-casting. Later in the afternoon he said that he needed to drive into Harrison, Arkansas, some 40 miles, to wire his story back to his newspaper. He said, "I know what my story is going to be; I fished with one of the top bass fishermen in America, in one of the top bass lakes in America, and we got skunked!" I don't mind not getting a string of fish, but I hate to get skunked!

I asked Bill Rose, our guide, to please stop by Big Sister Creek on the way in. He did and I caught a 3-lb. Kentucky bass. I turned to my friend and said, "I don't know about your story, but I caught one." That night at dinner he expressed great disappointment in the fishing, having herd of the big bass in Bull Shoals. The next morning he fished with his companion, and me by myself. Bill rose, who passed away since then, was my guide, and he was one of the best! We caught several small fish, but nothing of any consequence. After lunch the man and his companion went in to wire his story.

We were fishing in Big Music Creek, one of my favorite spots. At that time I had a throat infection and was on antibiotics. Bill was fishing with me and we were catching some small bass. He looked at me and said, "You're sick, let's head for the barn." I said, "Bill, I want to save 20 minutes to prove to my friend that there are still big bass in this lake." He said, "No one has taken a big bass in the last six weeks, where would you do it?" I said, "The Frost Bluff." He said, "Nobody ever caught a big bass along Frost Bluff." I said, "I know that, but I'm sure they are there." We got a few more small bass, and he said, "If you're going to get that big bass, we had better start in." We were in a cedar strip boat with a 25-horse motor and about 40 minutes away. "I said, "Bill, we'll just take a few minutes." It was almost sunset when we came to the bluff, and he asked me where I wanted to stop. I told him, he stopped, and I cast a Twinspin with a 6-inch black eel into the standing dead trees at the edge of the bluff. I got hung up on a snag the very first cast and started to break it off. Bill told me not to break it, we would go get it, and we did. It was almost dusk when Bill cast into the bluff, and he hung up on a snag. He started to break it off, but I said, "No, you got mine; let's get yours!" He paddled the boat in and I made a cast parallel with the bluff and the standing trees. I felt a tap, set the hook and said, "Bill, I got the one I wanted!" He said, "You're kidding me." He broke his line off and started to paddle out away from the timber. The bass got in the tree. He told me he was afraid to turn the light on, lest he scare the fish. We worked the bass out of the brush, and it surfaced. He said, "Man, you've got a hog!" But he missed it with a net. My heart sank as I only had 11-lb. test line. The next pass, he dipped the fish over into the boat. I put my hands to my face with my elbows on my knees. Bill turned his light on, pulled my right arm down and said, "I know you're hurting, but I want to shake your hand. I've caught one 10-1/2-lb. bass, and this one is larger." We took it in and weighed it, an even 11 pounds. Not large for a bass, but okay for our part of the country. My friend took a picture of it for his paper. He was happy, I was happy, and the American Legion of Miami, Oklahoma was happy! I had the fish mounted, and it also is on display with the rest of my fish in the Missouri Sports Hall of Fame east of Springfield, Missouri, on

My 11-lb. bass taken in Lake Bull Shoals on 20-minute stop

Highway 60. If Bill Rose hadn't had his lure snagged in the timber of Frost Bluff, I wouldn't have caught the fish. The answer! "Winds of Chance." That's the mystique that could happen to you.

Years ago plans were in the making to harness the mighty Colorado for power and for water for the desert lands of western Arizona and southern California. I don't know that anyone had any idea as to what would develop on the fishing side. Boulder Dam, near Las Vegas, Nevada, was a project of monstrous proportions. It was a tremendous engineering feat, but it worked. We had heard of the great fishing on Lake Mead and of the trout fishing below the dam on the river itself. Little did I dream that I would ever fish it. In the late '50s we received an invitation from the State of Nevada to explore the bass fishing on the lake. We were to stay at the Flamingo Hotel in Las Vegas and fish with one Abe Schiller, executive director of the Flamingo. He was the big fisherman on Lake Mead.

My wife didn't like to fly, so she rode a train to Las Vegas and I flew. There were no direct flights from Kansas City to Las Vegas, so I had to go by way of Phoenix. A passenger next to me on the plane was from Kansas City and worked for one of the Ford dealers, who were my sponsors on TV. He recognized me, and in the course of our conversation during the flight he told me that he didn't have reservations and wondered if I might help him find a place to stay in Las Vegas. I told him that the executive director of the Flamingo Hotel was to meet me at the airport and take me to the hotel. I told him I was sure that the man would take care of him. We arrived safely and got our luggage, which included my rod cases and camera gear. Schiller was nowhere to be seen as I stood by my luggage. A Red Cap asked me if I needed a taxi. I told him no, that I was going to be picked up. About 30 minutes later I was still standing there, and again the Red Cap asked me if I needed a taxi. I told him no, that Abe Schiller of the Flamingo was to meet me and take me to the hotel. He said, "I should have known that when I saw your fishing gear."

Mr. Schiller is the best fisherman in these parts. I was hardly prepared for what I saw, a man with a cowboy hat, cowboy boots and a sequined shirt and fancy Western pants. Gene Autry couldn't have dressed better! He was a big man, loud and boisterous. I expected Tom Mix or Gene Autry to come riding in. Sometimes first impressions can fool you, and I thought to myself, am I to fish with that? I told him of the passenger who needed a room. He said, "No problem, but where's your wife?" I told him she was coming in on a train about 10 p.m. that night. He drove us to the Flamingo and arranged for our rooms and invited us to his office. He had all kinds of pictures of him with fish he had caught, mostly taken with movie stars from Hollywood. One I remember, he was holding a string of nice bass, with Juliet Prowse, the dancer. As we were leaving, he said, "Trouble with all you outdoor writers, I have to catch all your fish!" The man with me said, "That may be so, but I want to be around when you come in the first day."

My wife arrived on time, but was worn out from the train ride. I told my wife that we might be in for trouble. Abe was very nice and told us to rest until about noon, and we would go out. He said, "I bought $25 worth of water dogs for bait, and we will catch some fish. The next day we drove to Boulder City to the marina where he kept their boat. It was a big new Chris-Craft, and certainly not what I was expecting for a bass fishing trip. He introduced us to his skipper and told us that this man could put us into fish if anyone could.

Lake Mead is a beautiful lake. The area surrounding the lake is what you would expect in the Southwest, barren and unforgiving, but with its own style of beauty. I wanted some pictures of the trip up the Lake, and to start the trip Abe and I sat on the seat in the stern. I had my wife Bonnie get some shots of Abe and me getting my tackle ready. I hadn't brought much in the way of lures, a few top water baits, some jars of pork eel, and some 1/2-oz. jig heads. Abe looked at the pork eel and laughed! He said, "Nobody here has had any success with that stuff. You have to use water dogs in this lake." Bonnie took the pictures of us as we went along. We also filmed the rugged countryside along the lake. After about an hour's ride the skipper found his pet spot, anchored the big pleasure craft and prepared to fish. I shot my preliminary stuff of the two of them, each one baiting up with a live water dog. I just sat there with my movie camera ready. Bonnie, my wife, is an excellent bass fishing lady, but was just observing the proceedings. It was almost dead calm on the water, and it was a hot day. Fortunately, in boats that size you have protection from the sun. Abe and his skipper were fishing off the stern, but Bonnie and I were sitting in the shade. Almost immediately Abe had a fish. He was a big "ham" and put on quite a show for our film. His skipper netted the fish, about a 3-1/2-lb. bass. We shot pictures of Abe holding up his bass, and I said, "Now release it, Abe." He said, "What?" I repeated it again, telling him to release the fish. He said, "No way; we are going to have a big fish fry for you tonight at the Flamingo. You have never eaten fish like our chef at the Flamingo fixes them!"

"That was just what we needed, a fish fry!" Bonnie looked at me as if to say why are they planning to feed us fish? We both love to eat fish, but were expecting something different in a place like the Flamingo in Las Vegas. We didn't say anything, but went on taking pictures of them catching fish and putting them in the live well. For a break in the action, I asked Bonnie to handle the camera and I would try my jig and eel. Abe laughed and said, "Are you really going to use that stuff? We have plenty of water dogs for you." I told him that I wanted to try it just the same. We were stationed in water about 20 feet deep. The only way I could fish was off the side of the boat. I dropped the jig to the bottom, lifted it up about a foot, and felt a fish take it. I was a little over-anxious and set the hook too soon, missing the fish. I told Bonnie that I did have a strike, but missed the fish. Abe said to his skipper, "That guy can't tell when he has a rock or a fish," and they both laughed. I dropped the bait back down, lifted it off the bottom a ways, got another strike. I let the fish run as I would with a plastic worm, set the hook and had a fish. Bonnie got pictures of me playing the fish, rod bending and such; then I asked Abe to net my fish. It was a bass that would go four pounds or better. Bonnie took pictures of Abe and me holding the fish, and I released it over the side of the boat. Abe said, "Man, why did you do that? We want to take fish in with us!" I told him that we used to keep bass, but had started a campaign to release the bass and eat crappie or other fish. I dropped the eel back down and for six straight drops caught fish. I heard a splat, and Abe had thrown his water dogs into the lake and asked if he could try a jig and eel. He did and immediately caught a bass. Then his skipper tried it and caught fish. We finished that part of the movie and headed for the dock.

Abe and his skipper had saved enough fish for his fish fry. On the way to Las Vegas, Abe said, "What time do you want to eat? How's 10 o'clock?"" Abe told us to rest awhile, and then we could try Pierre's fish. It was good, but no better than the crappie filets that we eat back home!

Abe said, "I have tickets for you for the 12 p.m. McGuire Sisters' Show and the 3 a.m. Giselle McKenzie Show." Bonnie looked at me, and I could see what was going on in her mind. We drive all night to get to Canada on our trip, but to be up most of the night in Las Vegas was different. We went to see the McGuire Sisters, as Bonnie always watched them on the Arthur Godfrey show and was thrilled to see them in person. She wasn't too excited about going to another show and said, "Do we have to go?" I told her we didn't have to go, but that wouldn't be very nice after Abe had gone to the trouble getting tickets for us. She said, "Maybe he forgot about it!" Abe didn't forget; I asked the maitre d' if he had tickets for the Ensleys. He said, "Yes, sir, right down on Kings Row." It was a good show and we enjoyed it, but it hardly prepared us for the next bass fishing.

We fished the water near the dam and from fishing boats instead of a big pleasure cruiser. Using top water lures, we had a great day catching a lot of nice bass. I don't think we caught anything over six pounds, yet a lot of bass good enough to finish our movie. Abe kept telling us about the great fishing on the Colorado below the dam. He said that we should be able to catch enough trophy trout for another movie for our show. The next day we put in below the dam on the Arizona side. We had guides using aluminum jon boats. Believe me, Boulder Dam is an awesome site, whether from the top as a tourist or fishing below the dam. It is one of the great engineering feats of our nation, and built before we had a lot of equipment that engineers have today. I was thrilled at the chance to fish there, but we caught nothing. I would like to try it again with the knowledge and methods we have learned through the years. I told Abe of the fabulous trout fishing we had on the White River before Bull Shoals Dam in Arkansas. At that time it wasn't unusual for boats to come in with limit strings of rainbows, running from five pounds up into the teens. I invited Abe to come back to fish with us. He did, and we had a great trip on the White River. My first impression of Abe when he picked me up at the airport was all wrong. We had become great friends in the short time we were there and remained friends through the years. Bonnie and I had found a fishing buddy in Las Vegas! "Winds of Chance."

My reporter for fishing conditions on the Gravois arm of Lake of the Ozarks, Gib Morgan, invited me down to fish and do a story for television. At that time we had reporters on most of the lakes in the four-state area, Oklahoma, Arkansas, Missouri and Kansas. In most cases we had four or five different areas in each lake reporting to us daily, Monday through Friday, for our radio show. We had fished many times on Lake of the Ozarks, but had never fished the Gravois arm. We arranged a date and invited a friend of mine, Buddy Baier, who operated a shooting preserve near Peculiar, Missouri, to go help me get a picture for my television show. Buddy was more of a hunter than a fisherman, but wanted to catch a big bass. We drove down to Versailles, picked up our reporter, Gib Morgan, at his tackle store near the Soap Creek arm, and then drove down to Washburn's point, a resort owned by Paul Washburn. Gib had arranged for Guido Hibdon and his son Teen to guide us. The Hibdon family had a reputation for being the best guides on the lake. Guido's dad before him may have been one of the first guides in the area. They had two 14-ft. aluminum boats with small outboards for us to use. Gib introduced us to Guido and his boy Teen, and we made ready with our gear and cameras to go fish.

I had intended for Buddy to be in the boat with me, but Guido said to me, "Get your fanny in the boat; me and Teen have heard of your reputation and we want you between us. We are going to whip your little ol' fanny!" Guido was a big man and a little gruff, but I found that he had a big heart! I said, "It will not make you a big hero to outfish me. Let's just catch fish have fun and make a movie." The motors were small and slow. Guido took us around to Soap Creek, and we started fishing, Teen in front, Guido in the back, and I'm in the middle. I asked them what they were using, and Guido said, "Black Lucky Sixty-Sixes." I had one in my tackle box and was going to tie it on, but I had left a 6-inch jig with eel tied on from a previous day of fishing. I normally would have taken the eel off the jig and put it back in the jar so that it would not dry out. I guess I got in a hurry and left it on. It had dried out and shriveled up! I was going to cut it off and tie on a Lucky Sixty-Six. Guido saw the dried eel and said to his boy, "Look, Teen, this guy is going to use one of those bacon rinds. I guided a doctor last week, and he put one on, and I laughed at him until he took it off!" I had planned to take it off and tie on a Lucky Sixty-Six until he said that. I had one jar of Lutz 6-inch pork eel in my box. They came three in a jar, and I had used one, so I just had two left. I cut the dried one off and put on a fresh one. They were already casting along the shoreline. I made a cast and felt a fish pick up the lure. Being a little over-anxious, I set the hook too soon and missed the fish. Guido saw me set the hook and get nothing! He said, "Teen, this guy can't tell when he has a stick or a fish." They both laughed and cast into the same spot but caught nothing. A few casts later I felt a fish, let it take it a ways, set the hook and had a 4-1/2-lb. bass. I yelled at Buddy and Gib in the other boat to come and take a picture. Back in those days we kept the fish. Sometime later I caught one that weighed 7-1/2 pounds, got a picture, then another about five pounds. Guido yelled at Teen in the front of the boat and said, "Son, can't you see what he's doing?" Teen said, "Yes, Dad, I'm eating my heart out." Then Guido asked if he could have one of the jigs and the last eel. I gave it to him; he tied it on and soon hooked a 7-1/2-lb. bass. I took the picture and told them that we needed to go back to the car and that Gib and I would drive into town and get some more eel. We did, and Teen also started using a jig and eel. Everyone caught fish! Big Guido caught a 7-1/2-pounder. We made the movie and boated 14 bass that weighed 56 pounds. From that day until he passed away, Guido never picked up his rod and reel in my boat while guiding me. He became one of my best friends and boosters. When his young son, whom we called Little Guido, started guiding, he guided us many times. He later became one of the top bass fishermen on the tournament trail. Now his son Dion is right up at the top of the list, but I have never fished with Dion. I need to do that to make it three generations of Hibdons.

I called Marge Carrington the other day to see if she had a picture of those bass that we caught with Teen and Big Guido. That day we ended up in front of their resort, Two Waters, where we weighed in the fish. Marge and Ed were some of the pioneer resort operators in the area. Marge told me she didn't take a picture that day. I knew somebody did, as I had seen it somewhere. I told her I was writing a book and wanted to use a picture of Big Guido. She promised to get me a picture and said, "In your book, tell about that day at Hot Dog Point." I had even forgotten about it! She added, "That was the first time you brought your reaper bait to this area." I said, "Yes, and that was a hot day." She said, "I remember it was on the 12th of July and the temperature was over 100 degrees. You guys had caught a lot of good bass on a black reaper at night but, of course, couldn't get any pictures for television."

That day we decided to fish daytime in spite of the heat. Dusty and Ed Carrington were in one boat, Little Guido and I were in the other. Man, it was hot. I was throwing a 5-inch reaper on a 1/2-oz. jig head with 4-lb. test line on my ultra-light spinning rod. We had fished for several hours with nothing. As we worked along the shoreline of the point at Indian Creek, three or four families were having a picnic on the point. They recognized us and wanted to know how we were doing. We told them no good, but that we might do better if we could have one of their hot dogs. They told us to come on in! We beached the boats and went up to where they were gathered in the shade. They shared their hot dogs with us and gave us something cold to drink. We thanked them, shoved our boats off and started fishing again. The first cast I caught a six-pound bass, and Dusty took the movie of it. We all started fishing and hooking nice bass. We made the movie right in front of their spot. To this day, it is known as "Hot Dog Point." Our thanks to Marge for bringing it to our attention! "Winds of Chance."

Alanska

ONE DAY in the early summer of 1962, the morning paper told of a prominent contractor of Nevada, Missouri, who had been rescued off the north coast of Alaska. He and his partner were polar bear hunting and became separated from their companion plane. They got lost, ran out of fuel and were forced to land on the ice. They evidently hit a soft spot in the ice and the plane broke through, but they were able to get out safely with some of their equipment, a little food and two sleeping bags. They made it safely to land, but were unable to make contact with anyone. They ate a snack and curled up in their sleeping bags. An Eskimo found them the next day. It was a harrowing experience, but they both survived.

I thought it would be nice for him to come on both radio and TV to tell his story and tell about their big game hunting operation. As I remember, their big thing was bear hunting, both polar and kodiaks, but they also outfitted for caribou and Dahl sheep. He asked me if I wanted to kill a bear. I said no, but if one of us had to go, it would be the bear. I also told them that I would like to fish in Alaska if I had the opportunity. He said his partner was not much of a fisherman, but they would be glad to fly me out to fishing waters, if I could arrange to get into Anchorage.

We set up the trip, and I flew to meet his partner to fish. It wasn't an easy flight, as I had to leave after my TV show at 10 p.m. with all my equipment, fishing gear, clothes and two movie cameras and film. I made the trip by myself, a real hassle, but really the "Chance of a lifetime." They had arranged for a young ski instructor, Gary King, an excellent fly fisherman, to fish with me. The first day the pilot took us to a small lake where we caught several trout, but nothing that I would call picture fish. However, the pilot flew us over the glacier country for some spectacular scenic beauty shots! Gary said, "Tomorrow we're going to take you to the Russian River to catch sockeye salmon." He told me that he had a special fly that was a killer. It was the only fly he had ever tied or used that consistently caught the sockeye. To me, it looked like he had used some Plymouth Rock chicken feathers.

The next morning the weather didn't look too promising, but we flew out to the Russian River. He could not land the float plane on the river, so we touched down on a small lake above the spot where we planned to fish. Usually the only access to the river was by fly-in or four-wheel-drive vehicle, five or six miles below the area, and hike up the banks of the river. The pilot suggested we put on our rain gear. If it started raining, it would be a long walk back to get it. We started downstream, and Gary was beating the water to a froth with his favorite fly. I followed him with the camera and my ultra-light spinning gear. It was a beautiful stream, and we saw lots of sockeye. However, the sockeye didn't take to Gary's fly. We reached his pet spot below a falls where there was a deep pool, where the water was fairly quiet. Then it started to rain. Not being able to shoot any movies, I decided to test the fishing. I tied on a 1/8-oz. white Maribou crappie jig. The first cast I hooked a salmon but couldn't handle it on 6-lb. test line. I was tying on another jig when I heard a man tell the pilot that he had put two letters in his plane and asked him to mail them when he got back to Anchorage. He then asked the pilot if someone in his party was from the states. The pilot pointed to me and said, "That guy in the rain parka." The young visitor walked over where I was fishing. I turned to speak to him. He said, "Harold Ensley, what are you doing here?" I said, "Who are you?" He said, "Bill Jennings from Joplin, Missouri. I went to school with your boys, Smokey and Dusty." I asked him what he was doing here. He said, "I'm the game warden and I'm here counting salmon on their run up the stream. I asked him if he were by himself and if that wasn't a pretty lonely job. I said, "Aren't you afraid of the bears?" He said, "Yes, but I watch carefully!" He went on his way back upstream. We caught some fish, but no pictures for my show. The rain stopped, and we were able to fly back out to Anchorage.

The next morning was the start of a beautiful day. They asked me where I wanted to fish. I said to take me back to the Russian River and let me get some pictures of the young game warden catching a fish for my show. We flew back into the spot near where he was working, counting salmon. I asked him if he would mind working with us for an hour or so. I told him what we had in mind. He told me that his parents watch me religiously on K.O.A.M. TV in Pittsburgh, Kansas. When we finished the picture of him, I asked for his parents' phone number and address so I could notify them to see their son. I asked if there was anything he wanted me to tell them. He said, "Tell them I'm fine, and tell that redheaded girlfriend that I'm going to come back and marry her." He went back to his work.

I told Gary that I needed to catch a sockeye and showed him how to run the camera. The day before I'd hooked several on my ultra-light gear but had them break off. I cast a 1/8-oz. Maribou jig into the swirling waters and immediately had a hook-up. The fish headed downstream with the current. The line was screaming off the reel. I yelled at Gary to get the camera and follow me. I was wearing a pair of borrowed hip waders that really didn't fit. I'd run down the brush-covered bank, hanging onto a tree here and there or running through water I could wade. The fish stayed ahead of me about 70 yards until it came to a still pool, and by the time I reached it, it would take off again. Gary stayed right after me. We had gone what I suppose was one-half mile or more, when I saw this fairly slow-moving stretch of water ahead of us. On the bank were five or six fishermen. I heard one of them say, "Look, there comes a salmon." Someone else said, "Yes, there is a guy chasing it." It turned out to be some airmen from the airbase in Anchorage, who had driven to the river in a four-wheel-drive vehicle and hiked some five or six miles up to this spot. By this time I caught up with the fish, and one of them asked me if I wanted him to net it. I said, "Do it, for I've about had it!" He waded out in the stream with a net, really too small for that size fish. He brought the net down on the fish like someone catching a butterfly and beat the fish off. He apologized and I thanked him.

As Gary and I walked back up to our spot, I told him that I was not going to chase another salmon. I tied on another jig, made another cast and hooked another fish. I said, "Gary, let's try one more time; grab that camera and let's go." We followed that crazy fish down the river, just like the first one. I heard one of the airmen say, "Look there comes another fish, and someone else said, "Yes, and that same guy is coming right behind him." When I caught up with the fish, they asked me if I wanted them to net it. I said, "No, but let me borrow your net!" We landed the fish, and Gary immediately started dressing it. He said, "I'll take these eggs and show you how to catch some big rainbows." One of the airmen came over and said, "Are you from the states?" I looked up at him and said, "Yes." He said, "You wouldn't be Harold Ensley, The Sportsman's Friend?" I said, "Yes, but who are you?" He said, "I'm Captain Jim Roberts and I watched your show when I was stationed at Richards-Gebaur airbase." I can hardly believe that in one day in a remote area of the Russian River that I met two men from our part of the country! "Winds of Chance."

We visited awhile, and then Gary and I hiked back up the river to fish for rainbow and fly back to Anchorage. That night our host held a big game dinner for us at his home. We had just finished our dinner when someone came into the room and said, "We have a phone call for a Harold Ensley," and took me to the phone. I didn't know anyone in Anchorage and wondered who in the world would be calling me. It was Captain Rutt, aide to General Bowman at the airbase. He said, "The General wants you to come out to the base tomorrow, he wants to see you." I told him that I would not be able to for I had to fly out in the morning to finish up my shows, then catch a plane back to Kansas City. My host heard me and asked if I had a problem. I said, "The General wants me to come out to the base in the morning." He aid, "That's no problem. I'll drive you out." So I told the Captain we would come out, but that my schedule was pretty tight. The next day we drove out to the base. I was puzzled by the turn of events and couldn't understand what he would want with me, nor how he even knew that I was in town. "Winds of Chance."

He wanted to fly me down to King Salmon to do a story on the Air Force rest camp. I told him I already had my airline schedule. He said, "I'll have my secretary change your flight back to Kansas City and you can fly down with me to King Salmon." "Chance of a lifetime."

We flew down the next morning in the General's plane to see the rest camp and to fish for big kings. I told the General I wanted to fish with him and shoot a picture of him with a fish. On the flight down the Captain said, "Ensley, he may not catch a big king. I'll hook one and hand him the rod." I said, "No, you will not, I don't do that with anyone, not even a General!" The Captain said, "Then we got a problem." I said, "No, you've got a problem!" General Bowman saved the day; he caught two big kings! What a thrill to get to fish with him and see him catch fish! People who fly in and out of King Salmon today would not believe what that place was like 38 years ago. I flew back to Anchorage in a cargo plane and just barely made my connection back to Kansas City in time to be on my TV show.

Years later I received a call from the Air Force Academy in Colorado from the General's aide. General Bowman was retiring, and they wanted to run the show I had made with him. I was honored to do so. But that doesn't close out my Alaskan saga. Many years later I appeared at Richards-Gebaur Air Base for their Operation Handshake. They had my red country sedan out by one of the planes where I could greet people. During the course of the day a man dressed in civilian clothes came up to me and said, "You don't remember me, do you?" I said, "Should I?" He said, "Did you ever fish on the Russian River in Alaska?" I said, "Captain Jim Roberts! What are you doing here?" He said, "I'm being mustered out here." "Winds of Chance," that we would meet gain!

But the story doesn't end there! Shortly after that I received a letter from a viewer, sent to K.O.A.M. TV, Pittsburgh, Kansas, and forwarded on to me. It was from Bill Jennings. He said, "When your show comes on, I tell people that I checked your fishing license on the Russian River in Alaska. Will you please tell them that I did, and by the way, I married that redheaded girlfriend and we have two little redheaded girls." I read his letter on the air to verify his statement. "Winds of Chance." But it doesn't stop there!

Years later I was doing a promotion, filleting crappie in the Wal-Mart store in Rolla, Missouri. We had several people watching the demonstration, and a man walked up and said, "I'll bet you don't remember me; I'm Jim Bell Jennings. We first met on the Russian River in Alaska, and this is my wife, the redheaded girlfriend I told you about." I believe that he said the two daughters were away in college. I hope someday to meet the four of them for a fishing trip for my TV show. "Winds of Chance."

It's the Little Things that Count

G.O. TILLEY, who operated a resort in the little town of Bull Shoals, Arkansas, also had a marina and float service below the dam, called me to come down for some spectacular trophy rainbow trout fishing. Below the dam they were catching rainbows weighing in the teens and some over 20 pounds. No one had heard of anything like it. They were catching them by lots of different methods. A revolutionary change came when a man and his wife were making a float trip from the dam to Cotter. The water was high and swift, as they had the flood gates open. I'm not sure if this couple was using Tilley's float service or Hurst's operation. The lady couldn't cast, but went along for the ride. After drifting some distance, she decided she wanted to fish. She said, "I can't cast, but why can't I drift a bait behind the boat?" Her husband told her that she probably would be snagged most of the time. Nevertheless, the guide rigged up a rod and reel, put a fairly heavy sinker about a foot up from the hook. He put a big night crawler on her hook. She couldn't cast, so she just dropped the worm over the side of the boat and let out some line. They had not drifted far until her rod bent double. Her husband said, "I thought that would happen!" About that time, a rainbow that would weigh nearly 8 pounds leaped high in the air. Then they realized the fish was on her line. She was screaming, "It's going to get away!" After quite a fight, the guide netted the fish. It was a real beauty. It may have been the first fish they had put in the boat. Her husband said that it was pure luck! The guide put on another night crawler and tossed it over the side of the boat. The lady let out some line again. They had not gone far when she yelled, "I've got another one." Her husband said, "Honey, you're hung up on a rock." About that time the fish leaped high in the air and the battle was on, and she landed the fish! It was almost as large as the first one. Her husband and her guide thought it was a fluke, until she caught two more. "Winds of Chance." Thus, a new method of fishing on White River below Bull Shoals Dam was born!

Soon came some modifications. The best method was to use a three-way swivel, attach on about a foot of line with a 1/2-oz. bell sinker, then another drop about three feet long with a hook and a night crawler. There were all kinds of wild tales of broken lines and big trophy rainbows. Tilley thought I might want to shoot a movie of it. My late wife, Bonnie, and I drove down to Tilley's. He said that it was not as good as it had been, but we should do all right.

We worked hard the first day, with the three of us dragging night crawlers. I caught one rainbow that would go a good five pounds. Bonnie took a picture of me catching it, but things didn't look good. The second morning she got tired of dragging a worm. She was a good caster. She asked Tilley if he didn't have a spoon that she could cast. I told her she should stick with the worm for that was the way they were catching them. She said, "How many have you caught?" Tilley laughed and asked her to hand him her line. He took off the worm rig and tied on a small silver spoon. Bonnie made a couple of casts. I heard her yell and saw a big rainbow give a spectacular leap, only to throw the spoon. Bonnie yelled, "I've got another one, get the camera!" I did and got movies of her fighting the fish and Tilley landing it. We weighed it when we came in that night — 7-3/4 pounds, not large in the sense of what they had been taking, but good enough for a picture.

The three of us started catching fish like crazy, casting silver spoons. We boated three limits of rainbow and made our movie. We had 18 nice fish, several 7 or 8-pounders, and I don't think any of them were less than 4 pounds. It was one of the greatest rainbow trout fishing days that Bonnie and I ever had. We had two of them that were blanks dragging worms and two spectacular days casting spoons. It seems ironic that it was two women who turned the trick. The lady who could not cast catching so many big trout on worms, and Bonnie being bored dragging worms for two days and nothing, then asking Tilley for a spoon. For two days, we had fantastic fishing, casting spoons. "Winds of Chance." How about a big hand for those two ladies on the White River in Arkansas.

Sometimes it's the little things that count. During our years of broadcasting fishing news, our TV series, The Sportsman's Friend, we received many invitations to fish some place new to us. In the late '60s I received a call from one of my sponsors, a Ford dealer named Dee Gorley in Lincoln and Beloit, in Kansas. Dee and some of his friends had made some trips with us to Costa Rica. I also had represented him and other Ford Dealers in north central Kansas, speaking to high schools, farming groups and others. We hunted pheasant and quail with him and the others. A young man from Alabama who operated a drug store and pharmacy in either Lincoln or Beloit (I don't remember for sure and I don't recall his name) kept telling Dee about the big bluegill and bass you could catch in his home area in Alabama. Dee called me and said, "We have one week we can go." I had already scheduled sales seminars for Abu Garcia at sporting goods outlets in Dayton and Cincinnati, Ohio, for the first two days of that week. I told him that if he and his friend and my son Dusty could pick me up at the airport at Birmingham that Tuesday night, that I could do my promotions in Ohio and we could still make the trip. They were going to drive through to Birmingham. I taught people to cast during a snowstorm in Cincinnati and barely made my flight at 9 p.m.

When I arrived in Birmingham, they told me that we had a problem. A cold front had moved into the area and dumped some eight inches of rainfall, flooding every place that we had planned to fish and get a program for my TV show. So we just kept driving south with floodwaters and a real cold front at our backs.

Every place we stopped we got the same answer, "You can't catch any fish with bad water conditions and cold winds." We finally came to the little town of Camden, not too far from the Gulf. It was late night, but we found a motel with a vacancy and put up for the rest of the night. Things didn't look good, but sometimes little things make a difference! We noticed a bass boat near the office of the motel and learned that the motel owner was a big fisherman. We asked to see him, thinking perhaps he might be of help. He also owned a cafe next to his motel. We went in for breakfast and asked for the owner. He was very nice, and when I told him that we were trying to find a lake or stream where we might catch some fish, he just smiled and said, "You're not going to catch any fish with the water and weather conditions that we have. We not only have floodwaters, but we had a hard freeze last night and it killed all our flowers." I asked if he knew anyone there that caught lots of crappie. He told me of an elderly gentleman who nearly every day caught 3 and 4-pound crappie. I asked him if he would call him to see if he might help me catch some fish for a TV show. He said, "He should be here anytime. He nearly always comes in for coffee."

The old gentleman came in, and he introduced us. I asked him if he would be willing to help us catch some big crappie for my TV show. He told me that we could try, but we might not do any good on account of bad weather conditions and the cold front. He had an old beat-up truck and pulled an old aluminum 12-foot boat with no motor. He drove us several miles out in the country. Dee and the guys followed him in the van. He pulled into a muddy flat near a bridge over a flooded stream on the downstream side of the bridge. The water backed into a spot about 80 yards wide and a mile up the river. As I remember, we had about four feet clearance to pass under the bridge. Dusty and the other two were going to fish from the bank. The water was discolored, but I've fished in worse. The old fellow didn't even have a paddle, so we used a short of piece of driftwood. He was using a cane pole and a minnow, and I was casting a crappie jig. It was a shallow brush area with lots of stumps. I was hung up almost every cast. I know that old fellow thought I had never fished before in my life. He finally caught a crappie about the size of your hand. We were only a couple of hundred feet from where Dusty and the druggist were casting for bass from the bank. Dee was not even fishing. He really wasn't a dedicated fisherman, but I heard him yell to Dusty that a fish had just surfaced. Dusty, who is an excellent caster, put the buzz bait just above the swirl, and a bass clobbered his lure. I grabbed the piece of driftwood and shoved the boat back to the bank. Dee had my camera ready, and I shot pictures of Dusty catching his fish. He held the bass up for the camera. The old gentleman said, "That fish will go 3-1/2 lbs." I told him I didn't think I'd want him weighing my fish. Dee Gorley went up to the van, got his Deliar and weighed the bass. It weighed 6-1/2 pounds, and Dusty released it. That changed our strategy. We quit the crappie and all went to bass fishing. We caught several more bass, but no picture fish. We thought we had found the answer. We would come back the next day and make the picture.

The next morning we drove to the spot. The editor of the local daily paper heard we were there trying to get a story for television and drove out to watch. When we arrived at the bridge, we found that the water had risen and therefore closed off our opportunity to fish our spot. It was a cold and blustery day with a 20 to 25-mile-an-hour wind blowing in from the north. Our only spot with water halfway decent was cut off from us.

I was sitting in the van with the newspaper editor. He wanted to learn about my show for an interview for his newspaper. I asked him if he knew of a farm pond where we might catch some fish. He said, "No, I don't know of any with conditions like this." He said, "This is nothing like fishing conditions, this is more like hunting conditions." He was an avid wild turkey hunter and deer hunter. We then got to talking about duck and goose hunting. He said, "I'd give my eye teeth to kill some Canadian geese." I told him that Kansas City was right between the central flyway and the Mississippi flyway. Two big federal game reservoirs, Squaw Creek and Swan Lake, both within two to three hours' drive. "If you will come to Kansas City, I'll put you up and guarantee a Canadian goose." I said at one time last winter over 200,000 geese passed through Swan Lake and nearly that many through Squaw Creek. I said I knew of many youngsters between the age of 12 and 16 years of age who have shot Canadians. "All you have to do is call me and we will put you into some of the finest goose hunting you could want." He said, "You would do that?" I told him I was serious and I would do as I said. He looked at me and smiled. He said, "I have a couple of big ponds you are welcome to try, but I assure you that you will not catch any fish in this cold wind." It was almost eleven o'clock. I asked him to lead the way, and Dee and the boys followed.

We drove about 20 miles, as I remember. There were two ponds. The lower pond covered about five acres and the upper pond was about twice the size. Dusty said, "Dad, you take the lower one, and I'll take a look at the other." I made a cast into the wind, and the Pomme special, a buzz bait with a big spinner, almost came back in my face. It was a lure designed and produced by the Mar-Lynn Lure Company that is more difficult to cast than most buzz baits, but it's the most productive for big bass that I have ever cast. The newspaper man told me again that I couldn't catch bass with that cold wind blowing hard from the north. I made my second cast and caught a small bass about 12 inches long. About that time Dusty walked back from the upper pond with a bass about the same size. He said, "Dad, let's go up there; it has a couple of aluminum boats. We can all four fish. The newspaper man told us that he had to get back to the office, but for us to go ahead and fish. We drove around to the other pond. The water was dingy but fishable. We tried several spots, but nothing. The water had backed up past the barbed wire fence almost to the top of the posts. I saw a bass swirl on the other side of the fence and cast past it about four feet to roll the buzz bait over the spot. There was an explosion as the bass hit, and I set the hook. I said, "Dusty, grab the camera; that's a picture fish." He said, "How are you going to get it through the fence?" We got the boat up to the fence, and I put my rod over the top strand of wire and put it under the water and brought it up free on our side of the fence and landed the fish. Dusty yelled to Dee to bring the scales. I asked Dee to be on the CB and call the newspaper man. That was when the CB craze was about like the cell phone is today. In fact, Midland CB's was one of our national sponsors on TV. My handle was Charlie Tuna. Dee got hold of the newspaperman, who told him he would be right out to get a picture. Dee brought his Deliar, and the bass weighed 7-1/2 pounds, not large as Alabama bass go, but good enough for the movie. The newspaperman came, shot some pictures and said, "What are you going to do with it?" I told him I was going to release it, that we hadn't kept a bass in many years. We will keep and eat the crappie and bluegill, but we release the bass. They belong to the same family and there's nothing wrong with eating bass, but we like to release them to be able to catch them again. The newspaperman went back to his office, but asked us to call him when we came in, and we continued fishing. He could not have reached town before Dusty caught a 9-pound bass. We filmed his fish and released it. We caught other bass and finished our movie. We stopped by the paper office, told him of Dusty's bass, thanked him and headed for Kansas City. What appeared to be a disastrous trip because of the weather was made successful because of a little thing. "Winds of Chance."

In the late '50s or early '60s, I cannot recall for sure, at the Kansas City Boat, Sports and Travel Show, a man from Chillicothe, Missouri, and his wife brought their daughter by my booth to meet me. Her name was Recil Skinner. She was a beautiful girl 10 or 12 years old, but a victim of polio. She was in a wheelchair, but not cast down, a very upbeat attitude toward life that would move you emotionally. They told me that she loved to fish. She had watched our TV show and wanted someday to go trout fishing on the White River in Arkansas. I promised them that if the Lord let me live until summer after Recil's school was out, we would take her on a float trip below Bull Shoals Dam. Summer came and I called G.O. Tilley at Bull Shoals and told him I wanted to take Recil on a float trip. G.O. operated a resort at Bull shoals and a float trip service on White River. He said that he would be most happy to arrange it. The Skinners drove Recil down, and for several days we floated the White River and fished for trout. Tilley and his guides used every precaution for Recil's safety. Recil caught a lot of trout just drifting a night crawler behind the boat. The last day at the head of the White hole, Recil hooked a good trout. That rainbow jumped all over the place, around the boat and under the boat. It was somewhere in the 5 or 6-pound class, but she landed it. A special moment for all of us. The courage of that little girl was enough to inspire everyone. "Winds of Chance and the Chance of a Lifetime."

I lost track of the family, but if I understood correctly, she graduated from high school, then college and was teaching school. When I planned to tell about this moment, for the life of me I could not remember Recil's name. It had been about 40 years ago. I called a duck hunting buddy of mine, Jeff Churan, at Chillicothe, Missouri, and he traced it down. My sincere thanks to a good friend.

Often we are asked by people who are just starting to learn to fish about the use of artificial lures vs. live bait. I caught my first bass on a minnow many moons ago. It's hard to beat live bait, and there's nothing wrong with fishing that way. The first bait I caught on an artificial lure was a small mouth on Indian Creek in southwest Missouri. I was using a tiny orange flat fish on a fly rod. Flat fish lures come in different sizes and colors, and I think they originated near Detroit, Michigan. It would still catch fish today. In fact, most, if not all the lures developed in the early years, would be as productive today as they were 40, 50 or 60 years ago. My generation will remember such names as Lazy Ike, Arborgast, Jitterbug, South Bend, Bassereno, Heddon, Chugger and Lucky Thirteen. Then came the stick baits: Devil's Horse, Gilmore Jumper and Zarah Spooks. Top water baits with propeller-like spinners: Heddon's Cripple Killer, Cotton Cordell, Boy Howdy, Heddon's Dying Flutter, and the like! Then I think of baits like the Swimming Minnow, Heddon Sonic, Bayou Boogie and Pica Perch. Then the soft baits like the Pork Eel, plastic worm and the Reaper. The first plastic worms were usually rigged worms, threaded with a piece of monofilament, two hooks and a small propeller-like spinner at the head. When they first came out, many of the good fishermen would not use them. The so-called rookies were catching bass like crazy on them. Later came the Squirmin' Jig by Dave Hawk and the ever-popular Texas Rig and the Carolina Rig. Jigs have been used in Arkansas. In fact, you would almost say there was a revolution in the sport fishing industry in the '50s and '60s. A revolution in tackle, boats and motors and the resort business in general. It also applied to new techniques in fishing.

Talking about artificial lures, I just remembered a story about one of my next-door neighbors in Independence, Missouri, years ago. He came to me one evening and said, "I've decided I want to learn to fish. Will you help me get started?" This was before the day of television, but he had listened to my radio show. He said, "I don't have a lot of money, will you go help me pick out enough tackle to get started?" I recommended the rod and reel to buy and a few lures and sent him to Sears, who were my sponsors on radio. He came back with a bait casting reel, a short steel rod, some line, a small tackle box and two Lazy Ike lures. I put the line on for him and went out in the backyard, and he learned to cast in a crude sort of way, enough that I thought he could get by. I didn't see him for about a week. Then the first thing he said, "Boy, those Lazy lures really worked!" I asked him where he had fished, and he told me of a fairly new state lake in north central Missouri. He said, "I caught my limit of six bass the first day." I asked him if he caught them from the bank. He said, "No, I was using a boat." I asked if he was casting the shoreline. He said, "No, I was trolling in the middle of the lake." I asked him how fast he trolled and he said, "Just as fast as I could row; I couldn't afford to rent a motor." I said, "The fish must have been hitting pretty good." He said, "I didn't see anyone else catching fish." Here he was on his first fishing trip, using artificial lures and caught his limit of bass! "Winds of Chance."

I can't remember his name or if he ever fished again. The first thing that ran through my mind was, this guy is a beginner, but he certainly doesn't need any more help from me. Maybe I should go with him! Luck or skill, who knows? That, my friend, is the magic and charm of learning to fish.

One Sunday afternoon I received a telephone call from a man in Pasadena, California. I don't recall his name, but he had seen one of my shows from Costa Rica. He said that he had a resort in Belize, and what would it take to get me down to Belize to fish at his camp? I asked him where he saw the show. He told me he had been staying in a motel in Bakersfield, California. I asked him where he was at the time. He told me Pasadena. I told him all he had to do was invite us. He did, and we set up a time. My wife and I took our daughter Sandy and her husband. We fished the river for snook, tarpon and the flats for bonefish. It was another "Chance of a Lifetime."

The next year we made another trip there. This time my fishing buddy, Dale Flaxbeard, wanted to take his wife and a contractor friend, Bill Beemer, who loved to fish for snook. Stan Kroneke, Bud Walton's son-in-law, also joined us. Our trip down was uneventful, and we got into the fish quickly. I chided Dale about giving his wife Charlene a pushbutton reel on a bass rod. I told him he was handicapping her for catching tarpon and snook. He said she had problems casting, and I gave her one of my five-foot casting rods and a 5500-C Ambassador reel. Fishing the river with 20-lb. test line, we got lots of snook in the 18 to 25-pound class, tarpon from 45 to 90 pounds, and Charlene landed a 22-pound snapper. Dale and Charlene had worked up the river that morning, and Beemer and Stan followed. In the meantime, Sandy caught a 22-pound snook. We had just finished taking the movies of Sandy's fish when Beemer and Stan came up quickly and yelled, "Charlene is fighting a big fish just around the next bend." I asked them what it was, and they told me they didn't know, but that she had fought it for over an hour. We hurriedly made it to the spot. Charlene was really giving the fish a battle. Dale said, "Let me help you." She said, "No way, I hooked it, and I'm going to land it!" After a long fight she got the fish up to the boat, the guide gaffed it and got it in the boat. We were shooting pictures all the while. Charlene's feet didn't touch the bottom of the boat as she jumped up and down. It was a great moment for her. She said, "It was just me and him, and I whipped that sucker by myself!" It was a 56-pound grouper, and if you don't think that's a handful on a light bass rod, try it yourself! "Winds of Chance."

In the early '60s Dean Edwards, one of my sponsors, called me to go to Cranberry Portage to help entertain some of his customers. Dean owned and operated Midwest Ford Truck Dealership in Kansas City. We drove up and spent a week on Lake Athapapascow. We had some great lake trout fishing. It's a deep lake, and we had two memorable incidents. One was a bad windstorm that forced us to take refuge for several hours on a small island. The other, to witness a long battle between one of the local guides and a big fish. Several boats of us were fishing a big hole out in the middle of the lake. Our people were using Reapers, but the locals were using a short piece of copper tubing with a treble hook and cut sucker meat. The water at that point was running from

75 to 120 feet deep. Our group was really catching more trout on Reapers than they were on cut bait. However, most of the fish caught were in the 7-10-pound class. One of the local guides was rather loud and boisterous. He knew we were shooting movies for television. Just after lunch he yelled, "Hey, television man, I've hooked a big one!" This guide had quite a reputation for catching record lake trout. In fact, if I remember correctly, at one time he held the world's record on a rod and reel. That fish was something over 60 pounds. I knew that he could tell when he had a big fish, so Dean and I had our guide move us over in position to film the sequence. It turned out to be quite a battle. The fish started pulling their boat, and we followed. He couldn't get the fish off the bottom. He would gain a little line and then lose it as the fish evidently went with the change in depths of the lake. The guide would alternately get cocky when he gained some line, and then be a little more subdued as the fish took off more line. Some two hours had elapsed, and the fish had pulled their boat about two miles toward the camp. The word spread like wildfire that he might have another world record trout. The local newspaper reporters and radio people started gathering at the dock, and with them a big crowd of local people. Three hours passed, then four hours, and he was no closer to getting the fish off the bottom. We kept following, staying close enough to get the picture. I told our guide to be ready to make a quick move if the fish turned our way. Both their boat and ours were powered with 35-horse motors. That was the largest they made at that time. We were moving away from the deep water, and he was gaining some line because of it. Dean asked me what I thought would happen when he reached a certain depth. I told him that I thought the fish would turn and head for deeper water. He asked me if I thought he was going to land the fish. By now, he had fought the fish for five hours. He was a big man and a little on the gruff side. I didn't think he was any closer to landing the fish than he was at the start, and if the fish makes a sudden move for deep water, he will have to start his motor and follow the fish. Since he hasn't started his motor for five hours, in that cold water it might not start quickly and he would be in trouble because the wind was now taking us toward the dock. At exactly five hours and 26 minutes the fish made its move and headed for deep water. I yelled at our guide to start the motor and get out of his way, and he did. The man with the fish pulled on the starter rope of the 35-horse motor, and it did not fire. The guy in the boat with him said, "Let me help you." He let out an oath, saying he could handle this by himself. All this time the fish was heading into the wind. The wind was moving his boat toward the dock. You knew it was all over; the fish took all his line. A five-hour, 26-minute battle, and he lost it because he got careless right at the last. "Winds of Chance."

We have fished the waters of Canada for almost 50 years. We have fished from the border to as far north as you can go in the Arctic and from coast to coast. However, no waters of Canada hold such a magic spell to me as the waters of God's Lake in Manitoba. I wish somehow I could learn who gave the lake its name and why. Maybe some reader, some time, some place, will get the word to me! The countryside scenery is beautiful, but no more so than hundreds of other Canadian lakes. It is a lake of sky- blue waters, but no more so than other Canadian lakes. There are other lakes in Canada where trophy lake trout and pike abound. There are other lakes in Canada where you can catch bunches of nice walleye. Yes, God created all the lakes of Canada! What makes God's Lake in Manitoba so special? For almost 50 years we have searched for the answer.

Milburn Stone, Doc of Gunsmoke, was as fascinated as we were, and in like manner everyone we have been privileged to take there has been cast in its spell. My friend, Paul Zanewith, spent a lifetime servicing the camps on God's Lake for fishermen and hunters. He passed away recently. He requested that he be cremated and the ashes be scattered over God's River, flowing from God's Lake. His family and friends took care of that for Paul. Our family has had so many wonderful times there over the years.

One I must tell you about happened about 35 years ago. My late wife Bonnie, Dusty, Sandy and I were at Elk Island Camp shooting a couple of movies for our television show. That particular day we had made a walleye movie where the Knife River empties into God's Lake on the south side. Never before or since have we had a day of walleye fishing to equal it. We were using ultra-light spinning gear and a 3-inch plastic worm. We all took limits, which at that time was eight. Sandy was 10 years old, and she caught her eight, running from 4 pounds to 8 pounds. We made the movie and had a great shore lunch. It was a family day of a lifetime! At the camp that night a lady came to us after dinner. She had heard about what we had done that day. She told us that she and her husband were school teachers from a little town near Dallas, Texas. They were not dedicated fishing people, but somehow heard of God's Lake. They evidently did not have a lot of money, but decided they wanted to see God's Lake. She said they hadn't caught any fish, but it really didn't matter. They just wanted to spend some time on God's Lake. She asked me if I could possibly take her husband one day and help him catch a few fish.

The next day I put her in the boat with me and my guide and Dusty in the boat with her husband and their guide. Bonnie and Sandy were going to stay at the camp and rest. Because of strong south winds, we could not take them to the Knife River. Our guides took us to Bailey Bay on the north side of the lake. We all caught lots of nice walleye. She was about the happiest camper you ever saw. I couldn't believe that catching fish that day meant so much to that couple. That night after dinner she came to our family and said, "I just knew that God had some purpose to lead us here to God's Lake at the same time you people were here!" They went their way and we went ours. I didn't ever expect to see them again.

A few years later I was called by a real estate developer in Florida to speak to the Woods and Water Club of Dallas, Texas. I flew to Dallas for the event, and to my surprise the school teacher and his wife were there. We had a nice visit before the meeting. She said, "We saw in the Dallas paper that you were to speak and just wanted to see you again and hear you speak." The Florida real estate developer who sponsored the event was giving away several nice door prizes, including a choice waterfront lot in a new development area. Names were drawn from those who registered. Guess who won first prize — the lakefront lot! The school teacher's wife. They were elated. She said, "I just knew God had some purpose in bringing us here today!" Winds of Chance."

I never saw them again, but I'm sure that God is still taking care of them. That's just some of the magic of God's Lake.

Crappie Fishing Special

PRODUCING A WEEKLY LIVE TV show forced us to fish winter and summer and hot or cold days. We started our career in the Midwest, where the temperature dropped way down, but we nearly always had access to open water. Occasionally we would have a season when we could safely ice-fish, but we could always drive a little farther south to Arkansas, Oklahoma, even Texas and Louisiana. We still had times when it was plenty cold. I realize the people of the North who fish through the ice may think we are "softies." We have done many ice fishing programs from Michigan west through Wisconsin to Minnesota and some here in Kansas. However, we are talking about the cold on open water, when ice would freeze on the guides of your fishing rod.

In the early '50s when I first started my broadcasting outdoor news and activities, we worked on our sales job Monday through Friday. Friday after work my wife and I would head off to Grand Lake in Oklahoma or Bull Shoals in Arkansas. It was a four-hour drive to Oklahoma and five or six to Bull Shoals. In the mid-winter when the temperature dropped down, we would mainly fish for crappie. Although those lakes seldom froze, yet it was too cold to fish from a boat. Many weekends we would fish off the dock at whatever particular resort we visited.

We told you about bass fishing on Lake Bull Shoals with Park Risley and Jerry Lumpe out of Buck Creek, crappie fishing when it was 9 degrees. At that time we didn't have the cold weather gear we have now. I got tired of all this, and the idea came to me, why not have someone build a heated fishing dock? Grand Lake of the Cherokee seemed the logical place to start. I called two of my reporters who gave me fishing reports daily, Monday through Friday — Sam Williams, who operated a minnow farm at Tiff City, Missouri, near the Cowskin arm of Grand Lake, and Floyd Long, who operated Long's Resort on the Honey Creek arm near Grove, Oklahoma. I told them of my idea for a heated dock. They liked the thought of opening up winter crappie fishing in comfort in a heated fishing dock. I suggested that they build it off the bluff at Long's Resort. We had caught lots of crappie fishing that spot from boats. In fact, it was to be over at Shelter #28. When Grand Lake was built, they cleared all the trees and brush, and the Oklahoma Fish and Game Department built a number of what they called fish shelters, composed of big piles of brush. They numbered them and put up signs to mark them. For a

117

Fishing in comfort with my friend, Tom Houston, in his private heated dock on Grand Lake

while people thought they were restricted areas, but when they learned that it was a marker to help them locate crappie, they became popular spots. No. 28, right at the bluff on the edge of Long's Resort, was one of our favorite spots. Sam and Long built a dock which still stands after 40 years and is still one of the best winter crappie fishing spots there. The dock is some 40 feet long and 20 feet wide, with two open fishing wells separated by a 4-foot walkway between the two wells. They put a wood stove in that spot and seats on three sides of each well. The open wells were about 15 feet long and 10 feet wide. The water was about 25 feet deep. It was anchored to the bluff, enclosed and lighted with electric lights. A group of us from Kansas City drove down to fish the first night. We fished all night in comfort. We caught a lot of crappie and white bass. The idea caught

Long's Fish Haven — first heated dock on Grand Lake in Oklahoma

fire, and heated docks sprang up all over the lake. It was a commercial operation. I think they charged a dollar per person. A group of us from Kansas City would fish the old year out and the New Year in. It was a four-hour drive, but none of us thought anything about that.

Now there are over 1200 heated docks on Grand Lake, most of them private. Also, most of them use gas heat and have comfortable seats, but there are still many commercial docks. It turned out to be a bonanza for the resort owners who had been closing down during the winter months. People learned to adapt to the art of dock fishing. It was great fun. We have fished many times when every seat in the dock was taken. Sometimes only a few caught fish; other times everyone caught fish! Sometimes nobody caught fish, but they had a good time! It also gave people who didn't own boats a comfortable place to fish. It was a good thing 40 years ago, and it's a good thing today!

At first, it was all minnow fishing until the advent of using tiny jigs. My wife and I had many wonderful weekends fishing there in cold weather. There was a special art to dock fishing, and I think the women adapted to it better than most men. But it wasn't always the best fisherman who caught the most fish. This amused me to no end. We would take a group of good fishermen with us, and two or three old ladies fishing there would catch more fish than the experts.

One time a good fisherman and I were shooting a quail movie in northeastern Oklahoma and the weather turned bad. We were about an hour's drive from Grand Lake. We generally take our fishing gear with us, so I suggested that we drive down to Long's at Grove, Oklahoma, and fish that afternoon. It was in the middle of the week and not many at the dock when we arrived. He said, "I don't want to fish in that dock; that's for the women and kids." I told him I was going to fish, so he gave in and went to the dock. It was mid-afternoon and a blustery cold day. Most of the day fishermen had gone home and the night fishermen hadn't arrived. We brought a bucket of minnows and climbed down the bluff to the dock. He reluctantly went with me. This was before monofilament line and spinning reels existed, so we were using our casting rods. The dock was empty except two honeymooners. We asked them how they were doing. The man said, "My bride here is catching some, but I can't do any good." We rigged up and started fishing. We had fished about an hour with nothing, and that young lady continued to catch fish. She smoked one cigarette after another. I started watching her closely and saw that she was constantly moving her fishing rod around, and whenever she stopped to take a puff of her cigarette she would catch a nice crappie. I watched her to see at what depth she was fishing and started fishing at the same depth, as near as I could ascertain. I started moving my line as she was doing, and when she stopped to take a puff, I stopped and caught a nice crappie. Naturally, I didn't say anything to my fishing partner. The lady caught her limit, which I believe at that time was 25. Her husband didn't catch any. I caught my limit, and my friend caught none. When we went up to the car, I asked him if he still thought dock fishing was for the women and kids. He said, "Well, that's the first time I ever fished in a heated dock." I said, "That's true, but it was that lady's first time." "Winds of Chance."

With advent of crappie jigs and spinning gear, things changed. Fishermen have their special way, size of lines, size of jigs, and so on. Believe me, there are many people, both men and women, who have become experts of jig fishing for crappie. Some contend you have to use this or that; then someone will come along, not do it right and catch a lot of fish. God made it this way. That's fishing; it's the little things that make a difference!

When we first started in the early '50s, many of the resorts would close right after Labor Day and reopen in the spring. When we started broadcasting fishing reports, we had reporters on all the lakes around the four-state area. Interest in winter fishing developed quickly, and many resorts started staying open year round. We fished in a lot of cold weather. In fact, we did a lot of cold weather bass fishing out of Bull Shoals Lake in Arkansas. Once in the dead of winter I called Bob Bright, one of my reporters, about shooting a black bass picture for my show. Bob operated the marina at Highway 125. He and Johnny Wiggins, who operated the marina at Lead Hill, Arkansas, were two of the finest marina operators that I had met. Both of them reported regularly about fishing conditions. You could always rely on them to give you true conditions. Bob told me that fishing was tough, but to come on down, that he would have Park Risley to guide us.

We drove down and the fishing was tough. A cold front came in from the north; my buddy at that time went home, but I needed a program so I stayed on. The next morning the temperature had dropped to 6 degrees. That was not wind-chill, because back in those days the radio weather people only gave the actual temperature. Park Risley, who has now passed on, was my guide. The lake was not frozen, but there were huge icicles hanging from the bluff rocks where the water had seeped down. In one case I asked Park to back the boat back to where I could get a picture of him and the huge icicle. The chunk of ice was about 10 feet across hanging down from a ledge about 12 feet. The wind moved the boat back toward the ice hanging from the cliff, and Park reached up with his paddle to shove the boat away. When he hit the ice, it came tumbling down, almost hitting Park and the boat. It would have probably weighed a ton or so. We could have lost our lives, and it scared the soup out of both of us! I said, "Let's not try that again!"

We moved up the lake past Buck Creek casting along in some of my favorite spots, to no avail. Then we were using braided line, and it would freeze on the spool. The lake level at that time was about 70 feet below power-pool level. You could see the treetops just barely out of the water along the old channel of the river. Park pulled up to the tree line so that I could cast into the treetops. The first cast I felt a slight peck, set the hook on a good fish. Park asked me if I wanted him to try to handle the movie camera. I told him no, that I had all I could handle with the fish in the tree. Park said, "Harold, that bass will go 10 pounds." I told him I didn't think so, but we put it on the stringer so that we could get a picture at the dock. I was using a twin spin with a 6-inch eel. The very next cast I caught another, but not nearly as large. We fished until late afternoon, but not another strike. We went back to the dock, weighed the fish and got the pictures. One weighed an even 9 pounds, the other 6-1/4 pounds. I have fished other cold days shooting ice fishing movies in Michigan, Wisconsin and Minnesota, but that was my coldest day of bass fishing. "Winds of Chance."

I'll always have a warm spot in my heart for Park Risley. He guided me many times when I fished out of Highway 125 boat dock. It was amazing to me that he put three of his kids through the University of Arkansas guiding for $8 or $10 a day. He made one remark I'll always remember. One afternoon when he was guiding me and we weren't catching any fish, I asked Park what time it was and he answered that he didn't know. I asked him if he didn't have a watch. He said, "Yes, but I never wear it when I'm guiding; I might be worrying about what time it is." I remember many cold days being on Bull Shoals. Jerry Lumpe, who was playing second base for the New York Yankee, and I had planned a fishing trip to Bull Shoals. I was to pick him up in Springfield, then drive to Buck Creek to crappie fish. It was 11 degrees in Kansas City when I called Jerry in Springfield to see if he still wanted to go. He said it was the only time we could make it before spring training. He told me he would be ready when I got there. When I arrived, the temperature had dropped to 9 degrees. We drove to Buck Creek and got out on the lake about mid-afternoon. It was really cold, and I was trying to get a movie for my TV show, but the fishing was tough. We didn't have a guide. The next day we were fishing along a timbered bluff bank to keep out of the wind. I noticed the line freezing in my rod tip and thought it might be a good thing to show how cold it was. We were using crappie jigs. I handed Jerry my fishing rod and picked up my camera to shoot a picture of the ice freezing in the rod tip. The rod tip bounced, and Jerry had a 2-1/2-pound crappie. We shot the picture and laughed about the fish getting on at that particular time. It was the largest crappie we caught in the three days that we fished. "Winds of Chance."

The next day we got into the bass and crappie and made the movie for the show in spite of the cold.

Many years later, my wife and I were walking down the ramp at Starrit Creek Marina on Truman Reservoir where I kept my boat. Jerry saw us and came up to greet us and asked us if we were doing any good. I told him that we really hadn't located any numbers of crappie and needed fish for a demonstration in the Wal-Mart stores. He told me of a cove up the Osage by Berry Bend where they had been doing well. It was a pretty good boat ride, but I knew the cove Jerry was talking about. We found the crappie and caught our limit, thanks to our friend, Jerry Lumpe. Jerry, I owe you one! "Winds of Chance."

Just as the development of Corps of Engineer reservoirs came in the Midwest, it opened up a whole new world for the bass fishermen. The advent of light and ultra-light spinning gear opened up a whole new venue of sport fishing for crappie. We had always loved to catch crappie using live bait, but with the advent of small crappie jigs it started a revolution. Ultra-light spinning gear, monofilament line in 2 and 4-lb. test sizes made it possible for fishermen to cast crappie jigs from 1/8-oz. on down to sometimes an 80th of an oz.

The crappie is a fascinating creature, but it really wasn't until the big reservoir came into existence that the amazing movement came. Kentucky Lake in Tennessee and Kentucky, Lake of the Ozarks in Missouri, Grand Lake in Oklahoma, Norfork Lake and Bull Shoals in Arkansas, Toledo Bend on the Texas-Louisiana border, Sam Raybourn in Texas, Melvern, Pomona, and Perry in Kansas and Powell Reservoir in the Rockies — all became meccas for giant crappie. This, in addition to the Minnesota lakes and the southern lakes of Ontario, brought forth crappie in size and numbers beyond anyone's fondest dreams. Even in the Mexico reservoirs we caught big crappie.

In fact, on one bass fishing journey to Lake Novillo, near Hermosillo, on top water bass lures we caught many 18" or 19" crappie. I wish I knew what it was about crappie fishing with jigs that is so fascinating!

Sam Walton, founder of Wal-Mart, loved to hunt, but I don't recall him fishing much. Sam loved crappie fillets. When he introduced me to Paul Harvey, he told Paul that he should taste the crappie that I brought him. He said, "You have never tasted anything like it, no odor or fishy smell." Sam was my friend and hunting partner for many years. We took Sam and Helen crappie fillets down through the years, until he passed away.

When we were fishing in Costa Rica for the first time, *Sports Illustrated* was doing a story on Ted Williams. Ted and I had been friends, but had never fished together. One night after dinner Ted asked me what was my favorite fish to catch. I said, "Ted, if I had to fish for one species, six days a week, year round, I would choose bass." However, for excitement and challenges occasionally I would take tarpon. He said, "I never thought of it in that light. I would have to think about it." That was in the mid '60s, and I've changed my mind. If I were asked the same question in the year 2001, I would say, "Crappie on ultra-light spinning and tiny crappie jigs." That might surprise some, but that's my present answer! Then the development of soft plastic crappie jigs, like the puddle jumper, has added a new dimension. To me, it presents a fascinating challenge, and its availability is almost limitless. An added attraction is the fact that crappie fillets are so great on the table. If the fish are cared for properly, dressed carefully and cooked in the best manner, God didn't give us anything finer for the table!

One time I was amused at my friend and publisher, Tom Leathers in Overland Park, Kansas. I called him one morning to tell him I had a mess of fish for him. Very quickly he said, "Our family doesn't eat fish much. What kind do you have?" I said, "Fresh crappie fillets!" Tom said, "Crappie fillets, bring them on!"

Crappie do not grow to large sizes, but are still fascinating to catch. During the years of live television, I think the largest trophy crappie brought into my show was a 4-1/2-pound black crappie from southeast Kansas. It was caught in one of the strip pits near Pittsburgh, Kansas. I just vaguely remember another 4-1/4-lb. crappie by a viewer, but do not remember who caught it or where. I have one special crappie story to tell.

In the early '70s, one Monday morning I received a telephone call from a man in Kansas City. He said that he was dressing some crappie in his backyard. His neighbor saw him and came over to see what was going on. He had said that he just had three crappie left to dress. When the neighbor saw the fish, he said, "Man, you should call Harold Ensley and show these big crappie on his television show." I asked how large his crappie were. He said, "A little over 3 pounds each. Are they big enough to put on your show?" I told him that my show was already planned and formatted, but if he wanted to bring the fish in and they did weigh 3 pounds or better apiece, we would use them for a few minutes. I also said that we would weigh them on the station's mail scales. If they didn't weigh 3 pounds each, we would not show them and there would be no hard feelings. He said, "That sounds good to me; I'll plan to be there." Late in the afternoon they called me, saying that there was a man there at the switchboard with some fish for my show. I went to the front desk to greet him. He had the fish in an ice chest. He opened the lid, and I nearly fainted at the size of his fish. I knew we didn't need to weigh them, but we took them back to the mailroom. Scotty Nelson, who handled the mail and memos for the station, weighed them. The three crappie weighed a total of 11 pounds. He said he had just dressed four more like them before his neighbor told him to call me. I had no reason to doubt him, since they were what he said they were. I asked him where he caught them. He told me that he caught the seven crappie out of Turkey Creek on Lake of the Ozarks, near Warsaw, using minnows for bait. I asked him how long he had been crappie fishing. He told me that he had just started, and that was his first time out. Since he had not lied about his big fish, I had no reason not to believe him about that. I told him that he might fish the rest of his life and never see anything like that, much less catch them. I proudly used him as a guest on my show. Really, that's one for Ripley! "Winds of Chance."

Short Takes and Best Brookie Ever

IN THE MID '70s I received a telephone call from Rack Pace, a good friend of mine at Flippen, Arkansas. Rack operated a float service on White River and the Buffalo River. We had fished together for years on Lake Bull Shoals and below the dam for trout. Rack asked me if I had any more shows left to do. I told him that I had three more to do. Why? He told me that one of his guides, Leon Wagner, had caught a big trout and they would like to show it. I said, "It would have to be a pretty big fish, as they would have to bring it to Wichita, some 300 miles." He told me that it was a 33-1/2-pound German brown, and had been certified as a new world's record. Rack is one of my special friends, and I would have used the fish had it only weighed 10 pounds!

They brought the fish to Wichita. I didn't ask Leon a lot of questions before we went on the air. I learned that people not accustomed to being interviewed do better the first time they tell their story. If you went over a lot of questions beforehand, they would be thinking too much about what they said the first time. We started the show and asked Leon to bring on his fish. It was frozen and in good shape. What a tremendous fish! Leon had caught it while fishing on his day off. He and his buddy were fishing from the bank at the White Hole, one of our favorite spots for big trout on White River between the dam and the little town of Cotter, Arkansas. I asked a few questions. He was holding that big rascal in his arms. Believe me, it was an armful! I asked him what he caught the fish on, meaning what kind of bait. He said, "I caught it on my Harold Ensley ultra-light spinning rod, my Abu Garcia Mitchell 408 and 6-lb. test Abu Garcia Royal Bonnyl line." I said, "Yes, but what were you using for bait?" Very calmly he said, "A worm." A world record brown trout, fishing from the bank on his day off, with the ultra-light spinning rod and reel and no net! "Winds of Chance."

Rack Pace and Leon Wagner were the last ones to bring fish in for my show. We went into national syndication, doing 20 weeks in a 70-station market. We chose KSN Channel 3, the NBC affiliate in Wichita, Kansas, to produce our show. They had the syndication expertise I needed, as they were doing a 150-market syndication for a religious group. We drove to Wichita to tape the shows, and they did the shipping. It changed our pattern somewhat, and we just didn't show strings of fish and local things as we had before.

Several years later, I was visiting Wal-Mart stores in northwest Arkansas, checking on my fishing rods and fillet knives. Years before, I had given Sam and Bud Walton the exclusive rights to both the rods and the knives. The Wal-Mart stores still have them. I stopped at the store in Springdale, met with the manager and asked him if it was okay to go check on the rods. He told me that it would be fine, but he was tied up at the moment and would come back later and visit with me. I walked back to the sporting goods department. A young man was busy stocking shelves with a shipment of lures. He had his back to me, and I asked him if he had any Harold Ensley rods. He told me that they did, and that they were on the other side of the rack. He turned to look at me and said, "Why, you are Harold Ensley!" We checked on the rods and knives and visited a moment. He told me that he worked for Wal-Mart three days a week, and three days a week he guided for striper fishing on Beaver Lake. He said that he and one of his buddies ran a guide service, and asked me if I could come fish with them and shoot a movie for TV. In the past I had done programs on fresh water striper fishing at Santee, Cooper, in South Carolina and Lake Texoma in Texas, among others. I also did a saltwater striper picture at Martha's Vineyard on the East Coast. However, for some reason or other I had never done a striper movie out of Beaver Lake. I have known for years that Beaver was one of the top freshwater striper spots in the nation. Here was my chance! "Winds of Chance."

He gave me his card and told me to call him. His name was Brad Wiegman. I told him that if it were okay we could just go ahead and schedule it. So we did, and three weeks later my fishing buddy, Jim Higgins, and I made the trip. Brad and his buddy were fine young men. They had good boats, properly equipped for striper fishing. They used live shad as most of the guides do at that particular season. There are times when they catch them on top water, but this wasn't that time. We fished three days, caught a good number of stripers, but couldn't get anything over 22 pounds. I told Brad that it wasn't fair to them or to Beaver Lake to put the show on without a striper larger than 22 pounds. He asked me if I'd come back the next week and try it again. We did, but again didn't catch the big one we needed! I asked Brad if he had some still pictures of big fish he had taken in the past. He wife had caught a 38-pounder, and a teenager fishing with him had taken a big one. He gave me the pictures, and I planned to use them if the film we had was okay. The movies came out all right for the show. I had planned to put the show together at Wichita. My nephew, Roland Stewart, a high school teacher at Claflin, Kansas, was a dedicated striper fisherman. He had caught lots of big stripers at Lake Wilson in central Kansas. He kept telling me how well he could prepare stripers for the table and how good they were. I called him and asked him if he would like to be on the striper show I was doing.

Sunday night before we were scheduled to do the TV show on Tuesday, I received a call from Brad in Arkansas. He said, "You probably won't believe it, but today I caught a 45-pound striper! I asked him where he had it. He told me that he had it in the freezer. I asked him if he or his buddy could bring it to Wichita for the show, and that it was just what I wanted. He told me they had to work and couldn't do it. I asked him if he would meet me the next day at Wal-Mart's home office in Bentonville. I told him I would get the

Brad Wiegman with his 45-lb. 9 oz. striper for Beaver Lake, Arkansas

fish and take it to Wichita for my show. The next day we met at Bentonville; I picked up the fish and drove to Wichita. My nephew and his wife came down, and I thought he would pass out when I showed him the fish! He said, "That fish will weigh 50 pounds!" It really was a beautiful specimen. We did the show with the movie we had made with Brad. My nephew gave his special recipe for cooking stripers and held up Brad's trophy for the camera. A perfect ending to our story! "Winds of Chance." I had a taxidermist friend, Neil Smith in Kansas City, mount the striper and gave it to Brad and his family. Brad and Kyle still have their guide service.

In the early '80s I received a phone call from Charlie Shaw in Chanute, Kansas. He was district manager over 10 Wal-Mart stores in southeast Kansas. Wal-Mart had been selling my line of fishing rods and fillet knives for some time. Charlie had watched my TV show and asked me what I would charge to hold a sales seminar for his sporting goods department heads. I told him that I would not charge anything if he would get them all together in one place. We agreed on a time and place. I don't remember for sure if it was at Chanute or Fort Scott Wal-Mart. Anyway, my wife and I drove down. Charlie had dinner for his department heads and us. He also brought the managers of each store in his district. After dinner we went to the store and had the seminar. When we finished,

Charlie said that each one of the store managers wanted me to come to their store for a personal appearance. We worked out a schedule and started a chain reaction that has continued to this day. I would do from three to four stores each week during the spring fishing season, beginning the last week in February to the first week in June. We scheduled the weekday seminars from 1-9 p.m. and Saturday from 10 a.m. 'til 6 p.m. At the first store appearance I worked in the sporting goods department, greeting people, helping select tackle and giving fishing tips. After the first appearance I told my wife I needed to work out something in addition to make it more interesting to the Wal-mart customers. She asked me what I planned. I told her that I decided to demonstrate to people how to take better care of their catch and how to fillet fish! This forced me to fish two or three days each week to get fish to fillet.

In early years I had started a campaign to get people to catch and release bass, but to eat the crappie. I decided that crappie and bluegill would serve the purpose. I called my friend, Blair Flynn at Overbrook, Kansas. We had done a lot of fishing together in Kansas lakes. At that time there was no limit on crappie in Kansas. I told Blair I needed some crappie for a Wal-Mart promotion. He said, "I wish you would have called me earlier; I just dressed out 110 big crappie that I caught at Lake Perry." He told me to come on out and we would catch the fish. I drove out to Overbrook, and we drove to Perry. We took an ice chest along and put the fish on ice. We put some ice in the bottom of the chest, then the fish, then more ice on top of the fish. I don't remember what Wal-Mart store I worked, but it was an instant success. I found people hungry to learn more about caring for their fish and how to dress them. It took a few weeks to learn how best to manage the demonstration and not make a big stinky mess. After a few weeks, I learned that I could fillet crappie and have it ready for the pan with no fish odor.

The fact is that there is no odor in any fish's flesh; in fact, there is no odor in any flesh God created, man, beast, fish or fowl! Each store would advertise my coming and what my demonstration was about. I still answered questions and helped people buy tackle. I might have a fish half filleted and see a man looking for a fishing rod. I would excuse myself, go help the customer, then come back and finish filleting the fish. People everywhere were amazed that you could fillet a fish without any odor. Most women don't like that fishy smell. I don't either, for that matter. My wife Bonnie used to make me cook fish in the garage. Now I could cook it in the living room and not smell up the house. The word spread, and I had calls from all over. I did stores as far away as Forth Worth, Texas to the southwest and east as far as Dayton, Ohio. Day after day, I learned more. Customers were surprised and pleased because I had caught the fish. And I enjoyed it. That makes me think of the old Chinese proverb, "If you give a man a fish, you feed one person, but if you teach a man to fish, you feed a thousand."

The years wore on and the program gained momentum. My wife and I were in the McCook, Nebraska Wal-Mart store on a Saturday. I finished about 6 p.m. that night, and we drove to York, Nebraska, to do a demonstration there. I had just filleted the last fish and was cleaning up the table when a lady came rushing in. She said, "I saw in the paper where you could show how to fillet a fish so there is no fishy odor. I can't stand that fishy smell in my house!" I told her that I had just filleted the last one. She said, "Can't you do just one more? I have driven 60 miles to learn this!" I told her how we did it, and she was happy. She said that they had a big ranch with lots of pheasant if we ever wanted to hunt it. "Winds of Chance."

In later years I got to thinking about cleaning fish, cooking and eating them, and food in general, and I remembered when I was a youngster my dad butchered a hog or a steer, and he always bled the animal before he butchered it.

I remembered in the Bible when Noah and his family stepped out of the ark, God said, "Be fruitful and multiply and fill this earth, and the fear of you shall be on every beast of the earth, and on every bird of the sky, with everything that creeps on the ground, and all the fish of the sea, into your hand they are given. Every moving thing shall be food for you. I give all to you as I gave the green plant. Only you shall not eat flesh with its life, that is, its blood, and surely I will require your lifeblood; from every beast I will require it. And from every man, from every man's brother I will require the life of Man." Genesis Chapter 9:1 and 5.

Some may say, well, that just applies to Noah's day. Centuries later God, through his servant Moses, said, "And any man from the house of Israel, or from the aliens who sojourn among them who eats any blood, I will set my face against that person who eats blood, and will cut him off from among his people. For the life of the flesh is in the blood, and I have given it to you on the altar to make atonement for your souls, for this is the blood by reason of the life that makes atonement. Therefore I said to the sons of Israel, no person among you may eat any blood, nor may any alien who sojourns among you eat blood." Leviticus 17:10 and 12.

Someone may say that just applies to the children of Israel in Moses' time. Read Acts 15; some were trying to force circumcision on the Gentile converts. The apostles met in Jerusalem to discuss the matter. James speaking said, "For it seemed good to the Holy Spirit and to us to lay no greater burden than these essentials; that you abstain from things sacrificial to idols AND FROM BLOOD and from things strangled and from fornication if you keep yourselves free from such things. You will do well." Acts 15:28 and 29.

So you see God told Noah and his family not to eat blood. Through Moses, God told the children of Israel not to eat blood. The apostles told Christians not to eat blood. That being the case, where do we stand? I got to thinking about it along with my demonstrations of preparing crappie. How do you bleed them? Fishermen have been bleeding big catfish for years. I started asking biologists around the different states, men with Master's degrees cutting up toads, fish and snakes. I found no answer from any of them. In the early '90s two of my fishing buddies, Norm Troutman and Jim Higgins, and I were shooting a crappie movie on Truman Reservoir near Warsaw, Missouri. Norm has had a guide service on Truman for most of 20 years. He and Jim and I, with another great crappie fisherman, Max Casteel, have fished on Truman together since the reservoir was filled.

However, Max was not with us that day. We finished the movie about 3 p.m. Each of us caught a limit of nice crappie. We were fishing up the Osage that day, and I asked Norm to pull up in a cove, that I wanted to figure out how to bleed a crappie! I told him that it had bothered me for some time, and that there must be a way! He pulled the boat ashore, and I took a live crappie out of the live well and sat on the front seat of the boat. I thought at first I would cut the gills out. Usually if you injure the gills of a fish, it will bleed profusely. I placed the live fish on a board on the boat seat. I lifted up the gill plate, and there I saw the fish's heart. It was a dark purple spot about the size of your little fingernail. It was covered with a thin transparent membrane. I stuck the point of the knife blade in the spot, and blood spurted out. I told Norm and Jim that I finally discovered it! "Winds of Chance."

We then proceeded to bleed each one of our fish. We also found that you had to bleed the fish while it was still alive, put it back in the live well and the fish would then pump all the blood from its body. We discovered that water temperature made a difference. In cold water you needed up to seven or eight minutes. Normal water temperature, slightly less. As soon as the fish died, we put it on a bed of crushed ice. Shaved ice is best; however, regular crushed ice serves the purpose. It's best to put at least four inches of crushed ice in your cooler, then a layer of fish and a layer of ice. If you will keep the water drained, crappie and bluegill will keep in good shape for a week or so without being dressed. However, even if I'm not demonstrating, I never clean my crappie or bluegill the same day. Many times you fish hard all day and come in tired. Bleed your fish, put them on ice and then clean them at your leisure. You will do a better job and have better fish. But remember, you **cannot** keep walleye and catfish without dressing! God didn't make anything better to eat than crappie or bluegill fillets! Why not prepare them in the best way possible and enjoy it!

The old-timers used to hang their big catfish on a tree and cut off their tails to bleed them out. I don't know that it is the best way, but it is simple to stick a knife blade into a fish's heart and bleed it. It may not mean anything to others, but it's a religious thing for me. God told Noah and his people not to eat blood. He told the children of Israel not to eat blood, and he told Christians not to eat blood. For that reason, I will not knowingly eat blood.

In my demonstrations in Wal-Mart stores, I started showing people how to bleed their crappie, as well as the method where there would be no odor. The response everywhere has been amazing. They called me to Duluth, Minnesota, to do a fishing seminar across the lake at Superior Wisconsin. This I did for several years! They would have me stay at a motel in Duluth on the north shore of Lake Superior. Then each day a retired biologist from Wisconsin would pick me up and bring me home. He was a nice gentleman and we built a friendship. The year after I had learned, I asked him if he ever saw a person bleed a crappie. He said, "Certainly not, but would it be the same on a trout?" I said, "Let's go back to the kids' trout pool and catch a small rainbow." We did and took it to the restroom. He gave me his knife, and I stuck the fish in the heart and held it over the trash barrel. The blood spurted out, just as it had on a crappie. He was amazed! "Winds of Chance."

During my 50 years of broadcasting outdoor shows on radio and television, I have been privileged to fish a lot of different waters, lakes, rivers, reservoirs in fresh water, plus many places along the Atlantic, Arctic and Pacific Oceans. I'm often asked about my favorite spot or my favorite fish or perhaps my most special moment of fishing. To be truthful, I have many favorite spots, many special kinds of fish and many special moments. It would be almost impossible to decide which spot, which species of fish and which special moment would be number UNO. The "Winds of Chance" have blown from many directions, bringing incidents that are precious memories.

In 1955, as I stood on a cliff on Elk Island looking over the blue waters of the God's Lake in Manitoba, Canada, I never dreamed that in the year 2000 I would be standing on the same cliff, doing an interview by satellite for Radio America in Washington, D.C. I'll admit that the connections were not the best, but we made it! I have many precious memories of fishing God's Lake and God's River. In 1955, both the lake and the river offered some of the top fishing in North America. God's Lake for walleye, northern pike and lake trout; God's River for some of the top brook trout fishing anywhere. The thrilling part of it is that it is just as great in the year 2000 as it was when I first fished it in 1954. This is also true of Lake Athabasca and Great Bear Lake.

Sometime in the late '50s or early '60s, Barney Lamm called me and wanted me to explore God's River at his outpost camp. Bonnie and I had fished it several times out of his Elk Island camp, but mostly to fly to the river for one day of fishing. That really didn't give you enough time to test all the waters. Then also, the guides would take you to the same spots. This trip was to be different; we were to stay in the outpost log cabin and fish the river above and below the camp. It as almost like a campout except we had a roof over our heads. The first day we fished below the camp and caught some nice brookies, but nothing over 4 pounds. The second day they took us up the river. They used strong wood freighter canoes, two native guides to a canoe. Bonnie was in a canoe with two native guides, and I was in the other canoe with two native guides. The waters were so treacherous that they used one guide in the front of the canoe and the other handling the motor in the rear. These canoes were large, but they only had 25-horse motors. Bonnie had a camera in her canoe, and I had one in ours. We had to make one portage around the first rapids. I noted that they kept fishing the smooth water above each rapids. At first we were a little jumpy, but they were really good; they would always have one veteran experienced guide in each boat. They knew the water and they didn't take any chances. We passed one falls and several rapids. I suppose some 10 or 15 miles upstream from the cabin we came to a spot where the river split around some big boulders, dividing the river at a heavy rapids. The waters were churning by this little island of boulders. I'm sure they wanted to fish the smooth waters just past the rapids, but thought it too dangerous to try. They pulled each canoe up on the boulder, and we started fishing in the swift water below the rapids. Bonnie and I were using ultra-light spinning gear. I think she had 4-lb. test and I had 2-lb. test. We were using 1/8-oz. crappie jigs. We had learned in Alaska and in the mountain waters of the Rockies that we would catch more trout on a crappie jig than anything else. We caught a few nice brookies 3 and 4 pounds, when I looked up on an eddy of smooth water on the left side of the split above the rapids. I saw a big trophy brookie surface. I yelled at Bonnie to look! She did, and from her canoe she cast upstream over the rock. She got snagged on the rocks. I told her to just break it off and turned the other way to see if I could cast to the spot. I heard their motor start. I looked up, and to my surprise they had already started up the rapids on the right hand side of the rock. It scared me, but they made it and got Bonnie's jig loose. She was really in a position to cast to the rising brookie, but she was so nervous about the rapids she said, "I just want out of here!" I told her guides to ease their canoe down to the big boulder splitting the river and let Bonnie out on the rock, and I would jump in their canoe. They did; Bonnie stepped out on the rock and I jumped into their canoe and almost turned it over! It wasn't a dangerous spot to fish, as there was an eddy of smooth water at the edge of the raging rapids. I made a cast, and when I did I had a big wad of line boil off in a twist, but the jig hit the spot. That big old trout hit, and we battled it out for a while. I knew it was the biggest brookie I had ever hooked. A big highly colored male! I worked carefully to keep the fish in the quiet water. It was almost exhausted, but took another short run and the current carried that beautiful fish over the rapids. There was nothing to do but break my line.

I was just sick, but tied on another jig and made a cast to the same spot and hooked another big brookie! I played the fish ever so carefully. I had the feeling if I didn't put too much pressure on the fish it would stay in that eddy. After a long hard fight, the fish came up and rolled over on its side. The guide went to net it and spooked it. It made a short run, lay over on its side and washed over the rapids. I turned to the older guide who was running the motor and asked him if they had ever been over that rapids. He said, "No, but we go get him!" He started the motor and told the guide in front to keep the bow of the canoe upstream with his paddle, that we were going down the rapids backwards. I yelled at Bonnie to get the camera ready to get us going down the rapids. By this time my fish was about 100 yards below us, exhausted and floating on top out of the current. The two guides kept the canoe straight, and we went shooting on past my fish. Now we were about 100 yards below it. It was almost a game of hide and seek, but they finally managed to net it about one mile below the rocks. My guides were so happy they both stood up to shake my hand, and we all three nearly went in the "drink." That was at least 40 years ago, but in my mind's eye I can still see that brookie going over the rapids. "Winds of Chance."

That fish weighed 7-1/4 pounds, not a real big brookie, but the circumstances made it a big moment in my life. We brought it back, had it mounted, and you can see it with some of my other trophy fish displayed in the Missouri Sports Hall of Fame, east of Springfield, Missouri on Highway 60.

Everyone has had some special incidents and moments in life. The editor of *Missouri*

Outdoors, a fairly new publication, recently called wanting an interview with us for an article about our work. In the course of the interview he asked the question, "What incident or moment of achievement stands out during your 50 years in the outdoor broadcasting field?" I told him I would be hard-pressed to choose one, for there were so many precious moments that it would be difficult to pin it down. I suppose we could fill a book with just precious moments! It is not that my life has been so great; it's just that God has blessed me with many wonderful opportunities. I sincerely hope that sharing just a few will add to your reading pleasure.

Since I wrote about that brookie, I have one more story from God's River. When Barney Lamm ended his resort operation in the north, we quit going to God's Lake. We had found so many great places like Warren Plummer's operation on Great Bear Lake. Paul Zaniwith called me from Winnipeg, Manitoba. Paul was one of the pioneer fishing and hunting camp operators in Canada. He had managed Ruminsky's camp on God's Lake where the lake waters pour into God's River, then on to the Hayes River and on to Hudson Bay. We had met Paul for several years at the airport in Winnipeg. He was then working for Plummer's Great Bear operation. He would meet Plummer's customers as they came to Winnipeg on commercial flights and take them to the hotel for the night. The next morning he picked them up and took them to the airport to get on Plummer's charter plane for Great Bear Lake. He also met the fishermen coming back from the trip and helped them on their flight home. It was sort of a shuttle service. He helped us and our parties for many years, both coming and going. He told me the reason he called was the Canadian government initiated a program by which they would buy or build a camp and let the native tribe of the area manage it. The Cree tribe had a village on the northeast corner of God's Lake. The government had built a new lodge and several additional units on the site of the old Ruminsky camp. It was a great location right on the banks of God's River. They put up some beautiful units. They hired Paul to oversee the operation and to book fishing parties from the states. Paul hired an experienced camp operator and a good chef and his wife to deliver good food. Paul also supervised the supplies, food and equipment. Paul knew of my work promoting Canadian fishing with Barney Lamm and Warren Plummer. He asked me if I would bring my crew to God's River Lodge to shot some movies for my TV shows.

I called three of my fishing buddies: Jim Higgins, a deputy sheriff at Holden, Missouri; Norm Troutman, a professional fishing guide on Truman Reservoir in Missouri, and Walt Shublom, a retired basketball coach of Kansas City, Kansas. I told them the story and asked them to help. I called Paul and we scheduled the trip. We flew commercial to Winnipeg, spent the night and the next day, and we took a charter flight to God's River. We were really impressed with everything, good accommodations and excellent service. There were only two other customers in camp besides our four. We had five days of excellent fishing; big northern pike and walleye fishing on the lake that was out of this world. We spent a day and a half on the river for some wild brook trout fishing. We made three movies for television. They had good boats and motors, and the native guides knew all the good spots. It just couldn't have been better! "Winds of Chance."

We came back to Kansas City and told our fishing friends of this new facility. We spread the news on radio and television. That winter Paul and his son Gary worked the sports and travel shows in Chicago, Minneapolis, Omaha and Kansas City. They invited us back the next year. The camp was filled! Paul had really jump-started their operation! We made it a regular part of our schedule. A young native guide named Jimmy Yellowback guided Higgins and me. He was a sharp young man and put us in a lot of good fishing, both on the river and on the lake. It was because of him that I had two great special moments.

The first was on the lake that morning; I told Jimmy that I would like to take our crew to Submarine Bay. It was a shallow bay across the lake from the lodge where in the past we had caught a lot of big pike. It was a good long boat ride, and to our dismay, nothing but pike in the 12 to 15-pound class. Late that afternoon we started back to camp, with our other boat ahead of us. Jimmy said, "We still have about 30 minutes we could fish. I know a spot at East Bay that is full of northern pike, mostly in the 10 to 15-pound class. I don't think you'll get a big one, but do you want to try it?" I really didn't; it had been a hard day. However, I couldn't remember ever in the 40 years of fishing the North of having a guide say, "Let's stay out a little longer." Usually they are ready to "head for the barn" at the twinkling of an eye. To please Jimmy, I told him to go for it! It was a little out of our way home, but Jim and I were soon buzzing Pomme Specials in a little bay. It may have been 200 yards long and 50 yards wide. Almost every cast one or both of us would get a 10 or 12-pound northern. The northern should not really attack buzz bait, but it was fun. I saw something swirl after some bait fish, and it was within casting distance. Jim saw it, too! He cast across the spot and got nothing. I followed him with my cast. I had reeled the buzz bait over the spot and almost to the boat; there was an explosion as a big northern smashed into the lure. It sounded like someone had thrown a hand grenade into the water. I yelled for Jim to grab the camera; we had to have a picture of the fish. Jim did and started grinding. That northern took us all over that little bay. We finally subdued it! It was a beautiful specimen. We checked it out, held it up for the camera and released it. We estimated it at better than 30 pounds. I had caught many northern at God's Lake in the 20 to 30-pound class, but this one came at a time I needed it, but if my guide, Jimmy Yellowback, had not suggested we try 30 minutes more, it never would have happened. "Winds of Chance."

God's River produced the material for many TV shows for me down through the years and many wonderful incidents. I must tell you of one more. I wish I had the talent and word power to describe the moment as it really happened. A few years ago, maybe in the mid '90s, a group of us flew to God's River Lodge for a week of fishing and shooting movies for our TV show. We did our lake fishing for walleye and northern pike the first part of the week. Mid-week we floated down God's River to their outpost camp. We fished as we went downstream and caught lots of nice brook trout in the 3 to 5-pound class. The river was full of walleye, so we caught walleye for our shore lunch. I told our group not to eat the brook trout, just release them and eat the walleye. The brookies are just too beautiful to kill and eat. At first our native guides didn't appreciate my stand. I told them that they wanted to increase and keep their customers. You just cannot catch brook trout in that size and number many places. I said, "Many camps in Canada can provide good walleye and pike fishing, but you have something not many camps can offer. Just don't destroy it!"

The second day we fished some in the river below the outpost camp. We pretty well had our brook trout movie made. I told the crew that I wanted to save a little time at the next big rapids to get some shots of the boats fighting their way up the swirling, twisting current. It was a beautiful stretch of white water churning around a boulder-filled drop-off. It was not a true waterfall but a drop-off, possibly 50 feet, in a 100-yard stretch. It really took two highly skilled native guides, one in the bow with a paddle and one with the motor, to get the boat up the rapids. It was a great experience.

White water in God's River, Manitoba

I checked the camera about a mile below the rapids. There was just 50 feet of film left. I asked the other three boats to proceed to the base of the rapids, and that Jim Higgins and I would stop to run off the rest of the film and reload. I didn't want to start up the rapids and run out of film. You just had one shot at it, and you had to get it the first run! Jimmy Yellowback, the young native who was guiding me when I caught the big pike, was front man, and an older native guide was on the motor. We had never stopped at that particular spot to fish. I asked them if we could anchor at that spot just to run off the film and reload. The current was really swift, but there was a boulder sticking up out of the water right in the middle of the river. It was just a small boulder about the size of a small card table and stood out of the water about 8 inches. They eased the boat up to the boulder. Jimmy stepped out on it and dropped the anchor. He stood on the rock holding the boat in place. I moved to the back of the boat and asked Jim to take the camera and run off the rest of the film, while I was tying on a jig, bending down the barb and squeezing on a 3-inch purple reaper. Jim said, "Now make a cast!" I cast upstream at a 45-degree angle, and the lure got hung up in the rocks. Jim told me that the film had just run out. I started to break my line when Jimmy asked me to pass him my rod with the snagged jig, and when I got the camera loaded we would run upstream and save the reaper. I handed Jimmy my rod. He was still standing on the rock holding the boat steady. I loaded the camera, handed it to Jim and told him I would make a cast with my extra rod. He could then run off enough film of me casting; then the camera would be ready for the rapids. My other ultra-light rod was already rigged with a 3-inch, 1/4-oz. pink reaper.

Jim started the camera. I made a cast at a 45-degree angle downstream and let the reaper sink and I felt the line tighten. I said, "I got this one snagged in the rocks." Then I felt the fish shake his head; I yelled to Jim to keep the camera rolling, that I had a good fish. Using 4-lb. test line in that swift current with the boat anchored might turn out to be a real battle. If the fish is big enough and started with the current, we would have to pull the anchor and follow the fish downstream. I learned a long time ago in a situation like that to take it easy and not crowd the fish. Fortunately, the fish stayed in the current and didn't go downstream. After a long, hard fight the guide netted the fish. What a beauty! It was easily the largest brookie that I had ever landed. We estimated it at 8 pounds or better. Jim got all the action of landing and releasing the best! If Jimmy Yellowback had not taken my snagged outfit, it wouldn't have happened. "Winds of Chance."

That roll of film was finished. I reloaded the camera, and we met the other three boats at the foot of the rapids, shot the pictures of the boat making the rapids, and headed for the barn. The end of a wonderful day! If we had not stopped in a spot we had never fished to run off some film, and if Jimmy Yellowback had not been nice enough to try and save my line, I would never have caught the trophy fish! As my friend, Jim Higgins would say, "The Lord takes care of those who can't take care of themselves."

Special Coaches

PERHAPS the strangest and most unique material for one of my TV shows came from Wyandotte High School in Kansas City, Kansas. I'm not sure of the date, but must have been late '50s or early '60s. I received a call from a young man who said that he was equipment manager for their basketball teams. Wyandotte had just won their third state basketball title. I'm not sure if they were Class 3A or 4A, but the class of the larger schools. He said that after the championship game, in the locker room he heard the coach say, "I'd give my eyeteeth to go fishing with that Ensley guy on TV." He asked me if it could be arranged. I told him that I had been broadcasting basketball games for many of the Kansas City area schools, and had many friends among the coaches. I said that I would need some special reason to take their coach.

A few days later he called me. Six-hundred of the student body at Wyandotte had signed a petition to take their coach on a fishing trip. They had taped pages of notebook paper with all the signatures on one roll. All this, without the coach's knowledge for a surprise gift! I didn't know the coach personally, but wasn't about to turn these young people down!

In the first place, I have a warm spot in my heart for teachers and coaches. I remember how much Russ Kaminski, the basketball and football coach of Joplin, did for my two boys, Smokey and Dusty. I told the kid to bring the roll of paper with the petition names on it to my TV show. We would show it and tell the coach that he had a free fishing trip coming, as soon as we could arrange it. They were to make sure that Coach Shublom was watching that night. The kid came on my show and unrolled the petition with the 600 signatures of Wyandotte's high school students.

Come Easter, I called the coach to tell him that I would like to take him to Bull Shoals in Arkansas for a bass fishing trip. I wanted to do it over Easter vacation. I asked him if he could possibly take off a day early so we could drive down Wednesday night. That would give us Thursday, Friday and Saturday to fish. He told me that he had to ask his superintendent for permission. I never dreamed that they wouldn't let him take a day off. I was almost shocked when he called to tell me that they wouldn't let him off.

Here was a man who had brought several state championships to the school, and they wouldn't let him off for a day! I said, "Coach, because of this, I will plan to take you

Walt Shublom, one of the nation's top high school basketball coaches, Wyandotte High School, Kansas City, Kansas

to Canada for a week of fishing as soon as school is out." This we did! The first week of June we left Monday night after my TV show and drove all night to Kenora, Ontario, where my friend, Barney Lamm, picked us up and flew us to his base camp at Ball Lake. We have five days of fabulous fishing for walleye, small mouth bass, lake trout and northern pike. I had not met Walter before the trip, but he proved to be the class act that most of our coaches and teachers are. Before the week was over, Barney asked me if I thought the coach might be interested in working for him during the summer months. He told me that he would use him to recruit business in the Kansas City area. Walter accepted the job and worked for Barney several years. It was ironic that the school wouldn't give him a day off; yet it worked out to be a blessing. "Winds of Chance."

Walter and I formed a friendship that has lasted to this day. We made a lot of great fishing trips to Canada and here in the States. He kept his coaching job and became one of the "winningest" high school basketball coaches in the country! He also conducted basketball clinics on the college level, both on the East Coast and on the West.

I think he won 10 out of 11 Kansas big school championships. He's the kind of teacher and coach you would want to teach your youngsters. A few years later I received an invitation to explore the fishing on Great Bear Lake in Canada's Northwest Territory. I needed someone young and strong to make the trip to help me. I called Walter and he asked me the dates. He told me that he would go, but that he had scheduled a basketball clinic in New York City at Long Island University. I told him I also had to be back that night for my TV show. We decided to make the trip and left right after my TV show at 10 p.m. Monday night.

We drove all night and arrived at Winnipeg Airport about 10:30 a.m. There we met Tony Birch, one of Barney's pilots, who was to fly us to Great Bear in a twin-engine Grumman Goose. We parked my station wagon at the hangar and headed north. I had flown with Tony before at Ball Lake. He was a great guy and an excellent pilot. The Goose is a great airplane but slow, and we had some 1700 miles to Sawmill Bay on the south side of Great Bear Lake. We made it to Uranium City late that evening. We landed on the water, docked the plane and spent the night in a hotel there. We were up early the next morning and flew to Yellowknife, where we again landed on the water. Tony said that we were to get our fishing license there. Walter and I took a taxi to a cafe downtown that sold fishing licenses. I remember it well, for the taxi driver wanted to sell us an interest in a gold mine. In the cafe I was standing near the cash register filling out the paper, when a voice from the dining room said, "Ensley, what are you doing here?" It was Doug Cameron, the first bush pilot to fly my wife and me to God's River. I told him that we were headed to Sawmill Bay at Great Bear Lake to shoot some stuff for television. I asked him what he was doing there. He told me that he was flying lumber to the gold mining camps. He also said that Great Bear Lake was still iced in, and that we would have to land on the sand strip at the sawmill. It was the last time I saw him until he flew me into Chantry Inlet, for Barney. I don't know if Doug is still alive. He was a veteran bush pilot and had flown all over Canada. He was as good a pilot as you ever saw and a great guy. You think of the odds of meeting him that far out in the "boon docks." "Winds of Chance."

We took a taxi back to the plane and headed for Great Bear. Tony had never been there, and we had to navigate with a map and the lakes. There were just two camps on the lake, Sawmill Bay operated by a group of doctors from North Dakota, and Plummers at Gun Barrel Inlet. Both camps used the strip at Sawmill. The airstrip had been built on the Dew line in World war II, and the sand strip certainly was not well groomed. The Goose has small landing wheels for landing on land, but was used mainly for landing on the water. As we approached the lake, you could see miles and miles of ice-covered water. For some reason Tony was unable to contact the camp radio for instructions to land. He circled the field a couple of times trying to decide which runway to use. The air sac was limp, as there was no wind. Tony made his descent. I was up with him, and Walter was in the back. Tony said, "Boys, buckle up tight, I'm going in with a high nose." Although the Goose is a slow plane, it lands pretty hot compared to its air speed. The runway was sand, but pock-marked. We evidently hit a hard spot on the sand; the plane bounced and skipped some distance, then hit a soft spot and rolled up on its nose and stopped. No damage was done because the nose of the plane extends several feet in front of the props. We climbed out of the plane. "Coach" wiped the sweat off his forehead and said, "I never did like a high dribble." We walked down to the camp. They were expecting us but didn't see us come in. The camp manager told us about the ice and that he couldn't get the boats out to the open water. He said there was an open stretch of water toward Plummer's Camp. I suggested to Tony that we fly out to the open water, land the plane in a likely spot and fish from the nose of the plane. Tony agreed to try it. We took off from the sand strip, which in itself was a project. Tony circled the open water, which may have covered a few square miles. He told me to pick out the spot, that he wouldn't have any idea since he didn't fish. He flew lower over the water, which was as clear as the water you drink. I was looking for a reef where you could see the boulders, in water deep enough to land the plane. We found just such a spot! Tony landed the plane.

I got out on the nose of the plane and started casting a 1/2-oz. Maribou jig. In short order, I had a trout and called for Walter to get the camera. He did. Tony and I landed the fish and released it. It was a small trout, about 12 pounds. I regret that we didn't get a still picture of us catching trout, from the nose of a twin-engine plane. I asked Tony to drop anchor, which he did. It was a chain anchor. After about an hour, Tony said, "Harold, we'd better get out of here before our battery runs down, pull the anchor." Would you believe it, the anchor was lodged in the rocks. We tried every way to shake it loose. We were all about ready to push the panic button. It could have spelled disaster! It finally worked loose and we took off.

When we got airborne, Tony said, "Ensley, don't ever ask me to do that again" I didn't, nor did I tell him that I was shaken up as bad as he was! We landed back on the sand strip, happy to be back on "Mother Earth" again. The next day I asked Tony to fly me to Plummer's Camp at Gun Barrel Inlet, to see if we could find some open water. We landed on the water at Plummer's Camp. I told Warren of my situation, that we couldn't get the boats out at the other camp. I didn't want to go back to Kansas City without a movie. He was very gracious and told me that all his guides were tied up. If I wanted to take a boat, he would loan me one. Then said, "I have a dock boy that can go with you. He doesn't know the lake and is not a fisherman, but he can run the motor for you." We left Tony at the dock and started up the lake. Walter and I worked hard the rest of the day but caught no picture fish!

We came back to the dock, and one of the young Indian guides yelled, "Hey, Ensley, what are you doing here?" I told him that I was trying to catch enough fish for a movie, but haven't done much good. He told me that he was guiding two older men from Chicago and that they couldn't catch many fish. He knew that I didn't keep the fish, as he had guided me several times near Kenora, Ontario. He told us that if we would come back the next morning and follow him, that he would put us in fish, providing we would give them our fish. Sounded good to me, so Tony flew us back the next day. I asked Tony to go with us and help catch fish. He said, "I'm no fisherman, but if you will teach me, I'll try." We followed this guide to his pet spot and caught fish like crazy and made our movie.

At one time Tony , Walter and I each had a nice trout on. I set the camera for the boy handling the motor. He got a picture of us netting three trout at one time. We caught a tub full of trout from 10 to 15 pounds and gave them to the other boat. It had made our day! "Winds of Chance."

When we got back to camp, Warren asked Tony if he would mind to fly some of his customers back to the strip at Sawmill Bay, where the Charter DC-6 was to pick them up and fly them to Winnipeg. Tony did, and the weather really socked in. It was getting late, but Tony thought we could make it to Yellowknife and spend the night there. It was misting rain when we took off from Sawmill. Walter climbed in the back of the plane and went to sleep. I was up front, helping Tony navigate by using a map and checking the lakes. We were getting pretty well on our way, and the ceiling was getting lower and lower. Tony said, "Check the altitude of the hills in this area." I checked the map, and there were hills all around us at 1100 feet and we were flying at 900 feet. Tony said, "Let's get out of here. We are turning back to Sawmill Bay." Walter was asleep in the back and didn't know we had turned back. As we went in to land at Sawmill, Walter awakened and looked out the window. He saw the old wind direction sock. He realized where we

Safe return from fly-out, with Warren Plummer, veteran bush pilot and pioneer camp operator

were and said, "What's going on?" I told him I wanted to come back and fish some more. I thought he would have a heart attack; he wasn't very happy! "I'm supposed to be in New York at Long Island University Monday night!" Then we told him that weather had forced us back.

We came back to camp; it was probably 9 p.m. I asked the manager if Walter and I could try to get a boat out through the ice floe. He said, "Wait until these other guys go to bed or they will all want to go out. I know you know what you are doing, but I don't want everyone out this time of night." At that time of year there was no darkness except from mist and fog. About midnight he came to us and said that we could go. I've done a lot of stupid things, but going out at midnight on a strange lake with ice all around us was the worst I had ever done. We had to walk about a quarter-mile to reach the boats. Then we had to take the oars and shove the small icebergs out of our way. I had not planned to go far! I had seen this bay from the air and thought it might be a mile across to the point where we wanted to fish. It turned out to be about seven miles across. About halfway over I asked Walter to check the spare gas can in the front end of the boat. He did, and said there wasn't much in it. I didn't tell Walter of my apprehension. We were in a difficult situation, with not much fuel left. We reached the point; there were some trout there and we caught a few.

At that time of year there is no total darkness, but I was a little alarmed by what looked like a fog bank moving in between us and the camp. I said, "Walter, let's head for the barn," and started toward the camp. We were almost three miles from the shoreline that ran out from the boat ramp. The fog rolled in and just closed off visibility, like you would fade out a picture. The wind died down, so we had no wave action to give us direction. I wanted to push the panic button, but tried to keep my sense of direction. I knew if we went past the bay to the north we would have to have someone rescue us the next day, if they could find us. I have a tendency to pull to the right when I'm lost and have no bearing. Therefore, I pointed the boat in the direction I last saw land and kept going. I didn't try to tell Walter what the situation was. Imagine my thrill when I saw the outline of the trees along the shore. I immediately ran the boat up on the beach! Was I ever glad to have my feet on terra firma.

I told Walter we would leave the boat there and walk to camp, starting up the shore-line. The fog really settled in. I was leading the way, carrying my rods and tackle box, when two big Husky dogs leaped out of the darkness, right at my throat. Walter said I must have leaped two feet in the air and came down with my fishing rods pointed at the dogs. It so happened that the dogs were tethered and could not reach me.

We had stumbled into the camp where the Indian guides and their families were camped with their sled dogs. They showed us the way to the camp. When we arrived at camp, the manager said they were just getting ready to send out a search party for us. We rested a few hours, and Tony said, "Men, let's go!" The weather improved, and we made it back safely to Winnipeg. However, Walter and I both were in a time crunch.

I asked Tony to take care of my station wagon and gear, that I had to fly back to Kansas City to do my TV show and would come back for it. I did my radio show from a phone booth there at the airport and asked them to tell the TV crew to have my things ready for a last-minute arrival. Walter and I boarded a flight to Minneapolis. There we split. Walter ran one way to catch his flight to New York, and I ran the other way to catch a flight to Kansas City. He made it to New York City, just in time to do his basketball seminar at Long Island University. I made it 30 minutes before time to go on the air with my TV show. "Winds of Chance."

Walter and I have fished together since then, but nothing as wild as that trip! Walter was also assistant coach to Norm Stewart at Missouri University. Our teachers and coaches are so important to our kids. They generally spend more time with them than the parents during the character-molding periods of their lives.

I shall always be grateful to Russ Kaminski, head football and basketball coach for so many years at Joplin High school in Southwest Missouri. His teams won many championships. Smokey, our oldest son, played both basketball and football. During his senior year Joplin won the state basketball championship over Beaumont of St. Louis. We were at the game, and I had my camera to get some pictures for my own use. The score was tied with just a few seconds to go. Joplin had the ball. Their little guard, Dailey, brought the ball down the court. He was a good ball handler and quick. All of us were expecting him somehow to drive on in for a lay-up. Three St. Louis players moved out to cover him. Russ didn't have any real tall players, so he was using a double post. When St. Louis moved out to stop Dailey, Smokey was standing wide open under the basket. Dailey passed it to him, and he laid it in with two seconds left on the clock to win the game. I just sat there with my camera in my lap and my teeth in my mouth and missed a shot of a lifetime.

Kaminski loved to fish, and for what he had done for my boys, I called him to see if he wanted to go sometime. We arranged a trip, and I took him to Bull Shoals for some bass fishing. The next year I called and asked him if he wanted to go again. He told me that he did and asked me to take Dusty, our youngest son. He said, "Can we go crappie fishing? I need some fish for a fish fry." We set the date for Easter weekend, and the three of us drove to Buck Creek on Bull Shoals. The weather turned bad, but we caught a lot of big crappie and some nice bass. The second day we were going down the lake to one of my favorite spots. We didn't have a guide, but Robbie Robinson, the camp owner, said, "I don't know much about fishing, but I'll run the boat for you guys." It was a chilly morning, but the sun was shining. Russ was in the bow with his back to us, and Dusty and I were side by side on the middle boat seat. Dusty had slumped down. I slapped him across the back and said, "Straighten your shoulders." I didn't do it roughly. He straightened his shoulders but soon slumped down again. I said, "Straighten up, Dusty." Without turning around, Russ said, "Leave the kid alone. I got Smokey to straighten his shoulders, didn't I?" I said, "You surely did." He said again, "Leave the kid alone, I'll straighten Dusty up." It made me realize how much a good coach cared about his players. We caught a lot of big crappies. That night I filleted fish in the cold until the wee hours of the morning for Russ Kaminski. I was honored and thrilled to do this little bit for a coach who had done so much for our boys and thousands of others. Dusty's senior year, Russ' team was second in the State, but he will always be first in the hearts of all he touched! Smokey went on to play at K.U. his freshman and sophomore years, and Dusty went on to play four years of Division One basketball at Centenary College at Shreveport, Louisiana.

So to Coach Walt Shublom and Russ Kaminski and all the other teachers out there, keep up the good work, and may God bless you in so doing.

After a time, we fished so much that I hurt my right elbow, and then I fished and cast until I hurt the left elbow. My doctor recommended surgery. When I learned that the doctor wanted to perform surgery on my right elbow, we chose to do it just prior to the annual sport show in Kansas City, so that I would have the extra ten days for healing. The surgery was a success, but they hadn't taken the stitches out, so I still had my arm in a sling. My wife said, "What are you going to do; you can't sign autographs or shake hands with the people." Nick Kahler always put my station wagon at the entrance of the auditorium where almost everyone had to pass by my position. My wife suggested that I have people sign their name for a chance at a fishing trip, with the winner to be our choice. It was an excellent idea; we brought a notebook for the event. Several thousand signed on.

One evening, with a crowd about our table waiting their turn, a young man reached out with a hook on his right arm to sign his name. He said, "Harold, I don't write so well with this hook, but I can still fish!" When he moved away, I asked his wife if he really liked to fish, and could he fish with that right arm off at the elbow? She told me that he was a school teacher in Independence, Missouri, and that he did love to fish. Immediately, I knew who my first choice would be. I told her not to say anything to him, but I would try to take him fishing. Just before Easter break, I called to tell him he had a free fishing trip to Bull Shoals. I asked him if he could possibly get off Wednesday from school so we could have an extra day. He said that he could because the school board told him that if he needed it for business, he could have it. He said, "This is a business!" I called my friend, Everett Crow, who operated Crow Barnes Resort on Lake Bull Shoals. I told him the circumstances. He told me to bring him and come on down after school, a six-hour drive, and it gave us an opportunity to get acquainted. He was one of the Rangers to hit the beaches in North Africa during World War II. He came through that combat zone without a scratch. He was instructing at one of the Army camps in Virginia or the Carolinas, and a booby trap with a faulty switch exploded in his hand and blew his right arm off at the elbow, mutilating his left arm, just leaving two fingers, and put out one eye. He lived through that and graduated from college and was teaching school in Independence. What a courageous young man with a great attitude. He asked no favors, and I never heard him complain. We arrived at the camp around midnight.

The next morning in the dining room we were seated along with some 15 or 20 other guests. They served us all at one long table together. He picked up the small glass or orange juice with his hook and spilled it all over. He picked up his fork and dropped it on the floor. Naturally all eyes were on him. He turned to me with a smile and said, "Boy, am I awkward this morning." My heart went out to him, but I knew then and there that everything was going to be all right.

We got a lot of fish, and he caught his share. One day we had taken a good string of bass and put them on a chain stringer for the picture, although we had a live well in the boat. He caught a bass that would go close to five pounds. I had one on the stringer about the same size. He was having a problem getting the fish on the stringer. I asked him to let me do it, but no way, he would do it himself. He put the string of fish over the side of the boat and was busy getting his lure ready for another cast. He had his back turned to me, and while he wasn't looking, I unsnapped the metal catch and hid his fish in a live well, but left the snap open. Sometime later, we decided to move. I asked him to put the string of fish in the boat. He smiled, to think I had asked him to do it, rather than do it myself. He lifted the stringer of fish and said, "Wait a minute, one of those fish is gone." Then he said, "That was my fish." You could see the look of disappointment on his face, but he said, "Well, I had the fun of catching it." I said, "I'll bet your wife will be proud to hear that you caught a five-pounder." He said, "When we left, my wife said, 'Honey, you won't think of me when you are down there,' and come to think of it, I haven't!" Our guide couldn't stand the pressure any longer and showed him his fish in the live well. So much time has passed, I cannot recall his name, but I shall always remember his courage in adversity.

144

Fishing Canada

MY WIFE BONNIE lost her fight with cancer in January of 1992. The Sunday following the funeral, a friend at church, Dale Flaxbeard, approached me and said, "I'd like to take you to Lake Athabasca in Saskatchewan for a week of fishing. I have two tickets, and it won't cost you anything. However, you cannot take your cameras." I told him that I could pay my own way, but if I couldn't take my cameras, I wouldn't go! He said, "Then take your cameras; I just want to do something nice for you!"

For some 30 years I'd flown over the lake enroute to Great Bear. I always thought of trying to fish there, but had no contacts. We made the trip, cameras and all. It turned out to be a dream trip. We flew commercial to Saskatchewan, and then charter flight to Stony Rapids where Cliff Blackburr, owner of Athabasca Camps, picked us up in his float plane and took us to his camp. I was hardly prepared for the quality of fishing we found. The first few days we fished for walleye and made a movie for TV. Cliff flew us to the Engler River one day and Richards Lake the next. In years past we had been fortunate to fish Canada's prime walleye spots — rivers and lakes in Quebec, Ontario and Manitoba. But in my life I have never had better walleye fishing in size and number than that. It was just fantastic!

One morning Cliff flew Dale and me into Richards Lake for walleye. It was a beautiful day, and fishing in the Otherside River flowing into the lake was unbelievable. I had fished Canadian waters for years and seen great walleye fishing, but there to catch walleye in the 6 to 8-pound class was run of the mill! We hadn't been taking movies; we were so busy catching fish. I thought that I had a good one on. I asked Dale to take the camera and we would start the movie. He started taking pictures of me fighting the fish. When it came to the surface, it was just a 4 or 4-1/2-pound walleye. Then I saw the big northern coming after it. I've seen many times when a northern would try to swallow a small northern, but never one that size. The northern stayed on the surface, swimming around with a 4-pound walleye in its mouth. Dale was taking movies of it. I tried to net both fish, but scared the northern off. It had killed the walleye. There was nothing unusual about it except the size of both fish. Dale had a pet spoon that he thought was the best northern pike bait out. I asked him if he would tie it on and try to catch that pike. I got movies of him tying the lure on and making a cast. The very first cast, the pike hit. We made the picture of him fighting the fish and landing it. It would go a good 25 pounds.

Dale had a big grin on his face. I asked him what his problem was. He said, "I was just thinking, if we had not had your movie camera and this had happened, you would have shot me!" He proceeded to take a 20-pound and a 30-pound northern. Imagine a 20, 25 and 30-pound northern pike in one day, while walleye fishing and getting it all on film. After Dale and I had made our walleye movie, he said, "Tomorrow I plan to show you some great pike fishing!"

Four of us flew to a place called "Ol' Man River" — a man and his son, Dale Flaxbeard and I. Cliff, the owner of the camp, kept several boats there. We made a few casts, caught several northern pike in the 20-pound class. The guide said, "I want to take you to a special bay," so we took off. We were impressed with what we had already caught, but the guide said, "You ain't seen nothing yet!" You know that old story; we went for miles and miles past one beautiful bay after another. Dale and I both were getting a little "antsy," thinking we had just gone for a long boat ride. The other boat stayed right with us, a father-and-son combination. As we rounded a point, we could see a narrow opening entering a small bay. It probably didn't cover an area much larger than a football field. A smaller bay that was literally alive with big pike. In over 40 years of fishing all over Canada, I had never seen anything like it. The water was crystal clear; you could see big pike all over the place. I'm talking BIG pike! Twenty-five pounds and up. You could cast in any direction with a buzz bait and have three or four pike try to get the lure at the same time. I hooked two that I'm sure would go over the 40-pound mark each. It was awesome! We were trying to get movies of the action. I had hooked a big one and asked Dale to grab a camera to shoot the action. The fish really put on a show, even jumped like a tarpon two or three times. Dale would say, "Wow, I got the jump and all!" The guide netted the fish, and we held it up for the camera. Dale told us then to release it. He said, "Man, I got it all!" I asked him for the camera. I said, "Dale, you picked up the wrong camera." We had already used that roll of film, and in the excitement I had neglected to load both cameras. He picked up the wrong one; we got nothing out of one of the largest pikes I ever had on my line. Dale was just sick about it, but we had big fish all around us. When we stopped for a shore lunch, the young man and his dad pulled up by us. He turned to me and said, "Ensley, I just died and went to heaven." I've had a lot of unforgettable days among the thousands I've been out, but that one had to go way up on the list. It was awesome! "Winds of Chance."

The second year David Glass, C.E.O. of Wal-Mart, and his grandson Dane made the trip with us and had a great time. We caught a lot of walleye and northern, but David and Dane had to fly out before we got to fish for lake trout. Cliff kept telling us about a new trophy lake trout spot they discovered, but it was a fly-out. We had planned to go there the next day. The four of us — Dale Flaxbeard, Don Maddux, Dusty and myself — got ready to fly out, but there was a strong wind blowing so the guide refused to go, saying that it was big water and too dangerous. Dale turned to me and said, "You don't need a guide, do you?" I said, "No, let's go!"

David Glass, CEO of Wal-Mart, and grandson Dane,
ready to fly to Lake Athabasca to fish

Cliff flew us about 70 miles to where he had some boats beached. The wind was blowing a gale when we took off from base camp, but when we arrived, the Lord took care of us and calmed the waves. It became almost dead calm as we got the boats ready and shoved off. We had fished the area one year before, but this was our first time without

Shore lunch — Lake Athahasca, with David Glass and grandson Dane

My biggest lake trout on 4-lb. test line — Lake Athabasca

guides. We tried our best to locate the reef where we had fished before. Dale was running one boat with Don Maddux, and Dusty was handling our boat. It was about 10 a.m. when we reached what we thought was the right location. We fished hard for nearly two hours without a peck. It was big water, but calm. Right out in the big nowhere, we paused to eat our sandwiches. Dusty had a sandwich in one hand, but just kept on fishing. He hooked a good fish, and I grabbed the camera and we got the picture. It was a nice trout; we estimated it at 25 pounds. We forgot about eating and went to work! We were using light spinning rods and 6-lb. test line. It was open water, I supposed about one mile from the nearest island on one side, but no land across the horizon the other way. My son, Dusty, is strong and was outcasting me by 20 feet or so. I picked up my walleye rod with 4-lb. test line.

We were really at a loss to know what to do, as we hadn't caught a fish for nearly two hours. We were casting reapers with 1/2-oz. jig heads. I was reeling in my line fast to make a cast in another direction. The lure was almost into the boat. I saw this big trout trying to keep up with the reaper. The fish saw me and spooked off. I yelled and said, "Man, did you see that fish that was following my reaper? I'll bet it will go 50 pounds!" They all laughed, and Dusty said, "Dad, you always get the big eye!" I said, "Dusty, I saw that fish, and it may be the biggest lake trout that I ever had follow my lure." We cast around for about a half-hour to no avail. I made a long cast back to the boat to let the reaper sink to the bottom and started reeling. I felt pressure on the line and set the hook. I said, "Dusty, grab that camera; I have a good fish!" We fought that thing for about 30 minutes, and when we got up to where we could see it, I said, "Now do you believe I saw a big fish follow me in?" We yelled at Dale to come over with their boat to net the fish for me. Maddux had the net and missed the fish the first pass. We were using a single barbless hook. All that fish had to do was roll over and the hook would fall out, but the fish kept its head down, and Maddux netted it. He said, "I lift weights, and that fish will go 50 pounds." About 30 minutes later, Don yelled that he had a good fish. We went to them and filmed the sequence. We estimated it around 30 pounds. A half hour later, Dale yelled that he had one. We went to them and filmed his fish! It was identical to the one I caught. I really think Dale's fish would have gone a few pounds more than mine. We saw the plane coming to get us and headed for the landing. Only four fish for our day's work, but all were trophies. We were probably never equal the three of them on 6-lb. test line, casting 1/2-oz. reapers and one on 4-lb. test, on a day when the native guides refused to go because of the wind. But to us, one day that will never be forgotten! "Winds of Chance."

In the summer of 1963 we were fishing in Canada for lake trout about 2:30 in the afternoon. I came up with an idea for a new lure to catch lake trout when they are down deep — maybe 60-100-ft. depths. It was an amazing discovery. We used the lure and the special technique from the U.S. border to the Arctic Ocean with unbelievable results.

Some 30 years later I received a telephone call from Morehead, Minnesota. It was from a man named Bud Bystrom, a teacher at Morehead State. He said that back in the mid '60s a television fisherman had come to the boundary waters of Minnesota with a new lure he had designed to catch lake trout. It was called the Ensley Reaper. He said that the man had a 5-ft. ultra-light spinning outfit. He was using 4-lb. test line and just revolutionized the way they were fishing for lake trout, walleye, northern pike and small mouth bass. He had traced me down and wondered if I was the right man. He wanted to order some of the reapers. He also said that he and his sons had guided our crew and me for many television shows in the boundary waters. I asked him where. He said, "Crane Lake, Minnesota." I said, "Bowser's Resort?" He said, "Yes!" I told him that Don Bowser had passed away and we quit going into that area. We had a nice visit. I gave him the address of the Mar-Lynn Lure Co. at Yellville, Arkansas, where the reapers were being made. We talked about the possibility of coming back to Crane Lake to do a TV show just for old times' sake. It was the first week of August and certainly not the best time of year to produce a show there. I asked him what they had to offer. He said walleye, small mouth bass and northern. I said, "Bud, I've fished those waters too many times; it would be next to impossible to do that in August! How about a crappie story?" He told me that no one fished for crappie there in August. He said that his daughter and her husband operated Nelson's Resort and would welcome us if we could come. His schoolwork at Morehead State was still going on, but he could come over for the weekend. I called my fishing buddy, Jim Higgins, and we drove to Crane Lake. Bud fished with us one day. We had three days of fabulous crappie fishing, made one movie and renewed old acquaintances. We didn't use the reaper for the crappie, but a take-off from it called the puddle jumper.

A friend of mine, Chuck Woods, had asked me years earlier if he could take my 3-inch reaper, cut it down and make crappie bait. He called it Puddle Jumper. Chuck was one of the best fishermen I have met in my lifetime. Earlier he had invented the "Beetle." His puddle jumper became an instant hit and is still one of the greatest crappie baits I have ever used. When we arrived at Crane Lake, they told us that the crappie fishing was slow and that we would have to use a jig tipped with a minnow. We caught our limits of big crappie on a 1/16-oz. yellow puddle jumper. I've never had a better day of crappie fishing than that last day with Bud. Since then, the Mar-Lynn Lure Co. has been making a 2-inch reaper in assorted colors. It is also a deadly crappie and trout lure. Getting back to Bud's telephone call, I don't know how he traced me down, but it was a great thrill to get to fish with him and his people after 30 years. Hopefully we will connect again somewhere down the line and fish with the reaper. Perhaps the "Winds of Chance" will blow that way. I wish I had the time to tell how many times things like this have happened. Maybe waiting in an airport or on an airplane or at a filling station waiting to buy gas, where we met someone out of the past or made a new acquaintance who became a fishing buddy or friend. That's the real meaning of "Winds of Chance."

I must share one more story with you. The following is a fisherman's testimonial and letter I recently received.

"Harold, just wanted to write to you a couple of my success stories that I have had with the reaper tail — the first one being the initial trip to Cree Lake in Saskatchewan. When we met on the airplane in July five years ago on the way to Saskatoon, we (Glenn Woodhouse, fishing partner, and I) would never have guessed that a particular fishing lure could be so productive. After we got through customs and you were nice enough to give us about a dozen of the 5-inch reapers, Glenn and myself proceeded to Cree Lake. We were ready to give the reaper a try. I will never forget the first night we tried the lure. We had found a drop-off in about 80 feet of water. I told Glenn, 'Let's see if these lures will work.' We both dropped the lures to the bottom, and using the presentation you told me, we both had lake trout on before I finished the sentence. Well, that trip was one of the most memorable trips ever. During the week I did a little test. I decided to try a normal white twister tail to see if the fish would eat anything put in front of them. I tried for half an hour without a bite, while my partner continued to catch lake trout on the reaper. I switched back to the reaper and had a fish on the very next cast. I was sold from that day forward. That week we caught and released hundreds of lake trout. We also caught several walleye and northern, but their teeth were taking too many of our precious tails. By the end of the week we were literally super-gluing the reaper tails to the hook so we didn't lose any of our last lures.

"Just recently I was in Colorado fishing a gold water trout stream (all natural trout, catch and release only, and lures and flies only). These trout have seen every lure known to mankind. I was throwing a 2-inch reaper and my partner was throwing a small spinner. Well, after three casts and three fish, we were both throwing the 2-inch reaper.

"I can remember an ice-fishing trip to Utah and fishing with a group for cut-throat trout. The lure and bait of choice was a small twister tail tipped with larvae. I fished with just a 2-inch white reaper. Some 30 trout later I had the group convinced.

"I have made several trips where many walleye, crappie and smallmouth bass were

victims to the reaper, but saltwater fishing for sea trout and redfish really stands out. One trip to the Texas coast near Port Aransus comes to mind. The group of people I was fishing with were having decent luck for sea trout and redfish with live shrimp, but the 3-inch pearl reaper was outmatching live bait 3 to 1. Another trip to the Tampa area was another success story. A cold front had moved through, so fishing was a little tough. The reaper out-fished the guide's best offering. I can remember fishing the Sanibel/Captiva area in Florida. The 3-inch reaper outmatched even live pelchers.

"By nature, I'm a very competitive person. I know fishing is more than catching fish, and I release more than 95% of my fish, but I have yet to find anything I would rather do than fish. (I think that's why my wife is usually upset with me.) I have an eight-year-old son that I hope someday has the passion for fishing that I do. (Not quite there yet!) That's one thing fishing teaches you is patience. In my youth I knew a priest who enjoyed fishing as much as I. He told me that every day you fish or think about fishing adds a day to your life. If that's true, I will never meet St. Peter at the pearly gates. Reaper tails have helped me immensely with catching more fish and can't thank you enough for introducing me to them."

The stories can go on and on, but one thing is certain, I will never go on another fishing trip without a stock of all sizes and colors of reapers, and without a stock of all sizes and colors of reapers and after fishing with several people, the end result is giving them the balance of my tails or shipping them some, once I have returned home.

"Dear Harold,

Per our conversation today, I just wanted to write to you to tell you how much getting to know you has changed my style of fishing. Meeting you on the way to Saskatoon was a once-in-a-lifetime opportunity. I'm sure you have met several people in your fishing lifetime, but I was lucky that you took time to share with me your fishing knowledge and adventures. The reaper tail! What a lure! I will never forget the conversation myself, Glenn Woodhouse (fishing partner) and Dusty had on that trip. We were both new to the lake trout fishing and were looking for some guidance. I thought I had heard of every fishing lure ever made, but when he mentioned he

Mike Loecker of Omaha, Nebraska, with laker taken in Cree Lake on a reaper

used a reaper tail, I responded with, what is a reaper tail? When he showed me the package with a familiar face on it, I had no idea I was going to meet the inventor. Well, after I found out you were sitting in the chair in front of me, the trip to Saskatoon was a very short one. It had to be the first time I ever wished for a longer flight, to hear even more adventures.

"Per your lures and instructions, we had one of the most memorable fishing trips ever. We caught more lake trout and northern pike than we could count. That trip was five years ago. I have had many other fishing trips since then with many success stories. The reaper tails are one of the biggest reasons for the success I have had. I have fished with many people since then. Usually, the conclusion is me sending or giving them a package of tails. Someday I hope we have a fishing trip together, so we have a chance to use reapers first-hand.

Sincerely, Mike Loecker"

I received a letter from a fisherman in London, England. He had fished with our mutual friend, Pete Perinchief, in Bermuda. They had used the Ensley reaper in Bermuda waters so successfully that he had taken numbers of them back to England. They had been so successful in the European waters near the British Isles that he wanted to try them on an upcoming fishing trip to the Canary Islands. He said that he had plenty of lead jig heads, but just to ship him an assortment of 3-inch and 5-inch reaper tails. We honored his request but never heard from him after that.

Just a few weeks ago we received a letter from a man in Escondido, California, wanting information as to where he could buy some Ensley reapers. He saw us on television catching lake trout on this lure and ultra-light spinning gear. We honored his request, telling him that for his area, he could order them through Cabello's catalogue at Sydney, Nebraska, and also gave him the Mar-Lynn Lure Co. address at Yellville, Arkansas.

Three weeks later while on a trip to Costa Rica, our guide was taking us out to sea at the mouth of the Parismina River, tarpon fishing. The sea was relatively calm, but we hit a breaker the wrong way. The slam of the boat, as it went high and dropped straight down, fractured my spine. We have been fishing this area each year for the past 37 years. There were over ten boats of us, three to a boat going out, but only in that particular spot did a breaker roll up that high. Ron Loveless from Bentonville, Arkansas, was my companion. I had caught a big tarpon the day before and wanted Ron to get one, so we stayed out two more hours, and I told Ron I needed to go back to the lodge, but he and the guide could come back out. I knew in my heart that my tarpon fishing for that trip was over. We have hosted a tour fishing group there annually for over 30 years. There was no doctor in the little village. I didn't want to go to the hospital there, so I toughed it out for five more days. Ron caught his big tarpon, as did every member of our party, and we flew home. It was the week of September 7-16, 2001, and we all made it safely home. It is now 2:30 a.m., as I am sitting on the edge of the hospital bed writing this and awaiting surgery on my spine, hopefully in just a few more hours. Right now, the Lord willing, I plan to go back to sleep for a few hours, and then after surgery I plan to tell you one more

Maurice O'Link with typicalCanadian walleye catch

story on the magic of a little bait called the Ensley reaper. "Winds of Chance."

In 1941 a man named Maurice O'Link started a manufacturing plant in St. Cloud, Minnesota, making flotation vests for people in the water. He had a passion to educate the public about the dangers of hypothermia. Especially those around water sports: water skiing, boating and fishing. He and a professor from the University of Duluth, Minnesota, wrote the book on hypothermia and also helped set the standards for safety for the Coast Guard. He probably did more than anyone to establish the criteria we use today in safety standards for the flotation vests, jackets and jumpsuits. Stearns quality was a mark of excellence that set the standard and still maintains it. They sponsored part of my national TV show for years. The agency man who bought the show called me from St. Paul. He suggested that I take O'Link on a fishing trip, as he loved to fish. He said that Maurice was an eccentric person and that he would need to make the trip with him. We took them on a special trip to Canada. I found out right quick that I didn't need the agency man. Maurice was eccentric, but he and I became great friends. We had a special friendship that lasted as long as he lived. He also had a passion for life and cooking. Once when I visited the plant in St. Cloud, he made me a French silk pie. He invited me to his home, where he had three or four complete kitchens. As I remember, a French, Chinese and maybe a German besides his American style. He was a storyteller excelled by no one. I just wish I had the time and space to tell you some of the incidents that happened on our many trips (I'll sneak one in).

A group of us were going to God's Lake to shoot a movie for TV, and I invited Maurice. We had caught lots of fish and had our movie almost made. It was a nasty, misty day, and we were fishing for fun. We stopped for shore lunch, three boats of us. As the native guides started to prepare lunch, we were just waiting when Maurice walked down to the boat. He always had a backpack on with survival gear. It didn't make any difference if were just going out for a few hours, he would put the survival backpack in the boat. He dug a bar of soap and a towel out of the kit, took it over to the native guides and asked them to wash their hands. We thought Maurice had met his match and would surely get scalped. To our surprise, the guides washed their hands. The next day the guides brought their own soap and towel. That was Maurice O'Link!

Bermuda Special

SOMETIME IN THE LATE '50s or early '60s I received a call from Joe Brooks, the famous fly fisherman and author in Baltimore. Joe was one of the great fly fishermen of his time and the author of several books on fly-fishing. He told me that he had been hired by the Bermuda Tourist Bureau to promote their fishing. He wanted to take a group of outdoor writers, and asked if I would go to represent the television side of the media. He said that the others were mainly newspaper columnists from he East Coast. I was thrilled with the invitation — another Chance of a Lifetime!

I told him I'd be happy to make the trip. Airline travel was not that simple then, first to Chicago, then to New York and on to Bermuda; carrying cameras, fishing gear and my clothes didn't make it any easier, but I did it! Bermuda is a beautiful place, surrounded by great fishing waters. Tropical fish of all kinds and colors! We got lots of fish, the usual barracuda, black fin tuna, yellowtail and triggerfish, but it was mostly trolling which doesn't excite me much. They would leave the dock about 10 a.m. and come in at 3 p.m. Joe and I spent a lot of time together, and we formed a bond of friendship that lasted until he passed on. I asked Joe if someday I could fish for something in the early morning and late afternoon. I told him that I was here in one of the great fishing spots of the world, and that five or six hours a day wasn't enough for me. He laughed about it and hired a taxi to pick me up at 4:30 a.m. and bring me back in time to go in the big boats. Then, again in the afternoon, to fish for a few hours. I had to fish from the beaches and had a daily battle with bone fish. They won most of the time, but it was fun to work for them. The taxi driver was a great guy, very British and always quoting Kipling. We managed to scratch out enough material for two 30-minute TV shows, and I was happy! I had made some new friends and fished in some great waters. A few years later I received another call from Joe. Cuba had hired him to do what he had done in Bermuda. He wanted me to join a group to go there for big bass. I declined, but some of the rest of them went on. I'm glad I made that decision.

I saw Joe one more time years later while fishing the Florida keys. A few years later while fishing on the Quanzi River in Africa, my guide, Louie, told a blue runner story. He was a Britisher who lived in what was Rhodesia at that time. He was one of those unforgettable characters you meet on life's pathway. He was small of stature, very British, and had a cigarette in his mouth constantly. He smuggled his rods and reels, but forged his own hooks. He wanted to learn all he could about fishing in the rest of the world and especially in America. He kept up a constant chatter. One afternoon as we fished, he talked about the sailfish that he had caught off the coast of Angola. He had read one of Joe Brooks' books, in which Joe said to use blue runners for bait. I did it, and it really worked. I'd been planning to write to Joe to tell him how much I had enjoyed his writing and his fishing tips, but I never seemed to get time to do it.

I told Louie that Joe and I had been friends for many years and that I would call him when I returned to the States. The sad part is that Joe passed away before I could call and tell him about his book being read in Africa. Another missed opportunity! "Winds of Chance."

By the way, in 1950 I caught my first sailfish off the Florida coast at West Palm beach, using a live blue runner, and I didn't get a chance to tell my friend Joe.

Several years after fishing with Joe Brooks in Bermuda, I told my wife Bonnie that I must have done something wrong in Bermuda. She asked me why, and I said, "I was not invited back." You'll not believe it, but three days later I received a cablegram from Hamilton, Bermuda, from Pete Perinchief, head of the Bermuda Tourist Bureau. He said, "It's about time you came back to fish with us." "Winds of Chance."

This time I got to take my wife Bonnie and daughter Sandy. It was another fabulous trip. I was privileged to fish with three members of the British Empire Tuna Team: Lou Moubray, curator of the Bermuda aquarium; Pete Perinchief, head of the Tourist Bureau, and one other whose name I cannot recall. One evening after dinner Pete asked what salt water fish was the toughest to handle. I immediately said, "Tarpon," for I had just returned from Costa Rica. Louie looked at Pete and said, "I wonder if he ever caught an Allison tuna." I told them no. Pete said, "You are going to find out tomorrow, for we have entered you in our National Tuna Tournament." They asked me what line class I wanted to enter. I had just recovered from an operation on my right elbow. I had cast so much right-handed that I ruined my elbow, then cast left-handed until I messed it up. The doctor performed surgery and warned me that might be my last chance. I had completely recovered, but tried to save it as much as possible, so I chose 20-lb. test category . They furnished me with a big Everol salt-water reel. I think it held 1000 yds. of 20-lb. test. Louie didn't go with us, but the other two tutored me. We went directly to where the challenger bluff dropped off in an unbelievable depth, about 35 miles out to sea.

The ocean was perfectly calm. Pete said, "I have lived here 45 years and I've never seen it like this." They anchored the boat just at the edge of the flat, before the depth dropped off sharply. They started chumming frozen anchovies off the stern. I hooked a black fin tuna, which wrapped the line around the anchor rope and broke off. The little mate yelled, "Hurry, Harold, let me have your line." He tied on a small hook I would have used for catfish, maybe a 4-0. He hooked a small frozen anchovy and threw it off the stern where a handful of chum was floating. I don't believe it was more than 15 ft. from the boat. I saw the tuna coming like a fighter jet making a pass. I still had the rod in my hands when that fish took that small bait and headed for the deep blue yonder. The line was screaming off the reel. Pete said, "Set the hook!" I said, "If that fish isn't hooked, I can't do anything but hold on." Pete asked me if I needed a harness. I told him no. I had seen the fish, and it wouldn't go over 100 lbs., and that I could handle it bare-handed. It seemed like that fish was going to run forever, and mainly down! If that reel held 1000 yds. of 20-lb. test, that fish took off more than half of it! I gained some line back and asked Pete to get my camera and start shooting. The fish made another run. Two hours later I asked Pete if it was legal in tournament rules to put on the harness. He told me that it was if no one touched rod in helping me put it on. Twenty-six minutes later we brought the fish up. It had taken two hours and 26 minutes, and I was about as far gone as the fish. It weighed 76 lbs.-plus and won the light tackle category. Why did that tuna take my bait out of the handful in the water? "Winds of Chance."

When the film was finished, I said, "Pete, you guys were right, that was the toughest battle I ever had."

The next day Pete and Louie took me out for what they called yellowtail, a small fish similar to bass. Louie needed them for an aquarium somewhere. They had a special boat with a sonar outfit on it. They located a school of fish, anchored the boat and started catching fish. They were using a frozen anchovy, with a hook like we had used for tuna. They were catching one fish after another, but they didn't rig me up. I didn't have any hooks or sinkers, so I took the 5-inch reaper tail off, put on an anchovy and I started catching fish. I said to the young mate, "I believe they will hit that reaper. Pete laughed and told me no Yankee bait would work in Bermuda. I dropped the white reaper down and immediately caught one of the larger yellowtail we had taken. It was just one fish after another. Pete asked the mate what I was doing and put on a reaper; then Louie took it up, and we caught the fish he needed. "Winds of Chance."

The next day Pete and I worked on the bonefish, and they had the largest bonefish I've found anywhere. Pete and Louie were two of the nicest people, and certainly two of the top fishermen I've met anywhere. Pete later sent me a tourist bulletin. In it I found written that the bait fisherman will catch more fish than the artificial baits, unless you have a reaper.

A few years later we received a letter from a man in London who had fished in Bermuda with Pete Perinchief. He had taken some reapers back to England and was so successful along the coast he wanted to order some! He was going to the Canary Islands and wanted to try them there. "Winds of Chance."

Fishing the Rivers and Impoundments of the West

In THE LATE '50s my wife and I, with another couple from Kansas City, were invited to fish in the Bridger wilderness area of Wyoming for golden trout. The Tourist Bureau of Wyoming had invited a group of writers from Denver, Salt Lake City, Dallas and Forth Worth and wanted us to cover the television part of it. We drove all night after my TV show, 1100 miles, to Pinedale, Wyoming. The first day we packed back into the wilderness area. My wife had never been on a horse, and you can imagine what it was like for her, 13 miles on her first trail ride. There were two other women in the party, and I don't remember how many of us, but it was quite a pack train, counting the pack animals with the tents and supplies. It was beautiful country over a rugged narrow trail to camp above the timberline, across swollen mountain streams and steep climbs.

As I look back, I don't know how the women stood it. We camped by beautiful snowcapped peaks at the edge of a lake. It was cold at night; it would freeze in. The fishing was absolutely unbelievable. Finis Mitchell and his wife were in charge of the camp. Finis was a member of the Wyoming State Legislature and a great outdoor photographer. Mrs. Mitchell was our cook, and since it was a wilderness area, she had to cook over an open fire. She did a good job; the food was great. The golden trout were something to behold. We caught a lot of goldens in the 3 to 4-1/2-pound class. I don't think that has ever happened again. We made two movies for our show and headed back home. The trail ride back was especially wild, but we made it down safely, and then drove 1100 miles back in time for our TV show.

The Tourist Bureau of Wyoming bought the film of the show that I had made to use in their promotional department. It was fortunate for us because a fellow contestant in the World Series in Michigan in 1960 wanted to run the Wyoming show on the Swedish television network in Stockholm. It was the original film and they never returned it! The State of Wyoming sent me a copy of what they had used. It made me sick to have lost the original, for that kind of golden trout fishing may never be captured again.

In 1991 my wife Bonnie lost her battle with cancer and passed away. In her memory, I used the Wyoming version as a rerun at my regular show. Two weeks later my office received a call from Rock Springs, Wyoming. A lady asked my secretary if she could get a copy of the show for her next-door neighbor, who was in the show. She wanted to make

Bonnie and I showing eight trophy golden trout from the Bridger wilderness area in Wyoming

him a present of it. I called her back to get the particulars and ask her who she wanted it for. She said Finis Mitchell and his wife had seen the show on the local station. I said I didn't mention his name because I couldn't remember it. She said, "Yes, you did." I guess that when I saw his face I remembered it. I asked her if she had their phone number. I called them, and Mrs. Mitchell answered the phone. I told her who I was, and she said, "It's so nice to hear your voice and to see the movies, but we were saddened to hear of Bonnie's death." I asked her if Finis was there and if I could speak to him. She said, "I'll get him on the other phone." He came on, and I said, "How are you, Finis?" He said, "I'm doing fairly well for a man 93 years old." His wife said, "Daddy, you're only 91." I told him I was sending him a copy of the show. I asked him if in his files he had a picture of Bonnie or me, or both of us with a golden trout. He said he would look for one. That Christmas, I received a card from him and this picture of the two of us with golden trout. "Winds of Chance."

In the early years of my TV career I was selected along with Thomas Hart Benton, the famous artist, and L.P. Cookingham, city manager of Kansas City, to judge the Junior Chamber of Commerce Christmas tree lighting contest. It was the first time I had met either of them, both giants in their own field. We were riding in a big limo, and I was a little guy sitting between those two great men. I didn't know if either of them knew who I was.

We covered the whole metropolitan area. We had been traveling sometime when Benton said, "Ensley, I want to go to the Bridger wilderness of Wyoming with you. I don't want to fish, but just sketch you doing it." My heart started pounding to think that this great artist wanted to go with me. I told him I would love to take him. We drove along for another hour or so, and he said, "I want you to take me to the Kimichi Mountains of

Oklahoma." I told him that I would. We drove on a ways, and he said, "Now I want to pay my way." I guess I thought he would live forever. He passed away before we got it done. The week before he passed away, I took him a mess of quail. He was working on the mural for the Country Music Hall of Fame. "Winds of Chance," but a missed opportunity.

Later on, we were invited to fish out of Bill Harrah's famous lodge on the middle fork of the Salmon River in Idaho. My son, Dusty, was in the Air Force Reserves at that particular time, and was on a mission to Saigon. I called my older son, Smokey, and asked him if he and his wife, Dodie, wanted to drive to Boise, Idaho, then fly into the camp on the river. He called me back saying that she didn't want to camp out. I persuaded her to go, and when she saw the camp, she said, "If I hadn't made this trip and then saw the pictures, I would have shot myself." Many of the Hollywood stars have stayed there. Jim Nabors just left before we got there, and Debbie Reynolds was coming in when we left. Ford was my sponsor, and they met the plane in a 1917 Model T hack. There were no roads, so they flew the parts in, flew the mechanics in and assembled it. Bill Harrah was there and asked me to come visit his casino and antique car collection. He also wanted me to fish with a banker friend. The man who operated the lodge told me of a lake in Utah that had 12 to 14-pound cutthroats. He wanted me to shoot a TV show there. This was my first trip to the Middle Fork and one trip I will never forget. Smokey's wife, Dodie, hooked a salmon. I was shooting the picture and saw the fish was going to jump. I had the camera on the fish, but should have had it on her face. She screamed, "Oh, my Lord, Moby Dick." It was a real thrill for me to be on the river. I had always loved the movie, "The River of No Return," with Robert Mitchum and Marilyn Monroe. I never dreamed I would ever fish this stream. "Winds of Chance.

Sometime in the late '50s or early '60s I was called to speak to the Soil District Conservation meeting in western Kansas near Garden City. That night I met a man named Harry Oswald. He was an avid hunter and fisherman. He was an inventive genius and had invented a high loader for cattle feeders to move ensilage. He also had many other patents on farming equipment. He had a special Canada goose hunting spot near Springfield, Colorado, and invited us out to do a goose-hunting movie.

My son, Smokey, and I drove to meet him and Cap Burtis, the Ford dealer in Garden City, Kansas. It was wintertime and pretty cold, but we drove on to Colorado to the goose hunting spot. We had a good hunt, made our movie and headed back to Kansas City in a terrible blizzard. Before we left them, Harry invited us to his summer home on the Gunnison River near Sapinaro, Colorado, and set a date for the next summer to shoot a trout-fishing movie. He had two sons and asked me to bring Smokey and Dusty. The Gunnison River was one of the prime trout fishing rivers of the Rockies, and I was thrilled with the opportunity. "Winds of Chance."

I don't remember exactly what time of year we drove there, but I think it was either late July or early August. His summer home sat on a high cliff, looking down on the river, not far from where the river pours into Black Canyon. It was a beautiful spot. The impounded waters of blue Mesa reservoir now cover it. As I remember, the river was not accessible from his home, but we had to drive up the highway above the little town of Sapinaro. Harry had three navy rafts for the six of us to float the river. He had invented a gadget where he could inflate the rafts from the exhaust of his pickup. We left my station wagon at the take-out point and hauled the inflated rafts up the river, several miles above what was called Moncrief Camp. The camp was made famous by the Hollywood stars that stayed at his place. Several great stories came out of there.

Bing Crosby, Phil Harris, Bob Hope and many others were to have rafted from Moncrief's place. Harry guided for him some. The story goes that one time on a float trip Bob Hope fell into the water several miles below Moncrief's. He decided he would hitchhike back up the highway to camp. The highway ran parallel to the river. He was soaking wet, and no one would pick him up, and he had to walk several miles to reach camp. I do not know if the story is true, but if it is, can you imagine what would have gone on in a motorist's mind if he stopped to pick up a hitchhiker and it turned out to be Bob Hope!

Harry and I fished together, and one of his boys was with Smokey and the other with Dusty. We were just learning to fish rivers for trout with ultra-light spinning equipment and 2-lb. test line and throwing small spoons. We didn't do as well as we did in later years with crappie jigs. We caught enough good trout for our movie. It was a beautiful day, and the water was just right. We only had to portage around one falls. Harry and I set out first and reached the waterfalls first and portaged around it.

I was just casually casting a silver spoon in the racing white water below the falls, when I saw this huge brown trout make two passes at my spoon, and each time the swift water washed the spoon away from the fish. I screamed at Harry, and he thought I had fallen in. Of course, no one believed how big I thought that brown was. I didn't lose the big one; I just didn't catch it. It was a great day for us, two fathers with our two sons. The next day we floated below Sapinaro. It was a little scary; you could hear the roar of the rapids echo up through the high canyon walls. We had another good day, and the third day we drove down the river on a little narrow gravel road. The scenery was spectacular! We had to fish from the rocks alongside the river, and we didn't catch many fish, but finished our movies and drove home.

I would love to fish the Gunnison one more time, since we have learned to use crappie jigs for trout. We will never be able to fish the same stretch of the river, as it is swallowed up in Blue Mesa Reservoir. This was just the beginning of our fishing the streams and impoundments on the Colorado basin. First, Lake Meade, then Powell Reservoir, and then Flaming Gorge, with the Bridger wilderness area of Wyoming for golden trout. The golden trout are a rare species, and most people have not even seen one. I had read about them and stories of fishermen in the High Sierras of the West; yet I was hardly prepared for what we found in the Bridger wilderness area. We caught a lot of 3-1/2 to 4-pound goldens. Males were spectacular at spawning time! On a 4-pound male it looked as though

God had taken a paintbrush with red paint and painted the sides of the fish with a 4-inch wide strip, from the gills almost back to the tail.

In 1966 I received a telephone call from Washington, D.C. — a man named Peterson, assistant to the director of the Bureau of Reclamation. He asked me if I would be willing to go to Dutch John, Utah, to do a story on the fishing in Flaming Gorge Reservoir and the river below the dam. I told him I hadn't heard of the place, but why did he call me? He told me that his boss in Denver heard me speak at the dedication of the Corps of Engineers project at Norton, Kansas. He had heard of all the TV and radio promotion on Corps of Engineer reservoirs throughout the country that I had given, and wanted to know why the Bureau of Reclamation couldn't get some of that free publicity. That was why he was calling me. He said that if I could get to McCook, Nebraska, they would fly me to Dutch John to fish. I was always looking for new material for my TV and radio shows, so we arranged a date.

My television director, Harry Francis, always wanted to make a trip with me. He wasn't a fisherman but would help me shoot some movies. We drove to McCook, where we met Mr. Peterson and his pilot, and we flew to Dutch John. It was my first flight over the Rockies in a small twin-engine plane. The weather was beautiful, and the scenery fantastic as always across Colorado. He flew us over Dinosaur National Park for some pictures, then on to Dutch John at the dam site. On the flight I asked him who we were to fish with. He told me a couple of his boys, meaning two of their employees.

The first morning he told me that we were going to float the river below the dam for rainbow trout. I had fished some below Boulder Dam on the mighty Colorado and many times on the river below Bull Shoals Dam. I was familiar with this type of fishing, but never from a rubber raft. It was an exciting moment for me, and I knew it would be quite a challenge. Can you imagine floating with five people in a raft, especially with my director who had never fished, and Peterson, who I think was in the same class. Two young men from the Bureau were handling the raft. It was a brilliant setting for a story. The sunshine was brilliant and the sky so blue. I took pictures of the dam from the top, and then we drove to a landing on the river below the dam, where two young men, Bobby Simpson and Mickey Maier, were waiting in a medium-sized navy raft. I had my director film me as Peterson and I walked down to the raft. I was carrying four ultra-light fishing rods rigged with white 1/8-oz. crappie jigs. Peterson introduced me to the two men, and my director filmed it and we started drifting down the river.

Mickey and Bob didn't appear to be excited about the trip and had asked me if I had any worms. I told them no, nothing but these crappie jigs. One of them said, "Then you'll not catch any trout!"

We had drifted about a mile and I was trying to show Harry Francis how to fish a jig, and we caught nothing in that mile. Bobby tells it that I caught on the first cast, but I didn't! As we drifted with the current, I saw a small rainbow in an eddy. I asked them if they could hold the raft and work it closer to the eddy; I cast and caught the fish. Then

Shore lunch at Dutch John, Utah, with Mickey Maier, Bob Simpson and Mr. Peterson from the Bureau of Reclamation

for the next 10 or 15 miles, some of the most beautiful canyon scenery we've seen. We caught rainbow trout like you wouldn't believe. All of us , my director, Peterson and even Bobby and Mickey! It was a day that I'll remember as long as I live. Rainbow trout jumping all over the river for our picture. Not large fish, but as I remember in the 2 to 4-pound class. Bobby tells it that we caught and released 50 by the time we ate our shore lunch at noon. I was busy making the picture and didn't worry about numbers. By mid-afternoon we arrived at the take-out point where they had left the truck to haul us back to Dutch John. Bobby and Mickey went over to the truck and asked me over. One of them, I don't remember which, said, "We want to apologize to you." I said, "What for?" Bobby said, "When you walked down to get into the raft this morning carrying four spinning rods with white Malibu jigs flashing in the sun, Mickey said, "I'll bet a filling station burned out and that guy bought all their tackle. We are in for a tough day! We have never seen anything like this. Can you do the same thing on the lake?" I said, "if the trout are there, like these are here, it will work."

The next day we fished the lake, but we had boats from the marina. It was absolutely unbelievable; I've never seen that many rainbows in one place in my life, still in the 2 to 4-pound class. We went back to the marina for something. The game warden, Roy Birrel, was there and asked if he could go back out with us. He didn't believe anyone could catch trout on a crappie jig. He wasn't fishing, just watching. I had just made a cast when my director hooked a nice trout. My jig was already in the water; I handed my rod to Roy and asked him if he would reel my line in while I shot a picture of my director. I had no sooner picked up the movie camera when I heard Roy grunt, and he had a fish on and landed it. The next day he went with us; it was either called Jack Rabbit flats or Antelope flats, and the trout were in there in numbers no one would believe. Roy was having a little trouble at first and said, "Show me what I'm doing wrong." I was loading a camera and told Bobby to show him what we were doing. Bobby must have done a good job, because years later I saw in one of the outdoor magazines where Roy Birrel was the best jig fisherman in the Flaming Gorge area.

The next day we fished down toward the dam, and you could understand why they called it Flaming Gorge. Beautiful canyon walls, very much like what you would find on Powell Reservoir. Before we started back to Kansas City, I asked Bobby and Mickey why they didn't start a float service below the dam on weekends, as there were no facilities at that time. They did and had a very successful operation for 17 years. I received a letter from Bobby wanting to know where they could order the Tiny Tot crappie jigs. He and Mickey had started a float service from the river below the dam on weekends. They called it Bull Canyon Guide Service.

Some 25 years later, one night I had just gone to bed and the phone rang. I answered it, and the man said, "Is this the fisherman Harold Ensley?" I said, "Well, I fish some, what do you need?" He said, "Does the name Simpson mean anything to you?" I said, "No," then said, "Wait a minute, you wouldn't be Bobby Simpson from Dutch John, Utah!" He said, "I'm the guy!" I asked him where he was calling from. He told me he was visiting his daughter in Grandview, Missouri, which is a suburb of Kansas City. We had a good visit, and he said he and Mickey had the float trip operation on the river below the dam at Flaming Gorge, but he retired after 17 years of it and that Mickey was running the salmon hatchery on the Columbia River. I wanted Bobby to come by to see me, but he and his wife were going home early the next day. He invited me to come back to Dutch John and fish the river with him. The next summer I called him and we set up a date. I called my director, Buck Bonner, in Wichita, Kansas, where I have produced my show the last 20-some years, and my fishing buddy of many years, Jim Higgins, a deputy sheriff at Holden, Missouri. We drove to Dutch John, fished with Bobby several days and shot a couple of movies for my TV show. Things have changed with many float trip operators and many boats on the river. It wasn't like the good old days, but it was just great to be back with Bobby after all those years. "Winds of Chance, but surely a Chance of a Lifetime."

In 1959 the Ford dealers of the Kansas City region expanded my program to an eight-station network, reaching into a part of eight states. They kept it in prime time for the next 18 years, some years at 6 p.m. on Saturday and other years at 6 p.m. on Sunday. It expanded our coverage in the Midwest to a point that it became necessary to reach out farther for program material, and it also brought in more requests for us to promote more outdoor recreational areas in many parts of North America.

Sometime in the late '50s we received a call from Phoenix, Arizona, to come to Fort Apache to help promote the Apache nation for their hunting, fishing and camping facilities, to draw tourists to the area. My son Dusty and I left K.C. after my TV program. We drove all night, straight through to Fort Apache. It was early morning when we hit the mountains of New Mexico, on through Lordsburg and Deming, to Apache land. We were really excited about doing a story with the Apaches! I was born in the West, and as a boy I was fascinated about the conquest of the West and the sad story of our treatment of Native American tribes.

When we reached Fort Apache, we were greeted by the representative from Phoenix. He introduced us to Ben Oliver, the elected chief of the Apaches. Ben was one of those unforgettable people that come your way as you go through life. He had attended Haskell Institute at Lawrence, Kansas. If I understood properly, he was the first of his tribe to get a master's degree and the first of his tribe to be selected as a delegate to a national political convention. Ben called a meeting of his business managers and introduced us. The tribe had managers in several categories. They had one for livestock, one for lumber, one for parks and recreation, and several others. He announced that we were there to help promote their fishing, hunting and outdoor recreational services. He told them that he wanted them to assist us in every way necessary. When he finished, I told him that we wanted to visit the camp for their cattle roundup, and that we wanted specifically to get a movie of him fishing with me in one of their lakes. He said that he didn't have time. I told the game warden who was in charge of the lakes, "Didn't he tell all of you managers to cooperate with us and give us what we needed?" Ben said, "Okay, I'll go fishing with you! What do you want to do first?"

They thought it best we go up to where they have the cattle roundup first. They have all their livestock together and separate them at roundup time for each individual owner. It was a unique experience. The country was beautiful and the weather perfect for our movie. The livestock manager (whose name I do not remember) was a big man and a most interesting individual. He had been a scout in the South Pacific during World War II. I asked him if he had any trouble getting riders for the roundup. He told me that it was no problem, for they loved to ride and yell. They invited us to have lunch at the mess camp. We did and had a delightful meal — chicken fried steak, mashed potatoes and gravy, corn and beans. To me it was a big thrill to be there with them. Their cook liked to fish, and before we left he took a willow pole and line, which he had evidently used before. He scratched out some leaves, picked up some worms and went fishing in a small mountain stream near the camp. In a matter of minutes, he caught several small trout.

It was great; we went back to Fort Apache where we had an opportunity to visit their school. The next day we were to fish with the Chief. First thing, he took us to see the lakes where we were to fish. They had built dams and impounded the waters. They had a nice area of campgrounds with hookups and water. There were several tourists there, camping and fishing. At noon, he invited us into his home for lunch. We accepted, and we met his wife and little six-year-old twins, a boy and a girl. At lunch I asked him if he had an Apache war outfit, and would he mind to put on his war paint for a picture with me. After lunch he went to his bedroom, donned his gear and put on his war paint. When he walked through the living room, the twins were watching television. The little boy looked up and said, "Look, Mommy, an Indian." We all got a big kick out of that! We went outside, where Dusty took pictures of us, both movies and stills. "Winds of Chance." He told me that he had a Comanche war-dress and would put it on. He did, and we got some more pictures. We told him that if it were possible we would like an Apache medicine man, in full dress, fishing with me.

I taught him to use a spinning outfit. We were fishing in a stream near the highway. Tourists would stop and wonder what was going on! It was scary to see him coming through the trees. I asked him to take off his mask. He told me that he was not allowed to do that. I then

Harold with Apache Chief, Ben Oliver, and his twins — Fort Apache, Arizona

asked Ben if we could use an Apache princess in a beaded dress. He arranged it, a beautiful teenager, one of ten children. Her mother came with her and watched, as I taught her daughter to use a spinning reel. Tourists would stop and want to get a picture of her. Her mother charged them 50 cents for each picture.

The next day Ben wanted to take his 12-year-old son with us to learn to fish. We were standing on the dock at one of the lakes, and I was teaching Ben how to cast. His first try went straight up, and the spoon landed on the dock. The next cast was about six feet off the dock, and a nice rainbow hit. Ben landed it and with a smile said, "I'll go get my boy and meet you at the lower lake."

It was just a short distance, so I walked on ahead. There were several people fishing from the bank. One elderly lady on the heavy side was sitting on a stump near the water's edge. She wasn't fishing, just watching the rest of the people. I asked her if it would bother her if I made a cast or two, and she told me to go ahead. I cast a brown crappie jig out about 30 feet and caught a rainbow trout about 12 inches long. She said, "You sure made that look easy; I wish my husband had seen that." I asked her where he was, and he had gone back up the hill. She said, "He just bought a new rod and reel for this trip and it wouldn't work." I told her if she would go get him I would see if I could help him, that I was just waiting for the Apache chief and his children and my son Dusty to get there. We were planning to shoot some movies for television. She immediately went up to the camper and got her husband. He had a new fly rod with an open-faced spinning reel on it and threaded with new fly line. Whoever threaded it up didn't put the line back on the bail. He would just wind without picking up the line and thought his reel was broken. I asked where he had bought the outfit. He said, "In California, before we came here for our vacation." I told him that you do not use a fly line on a spinning reel and that I had some extra spinning line in my station wagon. As soon as Dusty and Ben came back, I would get it. In the meantime, I cast out and handed him my rod. I heard him grunt and saw that he had a nice trout. He landed it and had a smile as large as the fish. "Winds of Chance."

Dusty, Ben and the kids came. I went to the station wagon, got a spool of 4-lb. test spinning line, filled his spool, threaded it up, tied on a crappie jig and told him to go to work. He started catching fish on his own outfit; although his fly rod didn't match his reel, it did work! He was now catching fish and was a happy camper!

By this time Dusty had rigged an outfit for Ben and his two kids. They caught fish and we made our movie. It was almost sunset when Dusty said, "Dad, we had better get moving if we're going to get back to Kansas City in time to do your show." We thanked Ben for being so nice to us. We considered it an honor and a privilege to spend a few short days with the Apaches. They are great people, and there is still a lot of history there. If you get a chance, I hope you will visit them at Fort Apache. I almost forgot to tell you of the big game warden. He told me that his dad or grandfather had been a roommate of Jim Thorpe. Every time I see a rerun of Jimmy Stewart in "Broken Arrow," I think of Ben and his people.

Exploring the Fishing of Africa

OFTEN I HAVE BEEN ASKED how I located the fishing spots for program material. It wasn't by any talent on my part, but most of it came from invitation, some from follow-up and many from return trips and many from recommendation of others. It is not likely that we would ever have made a trip to Africa had we not been invited by a group of businessmen from Pennsylvania to explore the tarpon fishing on the Quanza River in Angola. They asked us if we would make the trip to scout the area to see if they should put a camp there. To be truthful, I had never given it a thought and at first was a little cool on the idea. I told them that if I could take my wife and daughter I would go. It was to be a three-week trip. I knew of two couples that wanted to make the trip, Tom and Willie Wilhoit of Springfield, Missouri, and a wheat farmer and his wife, the Straeklejons from Garden City, Kansas. It was arranged.

"Winds of Chance."

We flew to Amsterdam, then to Rome, then to Johannesburg, where they put us on two twin-engine aircraft to fly us the rest of the trip. We flew first to Botswana to hunt and fish, then to Rhodesia. We fished for tiger fish on the Zambezi, then to Mozambique to fish, then back south to Durban to fish in the Indian Ocean. Of course, during that period we were privileged to see all kinds of African wildlife in the wild, not in national parks. We fished in one lagoon of about 180 acres that swarmed with hippos. We were fishing in a small aluminum boat with a bodyguard with an elephant gun and a native poling the boat. I didn't realize that the hippos are possibly the most dangerous animals in Africa. We didn't let the women go on the lake with us. I counted 52 hippos in the lagoon. My bodyguard had spent 17 months in the hospital after being mauled by a wounded lion. Some white hunter had wounded the lion, and the guide had to go after it. He sat there by me with his rifle in his hand. I heard him say, "We are too close. If they charge us, I may get one or two of them. If they turn the boat over, don't thrash around in the water." I said, "What do you want me to do, drown?" He said, "No, just swim silently and you might escape."

I wanted to get a shot of me taking a movie of the hippos. I asked Tommie if they would bring their boat over to ours and get my second movie camera. They did, and Tommie took pictures of me taking pictures of the hippos. It was a stupid thing to do, but we got it done without incident.

We flew from there to Durban, then to Johannesburg, and on to Luanda, Angola, to fish for tarpon. The political situation there was not good, and the natives in the little village on the river were not friendly. They had flown a British guide in from Rhodesia to fish with us on the river. He was of small stature, very British, and one of the most interesting people I've met. I cannot think of his last name, but his first name was Louie. He called me "Harry, for short." The temperature during the day was almost unbearable. We went to fish the river from the edge of the Atlantic upstream for some 20 miles. They were using boats made of native lumber. They were about 25 feet long with a live well in the center of the boat. It was simply a box about four feet long, two feet wide and 12 inches deep. It was built to keep their bait alive. Louie furnished the gear and hired two native guides for the other two boats. He bought live bait from the natives. The bait was a small fish similar to our bluegill and about the size of your hand. Louie had to smuggle his rods in. He made his own hooks. He used 30-lb. test line; with the last ten feet he doubled the line, then attached a ten-foot steel leader with two forged steel hooks tied about 12 inches apart. In the front end of the boat he had a big bucket of rocks about the size of a baseball, for sinkers. He also had a big rock on a rope to anchor the boat. I wanted to use artificial lures. He told me that if I wanted to catch tarpon we had better use live bait. We left my 16-year-old daughter at the hotel, and the three boats of us went up the river some 15 or 20 miles. We didn't see any tarpon rolling, but Louie stationed the three boats about 100 yards apart, and we started fishing. We had been told of 200-lb. tarpon in the river. Straeklejon hooked the first tarpon, and it broke the line. I hooked one and landed it, about 40 pounds, and I hooked another and landed it, about 10 pounds. I said, "Louie, I fly thousands of miles to catch a big tarpon and catch two of the smallest tarpon I have ever caught." He said, "Harry, they flew me thousands of miles, and those are the smallest tarpon to ever come in my boat." It was terribly hot, and the women were ready to give it up .

The Straeklejons went in, and the two boats stayed on until late afternoon. The two boats of us started in. There were a lot of floating bogs of high grass floating in the river. We ran through one, and Louie asked me to get up into the bow of the boat to watch for these floating bogs. I did, and I listed to the drone of the motor. I thought, man, what a privilege to be alive and fish in this wild country. It was getting late, and my wife was naturally concerned about Sandy being by herself at the hotel. Darkness comes in the jungle and closes in just as dissolving a picture on a movie screen. I could no longer see ahead, but I could see the glow of Louie's cigarette. He would light his first cigarette with his lighter; then the rest of the time from one cigarette to another. I suddenly felt jungle grass come up over the boat and heard the whine of the motor as the boat locked up on top of the bog. My wife became hysterical. She said, "I told you we should have come in early." Louie carried a long, heavy pole in the boat. I tried to use it to get back off the bog. I thought we were in shallow water. I stuck the pole straight down to push off the bottom. When I didn't reach the bottom, I almost became hysterical. The native guide who was following us either saw us in the darkness or saw the glow of Louie's cigarette. He tried to pull us off the bog but couldn't, so we all transferred to their boat. We made it in and found our daughter all right.

The next day we worked hard but caught nothing but a small sand shark. My wife and daughter brushed their teeth in the tap water and became terribly ill. My wife said, "Are you going to recommend that they build a fishing camp on the river?" I said, "No way." The next day she was too sick to go back up the river, so I went with Louie by myself and with the other two boats.

Early morning the natives had failed to have enough bait for the three boats. I suggested that the two couples take what bait we had and go on up the river to fish, while Louie and I tried to catch bait. Louie said, "No, let's keep some!" He took two live bluegill about the size of your hand and two live mullet about 15 inches in length. I asked him to take me where the natives trapped the bait with crude handmade traps. I told Louie that I had not been anywhere that I could not catch bait on a tiny crappie jig and 2-lb. test line. We fished for two hours with nothing. We ate our sandwiches and Louie said, "Let's go up the river to see how your friends are doing and use the bait we have." It was really hot and the sun was really bearing down. I asked myself, how do I get into these situations. Louie talked constantly and was so anxious to learn about fishing in other parts of the world. I couldn't hear too well from the front of the boat, so I moved back near Louie. All of a sudden he screamed, "Harry, I just saw a tarpon roll." I said, "Where?" He said that it was about a mile away near the riverbank on the left side. I turned to look and the tarpon surfaced again. He said, "Harry, mark him and we'll go try to catch him?" Can you imagine trying to mark a fish a mile away? We watched for this spot. Louie tied the boat to a tree limb at the edge of the water where we thought we last saw the fish. Louie had his pile of rocks in the front of the boat. He said, "The tide is at a standstill; we will not have to use a drop leader with a rock to hold the bait in place." He put the two bluegill on his forged hooks about a foot apart and let them over the side of the boat and said, "Harry, strip off the leaders and about 10 more feet of line." We were using 10 feet of double line, then 10 feet of steel leader. I stripped off the leader through 10 feet of line. I felt a heavy pressure, set the hook and was hung up on a log. We finally pulled it loose, but lost both the bluegill. I said, "Let's try one of those big mullet." He said, "They are no blankety-blank good." He started a tirade about the lazy native; however, he hooked the live mullet on with the first hook back of its head and the second hook back by the dorsal fin. He put the mullet over the side of the boat. He said, "Strip the two leaders and 10 feet of line." As the fish sank down into the water, I thought to myself that it looked pretty good. I stripped off 10 feet of double and 10 feet of steel leader. Just as I stripped off the last foot, I felt a strike. I set the hook, the line sang out, and this beautiful silver tarpon was leaping in the air on successive leaps down river. I have caught hundreds of tarpon in Costa Rica, Belize and Florida, but this was a magnificent fish whistling off line in spectacular leaps. I asked Louie to untie the boat, for I thought the tarpon was heading for the ocean. The line went slack, and I said, "Never mind, I lost him." He said, "Keep reeling, it may be coming back toward the boat." Sure enough, the fish was still on. I

My two biggest tarpon taken on back-to-back casts — Quanza River in Africa

asked Louie to grab the camera, held the fish and showed Louie what to do. He ran off the rest of the film on that roll but, of course, couldn't load the camera, and the other two boats were too far up the river to help. The fish finally wore down and lay on its side by the boat. Louie grabbed the gaff, and I said, "Louie, let me help you!" Louie would not weigh over 150 pounds soaking wet. I had seen big husky natives gaff a tarpon and almost get pulled overboard. I could just see Louie gaffing the fish and going over the side of the boat. I again said, "Louie, let me help you!" He told me no, to hang on, it might make another run. That time the fish bellied up, and Louie gaffed it. Somehow that little guy pulled that tarpon over the side of the boat. He sat back down on the boat seat and started huffing and puffing. He said, "Those blankety-blank cigarettes are going to kill me." He always used a holder that he called a filter. He started looking around and said, "Where is my filter?" I said, "Louie, you swallowed it." He laughed as he found it in the bottom of the boat and lit another cigarette. He said, "Let's use that other mullet." I told him no, that I wanted to reload my camera and go up to the other boats for some pictures.

We came first to the Straeklejons, who said, "You just lost a big fish down below us, didn't you?" We pulled up by their boat so they could see my fish. I told them I wanted to go to the Wilhoits so we could get some pictures. They pulled anchor, and we moved up the river to where they were anchored. It was just boiling hot, and they had put too much water in their live well and were almost losing what bait they had. Tommy asked me if I caught some bait. I told him that I had, as we pulled our boat up to theirs. He saw that big tarpon and said, "Man, you didn't catch that!"

We took some pictures, and I told them we should go back down the river and just might catch another. We anchored our boats about 150 yards apart. Somehow I didn't feel we were in the right spot. I was looking upstream when I saw another tarpon surface. I yelled to Louie and told him I had seen another fish about a mile upstream. He told me to mark the spot, and the three boats of us took off up the river, and I was skeptical as I only had one bait left. I told Louie where I thought the fish was, and he anchored the boat. We stationed the other two boats below us and started to fish. By this time the tide was moving toward the ocean. Louie told me he would have to use a rock to get the mullet down. I handed him a rock from his pile in the front of the boat. He tied it to a piece of monofilament line about six feet long and tied that to the steel leader about six feet above the hooks, with the mullet free on the line and the rock pulling the same way we rig a night crawler when drifting for trout on the White River in Arkansas. He told me to strip off the same amount of line that I used on the other fish until the rock hit the bottom. I dropped the bait down until the line went slack, lifted the bait, and you won't believe this. I set the hook, and that tarpon shot high in the air, reeling off line in acrobatic jumps down the river. It almost jumped in the Wilhoits' boat. I yelled at Louie to pull anchor as I was about out of line. He was pulling on the anchor one way, and the fish was going the other. I yelled at him not to do it, I was afraid I'd break my line, and then my line went slack. I told him, "Never mind, I lost him." He told me to keep reeling, that the fish might be coming back up the river. He was right; the fish was still on. I asked Tommy to come up to get my movie camera to shoot the action. He did and we landed the fish. It was almost identical to the other one. Both of them were beautiful mother of pearl silver. It was getting late, and I wanted to weigh the two fish and get a still picture. We weighed the fish on their loading scales at the dock. The first one weighed 150.4 on the scales, and the second one weighed 148.6. The two totaled 299 pounds. It made our pictures, the story and made the trip.

"Winds of Chance."

Louie told us the two fish we caught would feed the entire village. The natives instantly became friendly. Bonnie, my wife, said, "What are you going to recommend now?" I said, "I'm going to say, 'Build your camp.'" However, the political situation became so bad, nothing came. I would love to fish in the Quanza River one more time, but that's out of the question. We flew to Rio, then on to Miami and home. One thing I almost forgot to tell you — when we flew into Durban, South Africa, I wanted to fish one time in the Indian Ocean. Tommy and Willie wanted to go with me while the rest of them toured the city. There was a fishing pier extending out into the ocean. We went there and asked about it. They told us it would cost us $2 each and that we would need live bait. We would have to go downtown to get bait, and Tommy decided to go. Willie and I walked up the beach about a quarter of a mile to a rock jetty where we could see a few people fishing. The jetty was made of huge boulders which made walking difficult and dangerous. Willie decided not to try it. I had my casting rod and a handful of reapers, the bait I designed for lake trout in Canada. The jetty may have extended out into the ocean about 200 yards. I could see several natives fishing at the very end of the jetty, and I started working my way there. About two-thirds of the way out, I passed a man fishing with his two kids. Just as I was passing, I saw him catch a fish. I paused to visit with him. I told him I didn't have any bait, but wondered if that reaper would catch fish. He said, "It looks good to me, try it." I started on. He said, "Wait a minute. Are you from the States?" I said, "Yes, why?"

He told me to fish in his spot. He told me that where he was fishing was the only place anyone was catching fish. I told him that I didn't want to take his spot. He insisted that I take it, that he might be in the States someday and he might want my spot. I'll probably never see him again, but I'll never forget that man and the courtesy he extended to a total stranger in a foreign land. "Winds of Chance."

Oklahoma Catfish

IN THE MID-FORTIES, a carpenter friend of mine, Elmer Shackelford, called me from Miami, Oklahoma, and invited me to come down to fish with him and his family. He told me that they had discovered the craziest channel cat fishing he had ever seen. When I arrived in Miami early the next day, he told me that he had an emergency job to take care of, but that his wife and two teenage kids would take me down to the spot and he would be down later. They had a bundle of cane poles tied on top of their car. We bought a bucket of minnows and drove to Grand Lake. Mrs. Shackleford stopped the car at the side of the road just north of the bridge across Spring River. It's a place called Twin Bridges on Highway 60 just past Wyandotte, Oklahoma. The first bridge was across Spring River, then a few hundred yards another bridge crossed the Neosho River. Below the two bridges about one-half mile the two rivers converge to form Grand River. After the Grand River Dam was built near Jay, Oklahoma, the reservoir backed up past the junction of Spring River and the Neosho River. The waters on both sides of the highway were a part of Grand Lake on the Neosho River side and on the Spring River side. They called it Twin Bridges.

As they stopped the car, I looked out over the dingy water. It didn't look good to me; I was accustomed to the clear waters of the Cowskin Arm and the Honey Creek Arm, and it certainly didn't excite me about the possibilities. I asked Mrs. Shackleford where we were going to fish. She told me that we would fish off the rip rap at the base of the road bed. Rather reluctantly, I helped them down the embankment with the bundle of cane poles. The stretch of rip rap rocks extended from the edge of the bridge, up the road bed toward Wyandotte almost a quarter of a mile. Several other people were fishing along the road bed, having parked their cars at the side of the highway. Mrs. Shackelford, her son and daughter each took out a cane pole baited with a minnow and started fishing. Thus far, my fishing fever hadn't changed; then I got to thinking these people were nice enough to bring me here, I at least owed them the courtesy of trying. I picked out a small cane pole and line. I suppose it may have been about 10 feet long with the cork for a bobber set about three feet deep. I picked out a good lively minnow, tossed the line in the water, and the cork just went on down. I thought they had put a heavy sinker on this line and it pulled the cork under, but not so; I had a channel cat on my line. I just couldn't believe it. It might have weighed five pounds. I got the fish in, and each of them had a fish. We caught them as fast as we could get our lines in the water. By the time Elmer arrived, we had a big string of channel cats. No large fish, most of them from three to five pounds. Elmer said, "What do you think of that?" I told him that I had never seen anything like it.

By this time the cars were parked bumper to bumper along the highway, and people were standing shoulder to shoulder on each side of the highway. These people had spent the day at work and then came out to the lake. It wasn't like it is today, when retirees go fishing all day every day if they wished! You could have walked on the cane poles if they would've held you up! Actually, you could have walked on the cane poles for 200 yards along that rip rap; people were fishing that close to each other, and almost everyone was catching fish. People were coming down after work in the evening to fish. Many would come down before work of a morning. It was the month of June, and the channel cats were in most rocks along the roadbed spawning. No one will ever know how many thousands. Yes, I said "thousands" of fish were taken along that road fill. It became so bad with cars parked along the side of the road that for safety's sake they made it illegal to park there. People came from all over the four-state area. Some of them became experts, but nearly everyone caught fish. A cane pole with or without a bobber was the best rig, with a heavy clamp-on sinker and any kind of 4.0 hooks. Calcutta bamboo was the best, but hard to get. There were several men from Miami, a few From Joplin, and I remember three men from Granby, Missouri, who became real artists for that style of fishing. Everyone caught fish, but these guys were just deadly. The run usually started the first week of June and lasted through the 4th of July. Most of us would make the crappie run in April and May, then hit the channel cat about Memorial Day through the 4th of July. Some people have a tendency to look down on the channel cat and the channel cat fishermen. Let me tell you something, the channel cat is a great fish. You don't have to monster fish either; a 4 to 7-pound channel is something on the end of your line. The fishing at Twin Bridges was one of the greatest fish runs I have witnessed anywhere for any kind of fish. Most of us who learned what was going on started the first part of the run using a wad of worms. Then in a week or so we switched to soft-shelled crawfish, and the last part of the run we used shrimp. With a cane pole we would dunk the bait down in the holes of the rock bed. Occasionally you could get your bait through a crevice, hook a fish, and have to go in the water and roll the rocks off the hole. It was crazy. Sometimes the channel would hit so hard it would almost knock the pole from your hands.

I remember an incident when we were fishing on rip rap on the upstream side of the road. My little neighbor boy came running over the road from the downstream side. He yelled, "Mr. Ensley, come quick. A fish jerked the pole out of Peanuts' hand and is swimming off with it." Peanuts was his older brother, I would guess maybe 12 years old, a typical freckle-faced boy. I ran across the road and could see the pole in the lake going toward the river channel. About three feet of the butt of the pole could be seen. It reminded me of a submarine periscope as it bobbed along in a perpendicular position. I ran back across the road and down the embankment to get my rod and reel. I wasn't using it to fish with, as I always use a cane pole for this type of fish, but I always had my rod and reel handy. I ran down to the bridge, which was about 50 yards. I looked into the river on the downstream side. Sure enough, that fish was still taking that cane pole and was coming right up the river under the bridge. I ran to the upstream side and dropped my line with a heavy sinker into the path of the upcoming fish. After the second try, I hooked the line, but the fish took a run and straightened my hook. The last I saw of Peanuts' pole, it was still going up the river. No one had a boat nearby or we might have retrieved it. I don't know where my little friend, Peanuts, lives today, but I'll bet he still remembers that fish! Yes, I loaned him one of my poles to finish his day. "Winds of Chance."

I have no idea what fisherman found the spot first, but the place became the mother lode to thousands of fishermen. I'm grateful that I had the opportunity to see it and fish it during the prime years. I was amused at a crappie-fishing buddy of mine, Max Casteel, surely one of the best crappie fishermen that I have met. He has retired and now lives at Truman Reservoir. One day when we were fishing for crappie on Truman Reservoir, the subject of channel cat fishing came up, and Max told me that years and years ago his dad called and told him that Ensley on his radio show had told about a great channel cat run on Grand Lake in Oklahoma. He said, "Max, let's go down and check it out!" They did, and Max agreed with me that they had never seen anything like that. Max and I fished for crappie on Truman for several years, and he had never said anything about it before that day.

Recently in Kansas City people remember that 50 years ago one of the worse floods in its history swept through Kansas City, Kansas, and the industrial bottoms of Kansas City, Missouri. That took place in 1951. I was working for the radio station in Independence, Missouri. My wife and I had driven to southwest Missouri to visit her mother and dad. I drove on down to Twin Bridges to get in on the channel cat run. When I reached the area, I was surprised that there was not another car of fishermen. The water was high and muddy, but I decided to try it. I had to wade out into water almost waist deep to reach the rip rap. I caught a couple of small channel and drove back to pick up Bonnie, as I had a baseball game to broadcast in Independence. She told me that we couldn't get home. She said that 71 Highway was closed between Jasper and Lamar, Missouri. That four or five miles of the highway was under four to five feet of water, and that farther up the road was closed between Butler and Nevada with water over the road. I told her that if we couldn't get through I could just as well go back to Twin Bridges. She told me that they had just warned everyone on the radio from Miami, Oklahoma, on down to stay off the lake. It was rumored that a wall of water was coming down the Neosho River out of Kansas. It was my last time to fish that channel cat run, and it has never been the same since. We finally got into Kansas City in time to see the devastation of that flood.

A few years later I was doing a fishing seminar for Sears at Arkansas City, Kansas.

Lee Jeffery with blue cat caught on rod and reel — Grand Lake, Oklahoma

After the seminar, a tall can of corn came up to me and wanted to know where to take his basketball team on a good fishing trip. His name was Lee Jeffrey. He was head coach of basketball at Arkansas City Junior College. He was 6 foot 7 and stood out in the crowd. I learned later that he had played professional basketball for several years for the Denver Nuggets. I sent him to Big Hollow Resort on Grand Lake, run by Jess Leith. Jess and I had done lots of fishing together. I knew that he would take care of Lee and his basketball team. Years later I received a telephone call from Lee, and he wanted me to come to Sedan, Kansas, where he was principal of the high school, to speak at the high school commencement there. I did, and a few years later he called me from Pleasanton, Kansas, to speak at the high school commencement there. I did, and we became friends. Lee finally retired from the school business and bought a home on Grand Lake in Oklahoma. He started a daily fishing show on the local radio station in Grove, Oklahoma, and also did a fishing column in the Grove paper. I almost became family with Lee and his wife Norma. It was almost like I had a new home; Lee loves to fish and fished almost every day. He kept telling me about their jug line fishing and asked me to come down to do a catfish story for television. I called Jim Higgins, my fishing buddy who loves to catch catfish, and asked him if he wanted to go help me. We drove down to Lee's to do the story. Lee wanted his fishing buddy and next-door neighbor, Charlie French, to fish with us that night.

I asked Lee what we were going to use for bait on the jug lines. He told me that cut frozen shad were the best. In Oklahoma you are allowed five hooks for each jug and you had to have your name and fishing license number on each jug and set them spaced across the water on Okeegee flats, an area in front of Lee's home where the lake was about a mile wide. The main channel was along a bluff across from their place. We probably had the jug lines for a mile down the flats. We baited the lines, Charlie with his frozen shad, and Lee with his cut fresh shad. The next morning we went out to run the jugs. There wasn't a fish on Charlie's, and there wasn't a fish on Lee's. We were using Lee's pontoon boat to handle our camera equipment. We had shot the preliminary work the evening before, but now no fish. Charlie and Lee discussed the matter, and it reminded me of the show, "Grumpy Old Men." They were next-door neighbors and fishing buddies, but each had his own idea as to what the problem was. Lee said, "Let's pull into our neighbor's dock to see what they have caught." Their house was close enough to the dock that Lee called to them. The couple came down, pulled up their live box full of channel and blue cats. There we had nothing, and they had a bunch of fish. Lee asked them what they used for bait. They said, "We were using live black perch." That's what most people in our country call the green sunfish.

We took pictures of them with their fish, and I said, "Lee, let's go catch some blue gill and black perch and try it." They had caught their bait out of some farm pond. Lee took us around to Monkey Island. We bought a box of worms, some small hooks and caught a bucket full of small blue gill and black perch. To me that was almost as much fun as jug fishing. I guess that's the kid in me! We had the lines rebaited by noon, and by 5 p.m. had fish on them. We started filming. It was crazy; some jugs had four fish on, and most all of them had one to three. If I remember correctly, the lines on the jugs were about 15 feet long, with five hooks spaced about two feet apart. We caught most of the blue cat on the top hooks and channels on the lower ones. The fish would run from 3 to 12 pounds. We rebaited the lines for the night set. The neighbor couple also set their lines. The next morning we finished the picture. Almost every jug had at least one fish. It was amazing to me to be shooting a movie for my TV show just a few miles below where we had 50 years before had the fabulous and famous channel cat in the rocks along the road beds at Twin Bridges. "Winds of Chance."

Grand Lake has always been a great catfish lake, but until the past few years, it was channels and flatheads. Now the lake is full of blue cats. They catch them on trotlines, limb lines and jug lines and, of course, on rods and reels. It isn't anything to hear of 35 and 40-pound blues being caught not only from boats, but also from boat docks. I really don't know when or how the blue catfish came into Grand Lake, but it has added a new dimension to their sport fishing. Old-timers used to call the male channel cat a blue cat, but the blue cat is an entirely different fish. Yes, it had been great fun for Jim and me, jug line fishing with "Two grumpy old men." "Winds of Chance."

Remember also that Grand Lake is one of the top fishing lakes in America for bass, crappie, white bass and spoonbill as well as the catfish.

Where To Fish

IN MY WORK we had to fish under all kinds of conditions, but that's all part of the challenge. I have had to fish strange water, week after week. I do not like to beat my head against the wall in an impossible situation, but I love the challenge of fighting the odds. I always like to make one more cast after I quit; who knows, it might be the "Chance of a Lifetime!" Twice in my lifetime I have caught trophy fish on the cast after I quit. Solomon, the wise man of old, once said, and I quote, "He that looks to the wind will not sow, and he that looks to the clouds will not reap." Ecclesiastes, Chapter 11, Verse 4. "Whatever your hand finds to do, verily, do it with all your might; for there is no activity or planning or wisdom where you in sheol where you are going." Ecclesiastes, Chapter 9, Verse 10. The answer is simple: Do it while you live, or it can't be done! If you wait until it is just right, you will never go.

I was speaking to a group of boys at the McCune Boys Home, a correctional home sponsored by one of the civic clubs of Independence, Missouri. One of the club members brought his 12-year-old neighbor boy. As they drove along, the boy said, "I'd like to fish where Harold Ensley fishes! It's a cinch to catch them there!" I wish it were that simple! Really, it matters not how good you are or how bad! It matters little to the fish. During my lifetime I've been privileged to fish with people of all walks of life: the rich and famous, those not so famous, movie stars, beautiful women and handsome men, but they're all the same to the fish!

At a gathering where I spoke one night, someone asked the question, "Do you fish by the barometer?" My answer was yes. I fish when the barometer is rising, when it is falling, when it's low, when it's high and when it's steady! Certainly, there are times when it is easier to catch fish than others. There are many variables, but the best way to fish is whenever you can! When the time is opportune, fish!

We were exploring the fishing in Africa. One of our stops was a famous hunting camp in Mozambique. They had just opened up to groups other than hunters. I asked the outfitter about fishing for tiger fish in the river. He told me that the only time you can catch them was from 10 a.m. until 2 p.m. I asked him if I could go to the river late that evening. He told me I would have to have a bodyguard, but also told me that we would not catch any fish. I had never been anyplace in the world where fish kept office hours from 10 'til 2. To his surprise, we caught fish. Then it dawned on me, the reason for their thinking. The guides would take the hunters out in the early hours, come in about 10 a.m. for lunch, and then go back to their hunting from 2 p.m. on. The only time they staged was from 10 until 2.

My friend, if you wait for the right time, it may never come!

My dad never fished much; he worked hard and never had time to fish. In the spring of 1960 at age 80 he planted his garden and told two of his cronies that he was going to spend more time fishing with Harold. The next morning Mother went into his room to awaken him. She said, "Wake up, sleepyhead, breakfast is ready!" Dad had passed away in his sleep that night.

For 22 years Monday through Friday, I did a 15-minute radio fishing show on a 50,000-watt station in Kansas City, and was doing a live 30-minute TV show 52 weeks a year. I would close my radio show saying, "Ol' buddy, it may be later than you think; you had better take time out to fish!" Of course, fishing is not all that important, but if you're going to fish, do it while you can, when you can and where you can!

Someone might say, "What's the big deal about fishing?" I realize that fishing is not for everyone. But to the multiplied millions of us throughout the world who do fish, there is a mystique that defies explanation. We have seen it across North America, in Europe, in Central America, in South America, and we have seen it in Africa. To all of those of us all over the world that do fish, just mention the word "fishing" and eyes will light up! It may be a "want-to-be" fisherman, a casual fisherman, or a dedicated fisherman. Its scope takes in people of every walk of life and all ages. This book is not about how to fish. I merely want to share a few experiences with you from a lifetime of fishing in many parts of the world, both fresh water and salt. Every time I go fishing, I think something wonderful is going to happen.

There is an old saying that, "It is an ill wind that blows nobody good," and the "Winds of Chance" blow from many directions. At this point I would like to share with you a letter that I received in the spring of 2000.

Harold,

George Smetzer (born 1911) began taking me fishing in 1951 when I was 12. He was a neighbor and the manager of our 3 & 2 baseball team. His son Jim and I became good friends, and after taking a couple of the other boys on the team fishing and finding out that all they wanted to do was throw rocks in the water, they took me on a trip to the King's River. George gave me a bamboo rod, some poppers, a stick of ferrule cement and matches. It didn't take me long to figure out what the latter two were for. After showing how much I loved fishing, I was always invited on their fishing trips. Until this day, George and I still fish together whenever we can. He lives in a trailer on table Rock Lake in the summer and in Port Aransas, Texas, in the winter.

George caught these two fish at the same time October 8, 1987. We were on a late fall trip to try top water fishing at Pony Express Lake near Cameron, Missouri. As you can tell by the picture, it was a cold and cloudy day. George was using an Ambassador 5000 reel and his favorite lure, a white body, blue head, Woods #2000 Spot Tail Minnow. We always called them "Smokey Joe's," but that was really a favorite color we used.

After lunch, when I had given George my hooded sweatshirt and a pair of size 15 rubber boots that fit nice and snug with his shoes on, we headed for a tree trunk that was about two feet underwater. George placed a nice cast about three feet past the spot where we knew the tree trunk was, let the Spot Tail lay there for a few seconds, and then began working it toward the tree trunk. The lure sank in a big swirl and George set the hook. The water boiled as the fish sank a few feet and just stayed in the same place. George was fighting hard to just keep the rod tip up. My first thought was that he had one of the big muskie that had been stocked in the lake. Seeing the trouble he was having and knowing that we didn't have a net, I told him to guide

George Smetzer at 77 with two bass over 6 pounds each on one lure.

the fish toward the front of the boat where I was and I'd get him in when he surfaced. I wasn't ready for what happened next, as he pulled the fish to the surface. I was faced with not one, but two very large bass. Both with a single barb of a treble hook holding them. Both mouths were wide open, and I instantly clamped a thumb and forefinger down on the lower jaw of each fish. As I lifted them into the boat, the hook came out of their mouths, and my knees were shaking so bad I had to sit down. I had taken my camera to take a picture of George fishing. After weighing each fish (6-pounds 2-oz. and 6-pounds 9-oz.) with my Deliar which weighed things a little light if anything, I put them on a stringer so I could keep them in the water, while I calmed my nerves and readied the camera. After a few photos, George quickly took them off the stringer and released them, as I knew he would. We sat for a while talking, and I told George that I had just had my greatest thrill and I hadn't even caught a fish!

It has been 13 years since that day, but it still thrills me to relive that trip. While the years are taking a toll on his body, George's mind and spirit still make it easy to think of him as the same person I met 50 years ago.

Warren Platt

The following is a letter I received July 2, 2001:

Hi, Harold,

It was good talking to you on the phone the other day, and I am glad to hear that you are working on a book. You have had too many memories in your gifted life not to record a few to be shared with the rest of us. I was also pleased to hear that you wanted to include the fishing story about George Smetzer in the book.

George just celebrated his 90th birthday at a party given by his daughter, who lives in Kansas City north of the river. While I haven't fished with him the last couple of years, he still wets a line now and then in the summer on Table Rock and in south Texas in the winter. The desire to see that top water explosion, I believe, will never leave him. Please let me know about the photos.

Sincerely,
Warren Platt

In all this, we do not have all the answer. I occasionally meet people who feel they have all the answers. I've heard people say, "You have to be smarter than a fish and think like a fish." I don't even know if fish think, and until fish learn to read, write or talk, we will not have all the answers. If someone had all the answers, they would soon have all the fish, and you would lose the mystique and charm of fishing. Certainly through the centuries we have made great strides in equipment and techniques. Scientific research has taught us much about the habits of fish — spawning time, feeding habits, etc. I'm sure that there is much that we will never learn. For instance, why do Pacific salmon leave salt water to spawn in fresh water and die? Their fry go back to salt water to grow up, and then they come back to fresh water to spawn and die. Then the Atlantic salmon leave salt water, come in to spawn and then go back to sea to live and spawn again. God made them that way. Then tell me why tarpon leave salt water to spawn in fresh water, grow up in it, and then go back to sea. At the same time, I'm told that snook spawn in salt water and go to fresh water to grow up and start the cycle all over again. This helps us to determine the time and place to catch them. For instance, people have learned that it is much easier to locate and catch crappie as they move into the shallow water to spawn in the spring. They move when the water temperature is right for them. We have learned that in our part of the world the channel cat spawn around the month of June. You can almost set your clock by it. I can remember years back when in most states it was illegal to fish for bass during spawning time. I know of people today who schedule their vacations to coincide with spawning periods, whether it is crappie, bass, channel cat or what have you. This is a wise move, but there are a lot of variables — water levels, water temperatures, water discoloration, wind direction, etc. God made it that way! My advice is fish when you can, as often as you can and as long as you can!

As we have said before, the big problem is that many people do not have the luxury of fishing when the fishing is good. In our work for the past 50 years, we have been forced to adapt to the situation of the moment! How many times have you heard, "You should have been here yesterday," or "You should have stayed a day longer!"

I remember a situation at Grand Lake in Oklahoma one winter that illustrates the point. We were crappie fishing out of Long's heated dock on the Honey Creek Arm. There were perhaps 30 people fishing, some inside the dock and several on the walkway on the outside. We, along with many of the others, had fished several days. We were catching a few crappie, but it was a slow go. It was a beautiful winter day, sun shining brightly, and we were dressed for the occasion. I would guess in the sun on the south side of the dock the temperature was probably in the 50s. Jig fishing for crappie had not yet come on the scene. We were all minnow fishing. A man from Broken Arrow, Oklahoma, and I, along with several others, were fishing on the south side in the sun. He was on the southwest corner of the dock, and I was next to him. He had caught a couple of crappie, as we had fished most of the day. About 4 p.m. he said to me, "I've had it; I'm going home. You can have my spot." He left and I moved over in the spot he had vacated. To my amazement, the fish turned it on! He couldn't have been gone 30 minutes on his way home when I caught the first one. Everyone started catching nice crappie, and had he stayed an hour longer he would have been in on the good fishing. But he didn't! He probably went home saying, "Nobody caught any fish!" I never saw the man again to tell him the story.

I have people say to me, "When the fishing gets good, I want to go with you." Jokingly, I have a stock answer, "If you don't want to be with me when it's bad, I don't want you along when it's good."

"Winds of Chance."

There are many variables, but the best way to fish is whenever you can!

Thousands of years before satellite pictures of the world's weather, the source and destination of the wind had inspired the minds of poets and authors and all mankind. Solomon, the wise old man of old, wrote, "Blowing toward the south, then turning toward the north, the wind continues swirling along and on its circular course the wind turns" Ecclesiastes 1, Verses 6 and 7. I wonder what Solomon would think if he were to see today's television version of the wind. The wind, where does it come from and where is it going? As to the Winds of Chance, where does it come from and what does it bring? And what does it hold in store for each of us? Did you ever hear a person say, "I had my chance and blew it"? I thank God daily for the chances he has given me, and I think of the many wonderful people who have touched my life.

The source and destination of the Winds of Chance are just as mysterious as the winds that blow.

A few years back we were working at Elk Island Lodge on God's Lake in Manitoba. My crew, Jim Higgins, a deputy sheriff from Holden, Missouri; Norm Troutman, a guide from Warsaw, Missouri; Dwayne Paugh, a school teacher from Overland Park, Kansas, and I were working on a lake trout movie for my TV show. The weather had been good and the fishing excellent. We personally had fished this area almost every year since August of 1955. It took several years of trial and error before we came up with a technique to consistently catch lake trout on light spinning gear, when they are in water from 60 to 120 feet deep. For years people thought the only way to catch lake trout down deep was to troll hardware or jig for them, and some even went to downriggers. It would work, but I never cared for that style. We have covered this in several other places in this book, how we invented the reaper bait and the technique that we used. I make mention of this as a prelude to the story I want to tell.

The word passed around that our crew had been catching lots of lake trout. Over the years we had located several deep holes where lake trout would congregate as the summer weather advanced. They congregate in those spots around July 1st and stay there until cool wether moves in. You can almost set your calendar by it. That year was no exception. The lodge served meals family style, so it was a great time for the guests to get acquainted and really made it possible to share the day's experiences.

Late in the week a man from Chicago, Bill Keim, asked me if we would take him and his wife fishing one night after dinner. They hadn't been catching any lake trout and wanted to learn what we were doing. He said they would furnish the guides if we would just go along and show them what we were doing. I put Dwayne Paugh in the boat with him, and Elizabeth, his wife, in the boat with me. We had four or five good spots close to camp that were producing fish. We took them to the first one called Billy's Reef. The fish were in about 70 feet of water. Using reapers and light spinning gear, we started catching trout like crazy. We fished a couple of hours and came back to camp. Bill was so thrilled he asked me if we could do it again the next night, which we did with the same results. Their stay is a great story. We had not met them before this trip, but will always be thankful that our paths crossed.

When Elizabeth was 18, she was trapped behind the Iron Curtain in Poland. Desperate to get out from under the ironclad rules of the day, she walked across the country to Turkey, where she was to meet a contact, but somehow missed the connection. She became lost, and the Russians sent her back to Poland the next day. One year later she and a guide walked from Krakow, Poland, through Czechoslovakia and into Austria. There she applied for a visa to the USA. She arrived in Chicago with little or no money. She met a waitress who let her sleep in her apartment that night and later found a job as a manicurist. She met and married Bill Keim, and they now own one of the largest fur businesses in Chicago. Due to the "Winds of Chance," we had the opportunity to meet these two nice people. Can you imagine the courage it took for her to try again to escape to the United States? We in a free world can't begin to imagine the humiliation and suffering and the agony she went through!

Someone might say, "What's the big deal about fishing?" I realize that fishing is not for everyone. But to the millions of us throughout the world who do fish, there is a mystique that defies explanation. We have seen it across North America, in Europe, in Central America, in South America, and we have seen it in Africa. To all of those of us all over the world that do fish, just mention the word "fishing" and eyes will light up! He or she may be a "want-to-be" fisherman, a casual fisherman, or a dedicated fisherman. Its scope takes in people of every walk of life and all ages. This book is not about how to fish. I merely want to share a few experiences with you from a lifetime of fishing in many parts of the world, both fresh water and salt. Every time I go fishing, I think something wonderful is going to happen.

Each year for 47 years we have had a booth at the Kansas City Sports, Boat and Travel Show. We merely used our red Ford station wagon to display our goods, mainly the Abu Garcia fishing rods, which I designed and have given the exclusive rights to my friend, Sam Walton, and the Wal-Mart stores. Also, my fillet knives and the reaper lures I invented. It gives me an opportunity to meet many of the people throughout the Midwest who have watched my TV show through the years and visit with them.

A few years back the adjoining booth was manned by the K.C. Antique Tackle Collectors Club. They trade, collect and sell antique reels and lures. One of the mainstays was a man named Warren Platt. During the course of that week he told me an unusual story of his friend who had caught two bass on one plug at the same time. The fact that he had hooked two bass on the one plug at the same time was not unusual. It was the size of the bass and the circumstances that hit me! I asked if he had a picture that I might use on my TV show and tell the story. That he did, and it was an honor to have it on my show. While I was writing of eventful fishing experiences for my book, I thought of Warren and his mentor. I called him for permission to use the story and the picture. So this is the story from Warren himself and a picture to prove it. There is an old saying that: "It is an ill wind that blows nobody good, and the "Winds of Chance" blow from many directions."

Bible Connection

NOT MUCH WAS SAID in the Bible about fish and fishing. In the Old Testament, the first mention was in the story of creation. God created fish and underwater creatures on the fifth day. That was one day before he created man. It makes sense, that he created them for food. Certainly as a food source fish have played an important part in the advancement of civilization. It is still a major player in the world's food source. I don't know that you ever thought of it, but fish and underwater creatures were the ONLY creatures that were not destroyed by the flood, other than those Noah had in the ark with him. When Noah and his family stepped out of the ark, God gave them the cattle and the beasts of the field, and the fish for food. Not much is said about fish in the Old Testament. God told Moses that of the fish, only those with fins and scales were clean, for the children of Israel to eat — Leviticus 11, Verses 9 and 10.

When in the wilderness the children of Israel grumbled against the Lord, they said, "We had fish to eat in Egypt." When God told Moses to give them meat, Moses said, "For 600,000 people it would take all the fish of the sea." In the days of Ezra and Nehemiah, it tells of the merchants of Tyre waiting outside the walls to sell fish. Job mentions fish on one occasion. In the New Testament, it's a different story. Jesus is selecting his first four sales managers, and he selected four fishermen, Peter and Andrew, James and John. Jesus said, "Follow me and I will make you fishers of men." I don't know how much they fished after that. However, it appears that they were around the water a lot. We know the story of Jesus walking on water and calming winds. To me, the greatest occasion of fishing by the disciples is recorded by John, Chapter 21, Verses 3-14. This took place on the Sea Tiberius. It was just after the resurrection.

The apostles were still in a state of shock. Peter, Thomas, Nathaniel, James and John and two others whose names are not mentioned were gathered together. Simon Peter said, "I am going fishing." They said, "We'll also go with you." Do you think they went fishing to catch food? There must have been something special about being out fishing. John said that they got in a boat and fished all night, but nothing. Just at daybreak, Jesus appeared on the shore. He asked them if they had caught any fish. They told him no. Jesus said, "Cast the net on the right-hand side of the boat, and you will find a catch." They did and caught a net full of large fish, 153. Jesus had a charcoal fire with fish and bread placed on it. Jesus said, "Come and have breakfast." He took the bread and gave them and the fish likewise. Fish story? Not to me, I believe the Bible. Nothing was said as to whether Jesus ate some of the fish, but I'm sure he did.

Luke verifies the fact that he did eat fish after he was raised from the dead. In Luke, Chapter 24, Verses 36-43, you will find Luke's record as proof that Jesus' body had been raised from the dead. After the resurrection, the 11 apostles and others were gathered together in Jerusalem. Jesus appeared in their midst. They were startled and thought it was a spirit. In Luke 24:39 Jesus said, "See my hands and my feet, for a spirit does not have flesh and bones, as you see that I have. In Verse 41 He said to them, "Have you anything here to eat?" And they gave him a piece of broiled fish, and he took and ate it before them. Proof that God raised up his body. He appeared before the disciples — they were startled and frightened, while they could not believe it for joy and were marveling.

Yes, there was a reason Peter said, "I am going fishing."